Gregor Bachmann, Horst Eidenmüller, Andreas Engert, Holger Fleischer, Wolfgang Schön

Regulating the Closed Corporation

ECFR Special Volume 4

European Company and Financial Law Review

Ondernemingsrecht
RdS
Rev. prat. soc.
Rev. Sociétés
Riv. Società
SZW
ZGR

Edited by
Pierre-Henri Conac, Paul Davies, Yves De Cordt,
José M. Embid Irujo, Luis Fernández de la Gándara,
Guido Ferrarini, Holger Fleischer, Heribert Hirte,
Peter Hommelhoff, Klaus J. Hopt, Susanne Kalss,
Maarten J. Kroeze, Hanno Merkt, Peter Nobel,
Christoph Teichmann, Isabelle Urbain-Parleani,
Marco Ventoruzzo

Special Volume 4

Gregor Bachmann, Horst Eidenmüller,
Andreas Engert, Holger Fleischer,
Wolfgang Schön

Regulating the Closed Corporation

DE GRUYTER

ISBN 978-3-11-028643-4
e-ISBN 978-3-11-029527-6

Library of Congress Cataloging-in-Publication Data
A CIP catalog record for this book has been applied for at the Library of Congress.

Bibliographic information published by the Deutsche Nationalbibliothek
The Deutsche Nationalbibliothek lists this publication in the Deutsche Nationalbibliografie; detailed bibliographic data are available in the Internet at http://dnb.dnb.de.

Print: Hubert & Co. GmbH & Co. KG, Göttingen
♾ Printed on acid-free paper
Printed in Germany

www.degruyter.com

MIX
Papier aus verantwortungsvollen Quellen
FSC® C016439

Preface

Small and medium-sized enterprises* (SMEs) are the backbone of Europe's economies. More than 99% of all European companies classify as SMEs. These companies employ more than 65 million workers, and they account for more than 60% of the European Union's (EU) gross domestic product. The preferred company law form for an SME is the *closed corporation.* It offers the shareholders limited liability and thereby protects them from grave entrepreneurial risks. The number of shareholders is limited, and the shareholder composition usually remains relatively stable over time. Not less relevant is the role of the closed corporation for other uses such as private equity firms, joint ventures, or as a building block of corporate groups. This relates to the legal structuring of cross-border business activity in particular and is important for large businesses and SMEs alike.

The legal rules governing the closed corporation are relevant to how well this company law form can achieve its manifold objectives. Both the EU and its Member States have recognized this. In the last years, many Member States have modernized their closed corporation statutes, and on the EU level it is intensively discussed whether and under which circumstances a European closed corporation form (*Societas Privata Europaea*, SPE) should be introduced.

Against this background, in this book we attempt to develop a framework for *regulating the closed corporation:* We seek to answer the question of what the legal rules governing the closed corporation should ideally look like, how – in other words – the 'Volkswagen' of the law of closed corporations should be construed. There is a clear research gap here: legal research worldwide has devoted its main attention so far primarily to public corporations.

With this book, we would like to contribute to modernizing the legal rules for closed corporations in Europe and support both the national and European lawmakers in their reform endeavors. The specifics of a genuinely *European* closed corporation statute will be examined in a chapter of the book. However, these specifics are not our only or primary concern. We are as much interested in the closed corporation statutes of the Member States.

The starting point for our analysis is the structure of a closed corporation and the conflicts (of interest) that characterize it: conflicts between the shareholders, between the shareholders and board members, and between the corpo-

---

* According to a definition of the EU Commission, SMEs include firms with less than 250 employees, a turnover of ≤ 50 million Euro p.a. or a balance sheet total of ≤ 43 million Euro. Start-ups are usually SMEs within this definition.

ration and its creditors. Hence, after an introduction to the aims of our project and the problem it seeks to address (§ 1) and a presentation of our analytical and methodological approach (§ 2), we examine shareholder conflicts in closed corporations (§ 3), the role of the board (§ 4) and creditor protection in a closed corporation (§ 5). Following this analysis, we discuss rules on formation of a closed corporation, management and share transfer (§ 6). In a final chapter, we examine regulatory specifics of a European closed corporation statute (§ 7).

Our analysis is based on a functional-economic perspective that attaches significant weight to the economic consequences of legal rules. Important regulatory approaches of European Member States as well as those in the US are taken into account comparatively. We also take account of the historical experiences that different jurisdictions have had with certain regulatory approaches. Each chapter in this book concludes with a set of main findings. These might guide lawmakers that seek to construe an 'ideal' closed corporation statute.

A draft for each chapter of this volume has been prepared by one of the authors. All chapters have thereafter been discussed extensively within our group. The book we present now is a work of all of us as co-authors – in all parts.

The project that finally led to this book goes back to an initiative of Horst Eidenmüller in 2008. This initiative was made possible by a grant of a research professorship by Ludwig-Maximilians-University Munich as part of the 'excellence scheme' of the German Research Foundation (DFG). For this grant Horst Eidenmüller is very grateful to the DFG and Ludwig-Maximilians-University Munich. In the course of this project, various research assistants at the chair of Horst Eidenmüller have provided research support and helped with the production process of this volume. We are very grateful to all of them. Feedback and criticism are, of course, most welcome.

Berlin, Hamburg, Mannheim and Munich, October 2013

Gregor Bachmann
Horst Eidenmüller
Andreas Engert
Holger Fleischer
Wolfgang Schön

Overview

Abbreviations

AcP	Archiv für die civilistische Praxis
Am. Bus. L. J.	American Business Law Journal
Am. Econ. Rev.	American Economic Review
BB	Betriebs-Berater (Zeitschrift für Recht, Steuern und Wirtschaft)
BGBl.	Bundesgesetzblatt
BGHZ	Entscheidungen des Bundesgerichtshofs in Zivilsachen
BOE	Boletin Oficial del Estado
Bus. Law.	The Business Lawyer
C.com.	Code de commerce (France)
Colum. L. Rev.	Columbia Law Review
DB	Der Betrieb
Del. Gen. Corp. L.	Delaware General Corporation Law
DJT	Deutscher Juristentag
DK	Der Konzern
DStR	Deutsches Steuerrecht
DZWiR	Deutsche Zeitschrift für Wirtschafts- und Insolvenzrecht
EEIG	European Economic Interest Grouping
ECJ	European Court of Justice
EBOR	European Business Organization Law Review
ECFR	European Company and Financial Law Review
Eur. Acct. Rev.	European Accounting Review
Eur. Bus. L. Rev.	European Business Law Review
Eur. Bus. Org. L. Rev.	European Business Organization Law Review
Eur. Co. & Fin. L. Rev.	European Company and Financial Law Review
EuZW	Europäische Zeitschrift für Wirtschaftsrecht
EWS	Europäisches Wirtschafts- und Steuerrecht
FS	Festschrift
Games & Econ. Behav.	Games and Economic Behavior
German L. J.	German Law Journal
GmbHG	Gesetz betreffend die Gesellschaften mit beschränkter Haftung (Germany and Austria)
GmbHR	GmbH-Rundschau
Harv. L. Rew.	Harvard Law Review
HGB	Handelsgesetzbuch
J. Acct. Res	Journal of Accounting Research
J. Bus. & Tech. L	Journal of Business & Technology Law
J. Corp. Fin.	Journal of Corporate Finance
J. Corp. L. Stud.	Journal of Corporate Law Studies
J. Fin. Econ.	The Journal of Financial Economics
J. Inst. Theor. Econ.	Journal of Institutional and Theoretical Economics
J. Legal Stud.	The Journal of Legal Studies
J. L. & Econ.	Journal of Law and Economics
J. Pol. Econ.	Journal of Political Economy
JZ	Juristenzeitung

Komm. z. GmbHG	Kommentar zum GmbHG
LLC	Limited Liability Company
LLP	Limited Liability Partnership
MittBayNot	Mitteilungen des Bayerischen Notarvereins, der Notarkasse und der Landesnotarkammer Bayern
Münchener Komm. z. GmbHG	Münchener Kommentar zum GmbHG
Münchener Komm. z. HGB	Münchener Kommentar zum HGB
NJW	Neue Juristische Wochenschrift
NZG	Neue Zeitschrift für Gesellschaftsrecht
PLC	Public Limited Company
Q. J. Econ.	Quarterly Journal of Economics
RabelsZ	Rabels Zeitschrift für ausländisches und internationales Privatrecht
RIW	Recht der Internationalen Wirtschaft
SE	Societas Europaea
Small Bus. Econ.	Small Business Economics
SPE	Societas Privata Europaea
Stan. L. Rev.	Stanford Law Review
U. Pa. L. Rev.	University of Pennsylvania Law Review
Va. L. & Bus. Rev.	Virginia Law & Business Review
Va. L. Rev.	Virginia Law Review
VGR	Gesellschaftsrechtliche Vereinigung
VVDStRL	Veröffentlichungen der Vereinigung der Deutschen Staatsrechtslehrer
W. L. R.	Wisconsin Law Review
WM	Zeitschrift für Wirtschafts- und Bankrecht (Wertpapier-Mitteilungen)
Yale L. J.	Yale Law Journal
ZBB	Zeitschrift für Bankrecht und Bankwirtschaft
ZEuP	Zeitschrift für Europäisches Privatrecht
ZGR	Zeitschrift für Unternehmens- und Gesellschaftsrecht
ZHR	Zeitschrift für das gesamte Handels- und Wirtschaftsrecht
ZIP	Zeitschrift für Wirtschaftsrecht
ZRP	Zeitschrift für Rechtspolitik
ZVglRWiss	Zeitschrift für Vergleichende Rechtswissenschaft

Chapter 1 Introduction and Objectives*

This book attempts to develop and discuss legal regulations for the closed corporation without taking into consideration existing statutory law or legislative projects.[1] What would the "small" corporation form ideally look like? This is the core issue we attempt to answer. "Closed corporations" are those characterised by a limited group of shareholders, whose shares are not traded on public capital markets.[2] These corporations characteristically display organisational and regulatory structures distinct from those of public corporations.[3]

We pursue a conceptual approach that leaves aside a comprehensive comparative treatment of existing regulatory systems. However, the experience of and solutions deriving from individual legal systems are selectively taken into consideration and included in our analysis. The concept of a "regulation" indicates that our discussion extends – as far as possible – beyond the identification of significant problem fields, such as shareholders' and directors' liability, share transfer or flexibility of organisation, regulatory structures and approaches to solutions, and at least in certain cases proceeds to make specific proposals for the regulation of particular issues. Where this seems impossible, we at least discuss various regulatory options and their respective merits. We do not intend to

---

* The text is based on a draft by *Eidenmüller.*

1 For a "meta-theory" of the evolution of corporate law in different jurisdictions, see by contrast, for example, *McCahery/Vermeulen/Hisatake/Saito* The New Company Law: What Matters in an Innovative Economy, in: McCahery/Timmerman/Vermeulen, Private Company Law Reform: International and European Perspectives, 2010, p. 71 et seq. For a discussion of the development trends in various corporate law systems, see *Gordon/Roe* Convergence and Persistence in Corporate Governance, 2004.

2 In more recent legal and policy discussions, an emerging trend is to replace the distinction between open and closed or private and public corporate forms with the distinction between listed and non-listed corporate forms. See, for example, Report of the Reflection Group on the Future of EU Company Law, Brussels, 5 April 2011, p. 8 et seq. Such distinctions must always be viewed and justified on the basis of a specific heuristic or scientific purpose. Our interest focuses on the conflicts involved in closed corporations and legal regulations to resolve these conflicts. See Chapter 2 A and B below.

3 This characteristic distinguishes this project from the European Model Company Law Project, which aims at the development of model regulations for public corporations. See *Baums/Krüger Andersen* The European Model Company Law Act Project, in: Tison/de Wulf/van der Elst/Steennot, Perspectives in Company Law and Financial Regulation: Essays in Honour of Eddy Wymeersch, 2009, p. 5, 14.

produce a complete set of "model rules", such as those promulgated by the American Bar Association in 1984 for the U.S. closed corporation.[4]

The practical implementation of regulations for the closed corporation in a country presupposes that the applicable regulatory environment must always be taken into account. A meaningful regulation capable of being implemented in one jurisdiction in a certain environment may not be in another. At critical points in our investigation, we make explicit reference to such difficulties of implementation and/or adaptation. In any case, we presuppose that a corporate form capable of stock exchange listing is available as an alternative legal form alongside the closed corporation still to be conceived.

To a certain extent, our investigation focuses on the structure of closed corporations in Europe. Several years ago, the European Commission presented a proposal for the Statute of a "European private company" (*Societas Privata Europæa*, SPE).[5] The proposal aimed to create a European (supranational) legal form for closed corporations. With this, the Commission intended to provide a system of rules alongside the "European stock corporation" (*Societas Europæa*, SE) to be used particularly by small and medium-sized firms operating on a cross-border basis.[6]

Shortly after submission of the Commission's proposal, an intensive legal, policy and juridical discussion ensued – especially in Germany – about the merits and demerits of creating a "European private company" generally and the Commission's proposal in particular.[7] Following various proposed compromises, the draft failed before the Council on 30/31 May 2011 due to a lack of unanimity.[8]

---

4 American Bar Association, Model Business Corporation Act Annotated: Professional Corporation Supplement: Close Corporation Supplement, 1984.

5 Proposal for a Council Regulation on the Statute for a European Private Company, COM(2008) 396 final of 25 June 2008.

6 COM(2008) 396 final of 25 June 2008, p. 2.

7 See *Drury* EBOR 9 (2008), 125; *Davies* FS Hopt, 2010, p. 479; *Neville* FS Hommelhoff, 2012, p. 835. For the discussion in Germany, see, for example, the opinion of the "Arbeitskreis Europäisches Unternehmensrecht", NZG 2008, 897; *Teichmann* Gesellschaftsrechtliche Vereinigung (VGR) 14 (2008), 55; *Hommelhoff* ZHR 173 (2009), 255; *Siems/Rosenhäger/Herzog* DK 2008, 393; *Hadding/Kießling* WM 2009, 145; *Wicke* GmbHR 2011, 566; *Jung* in: Jung, Supranationale Rechtsformen im Typenwettbewerb, 2011, p. 49 et seq.

8 See Council of the European Union, press release PRES/11/146: 3094th Council meeting on Competitiveness (Internal Market, Industry, Research and Space) Brussels, 30 and 31 May 2011, available at http://europa.eu/rapid/press-release_PRES-11–146_en.htm. Currently, it is quite uncertain whether a new regulatory attempt will be made. The Reflection Group on the Future of EU Company Law appears to favor another model, within which Member States would be obliged by a Directive to make available a single-member corporate form in their respective national laws with an extremely simple structure. This structure could be used as a group

Academic and political discussion of the SPE will nevertheless continue. It compels us to focus on European legislative tasks in the area of corporate law and to contribute to improving the quality of the SPE "product" – if it ever reaches the "market".[9] At the same time, the discussion's focus on the SPE project also involves disadvantages: it narrows the perspective to *one single* specific set of regulations, its advantages and weaknesses, and opportunities for improvement. This makes us lose sight of two elements: firstly, what an SPE might and should look like if it is conceived from scratch; secondly – and more importantly –, which regulations apply, or at least should apply generally, to the closed corporation in Europe. Reform is necessary not only for the creation of a new European corporate form, but also in relation to relevant systems of regulations of the Member States. Recent endeavours in the United Kingdom, France, Spain and Germany to make the respective legal systems more amenable to closed corporations under the influence of regulatory competition in corporate law[10] make this very clear.[11] In some respects, the very liberal law governing the U.S. limited liability company (LLC) serves as a source of inspiration and an engine for reform.[12]

Chapter 2 establishes the analytical framework for our subsequent investigation. We identify typical conflicts (of interest) and regulatory requirements aris-

---

subsidiary or by start-ups. See Report of the Reflection Group on the Future of EU Company Law, supra (note 2), p. 30, 57 et seq., 66 et seq. In its "Action Plan: European company law and corporate governance – a modern legal framework for more engaged shareholders and sustainable companies", the European Commission does not take up this suggestion explicitly. Instead, it simply states that it "... will continue to work on the follow-up to the SPE proposal with a view to enhancing cross-border opportunities for SMEs", COM (2012) 740 final of 12 December 2012, p. 14. See also Ch. 7, note 31.

9 On vertical regulatory competition between the European Member States and the EU see *Eidenmüller* Regulatory Competition in Contract Law and Dispute Resolution, in: Eidenmüller, Regulatory Competition in Contract Law and Dispute Resolution, 2013, p. 1, 4 et seq.

10 Empirical studies have shown both for Europe and the United States that the incorporation decisions of closed corporations – and not only those of public corporations – are also strategically based on a cost-benefit calculation by the founders. See *Becht/Mayer/Wagner* 14 J. Corp. Fin. 241 (2008); *Dammann/Schündeln* 27 J.L. Econ. & Org. 79 (2011).

11 UK Companies Act 2006; Loi n° 2003-721 du 1 août 2003 pour l'initiative économique, JORF n°179 du 5 août 2003, p. 13449; Ley 25/2011, de 1 de agosto, de reforma parcial de la Ley de Sociedades de Capital y de incorporación de la Directiva 2007/36/CE, del Parlamento Europeo y del Consejo, de 11 de julio, sobre el ejercicio de determinados derechos de los accionistas de sociedades cotizadas, BOE Núm. 184, 2 de agosto de 2011, Sec. I, Pág. 8746; Gesetz zur Modernisierung des GmbH-Rechts und zur Bekämpfung von Missbräuchen (MoMiG), Bundesgesetzblatt (BGBl.) I/2008, p. 2026.

12 On the development of the LLC in the United States, see *Ribstein* The Rise of the Uncorporation, 2010, p. 119 et seq.

ing in closed corporations. We also discuss different regulatory goals, contents and forms. Chapters 3 to 5 then address regulations governing the relationships between shareholders, between shareholders and directors and between the corporation or its shareholders and third parties. Each section predominantly focuses on the issue that directs our research, namely the reducing or avoiding costs involved with the diverse conflicts (of interest). By contrast, Chapter 6 deals with the formation of a closed corporation, the transfer of shares, the costs involved and how those costs may be reduced. Finally, Chapter 7 is devoted to the special regulatory features of a European closed corporation.

Chapter 2 Analytical Framework*

Table of Contents

A Closed Corporations

The development of the "right" rules – or perhaps the most "convincing" rules – for closed corporations first requires a clear description of the object of investigation: closed corporations. For the *corporation*, the comparative-functional legal analysis agrees that it represents a type of company with the decisive characteristics of legal personality, limited liability (of the shareholders), transferability of shares, the possibility of delegated management and ownership of the capital providers where management and property rights are linked to the role of capital provider.[1] The first two characteristics, in particular, are functionally important: the legal capacity of the corporation protects the corporation's assets from recourse by shareholders, whilst the limited liability of the shareholders shields their (private) assets from recourse by the corporation's creditors, thereby

* The text is based on a draft by *Eidenmüller.*

1 See *Armour/Hansmann/Kraakman* in: Kraakman/Armour/Davies/Enriques/Hansmann/Hertig/Hopt/Kanda/Rock, The Anatomy of Corporate Law: A Comparative and Functional Approach, 2nd ed., 2009, p. 1.

making share trading and risk diversification possible.[2] These characteristics are in no way morphological features dictated by a legal system. Instead, they are endogenous legal characteristics that accompany critical discourse on particular issues – in the sense of framework conditions taken for granted – rather than forming the basis of it.

The same applies to the criterion of "closeness" as a characteristic of *closed* corporations. Closeness generally means that shares in closed corporations are not tradable on the stock exchange, i. e., the group of shareholders is restricted. In addition, the shares are – at least potentially – subject to restrictions on transfer.[3] If and to what extent these (or other) characteristics stand out as the constitutive elements of a closed corporation in a given legal system depends on the individual case.[4] We should also be mindful of hybrid corporate forms such as the American *limited liability company*; its internal affairs are derived from the *partnership*, and its liability limitations are conceived like those of a *corporation*.[5]

For many corporations, the legal characteristic of closeness results from a practical need: if an entrepreneur forms a corporation and also simultaneously manages the business, third parties are only permitted to become shareholders under restricted preconditions (management "suitability"). This is also true if a corporation – either from its inception or in the course of its development, e. g., through inheritance – is a family business in which individual family members perform management functions ("compatibility" with the family).

At the same time, the characteristic of closeness also produces a series of other typical features of this corporate form that are important for its legal treat-

---

2 *Hansmann/Kraakman* 110 Yale L.J. 387 (2000) (affirmative asset partitioning, defensive asset partitioning).

3 See *Armour/Hansmann/Kraakman* in: Kraakman et al., supra (note 1), p. 5 et seq., 11 et seq.; *Cheffins* Company Law: Theory, Structure and Operation, 1997, p. 49 et seq.; *Bainbridge* Corporation Law and Economics, 2002, p. 798 et seq.; *Easterbrook/Fischel* 38 Stan. L. Rev. 271, 273 et seq. (1986). From the point of view of German doctrinal discourse regarding the GmbH, see, for instance, *Fleischer* Münchener Komm. z. GmbHG, 2010, Introduction margin no. 37 et seq.; *Wicke* Komm. z. GmbHG, 2nd ed., 2011, Introduction margin no. 10.

4 In some legal systems, it is sufficient for the shareholders themselves to choose a *closed corporation status*. See, for example, the Companies Act 2006 for the United Kingdom, which restricts itself to excluding a public offer of the shares for a private *company limited by shares* (in contrast to a PLC) (s. 755 Companies Act 2006). Others, by contrast, stipulate objective preconditions for access to this form of corporation, such as a maximum number of shareholders, see for example Art. L223–3 C.com. for the S.à.r.l. for France (maximum of 100 shareholders) or Sec. 342(a)(1) Del. Gen. Corp. L. for Delaware (maximum of 30 shareholders).

5 See in particular in this context the Revised Uniform Limited Liability Company Act (2006) and the Delaware Limited Liability Company Act, 6 Del. C. Sec. 18–101 et seq. (in force since 1 October 1992).

ment: shareholders do not have the possibility of easily leaving the closed corporation and "cashing in" their shares.[6] This increases the desire for active involvement in the closed corporation, particularly since directors' salaries are often the most important form of remuneration for corporate participation.[7] However, from an economic point of view, this has a negative consequence: any advantages of specialisation through the separation of tasks and roles between the shareholders and directors are lost. Shareholders, who invest a significant part of their assets in the closed corporation, are less efficient risk-bearers than well-diversified shareholders of public corporations.[8] On the other hand, the restricted group of shareholders also bears economic advantages: negotiations and agreements between the participants are conducted at relatively low cost.[9]

Unsurprisingly, there is no single form of closed corporation in actual practice. Company founders and established firms alike – both small and large – use this legal form. Moreover, a closed corporation can be structured in either a more "personalized" way or in a more capitalistic way; it can be used as either a single-member corporation or as a group subsidiary; it can operate on either a for-profit or charitable basis, etc. Given this broad array of possibilities, the question necessarily arises whether the rules for this corporate form should be guided by a general concept and, if so, which. A closed corporation is often used in practice as a legal form for new or small/medium-sized firms interested in limiting their shareholders' personal liability.[10] In a closed corporation, the number of shareholders is comparatively low, and a change in shareholders seldom occurs. Consequently, the founder's perspective is of central importance for our investigation. It is also appropriately at the forefront of the Commission's proposal for an SPE Statute. This has consequences for the types of shareholders in question with respect to their behavior, their needs and the regulations meaningful for them. Facts and circumstances concerning groups of companies therefore will not be examined here. However, focus on the founder's perspective should in

6 Hence, they do not have a liquid exit option as described in *Hirschman* Exit, Voice, and Loyalty: Responses to Decline in Firms, Organizations, and States, 1970.

7 See *Bainbridge* supra (note 3), p. 798 et seq.

8 See *Easterbrook/Fischel* 38 Stan. L. Rev. 271, 274 (1986). However, the directors' risk aversion can also have (economic) advantages: directors may well then avoid entering into risks endangering the continued existence of the corporation and damaging the position of the corporation's creditors – at least at a stage in which substantive insolvency is still (far) away (see, by contrast, Chapter 2 B.III. regarding risk incentives close to insolvency).

9 See *Bainbridge* supra (note 3), p. 798; *Easterbrook/Fischel* 38 Stan. L. Rev. 271, 274 (1986).

10 Empirical evidence, for instance, on the use of the German GmbH, is provided by *Fleischer* supra (note 3), Introduction GmbHG margin no. 198 et seq.

no way involve a one-sided view of the regulations on closed corporations towards the needs of founders of corporations. Instead, these regulations must – at least in principle – also be suitable for enabling and structuring other uses of the closed corporation.

B Types of Conflicts (of Interest)

The clearest difference between open, capital market-oriented corporations and closed corporations is found in their respective types of conflicts (of interest).[11] The main findings of economic research on public corporations include the separation between the ownership (shareholder position) and control (management, directors) involving divergent interests and conflicts of interest that produce costs for the corporation.[12] Shareholders' interests are different from those of executive board members: shareholders incur costs by supervising the latter – e.g., establishing a supervisory board. Executive board members undertake expensive measures to present themselves as loyal agents. Finally, residual losses inevitably accrue which cannot be eliminated by increased supervision and self-committing signals.[13] These problems increase with larger numbers of shareholders, because it becomes more difficult for shareholders to coordinate their actions in relation to directors.

I Shareholders – Directors

Conflicts between shareholders and directors rarely occur in closed corporations. To the extent shareholders manage a business themselves, as is the case in four-fifths of all German limited liability corporations (GmbH),[14] opposing interests between shareholders and directors play either no role at all or – in the case of companies where not all of the shareholders are directors – only a limited role. In addition, a smaller group of shareholders can coordinate its actions more easily and is therefore better able to assert its interests against the directors.[15] Due to the shareholders' easier monitoring of the directors, specialised su-

11 For an overview of the economic structure of closed corporations, see *McCahery/Vermeulen* Corporate Governance of Non-Listed Companies, 2008, p. 6 et seq.
12 The seminal work is *Berle/Means* The Modern Corporation and Private Property, 1932.
13 *Jensen/Meckling* 3 J. Fin. Econ. 306 (1976).
14 *Fleischer* supra (note 3), Introduction GmbHG margin no. 203.
15 See *Bainbridge* supra (note 3), p. 798.

pervisory organs, such as a supervisory board, are seldom found in closed corporations.[16]

From a regulatory point of view, conflicts with shareholders therefore also carry less weight as regards directors' positions in closed corporations compared to public corporations. The primary focus, in closed corporations, is instead the duty-bound intermediary role of the directors (if the shareholders make use of the possibility of delegated management) between the different participants in the enterprise, particularly as between the shareholders and the corporation's creditors.[17]

II Shareholders – Shareholders

The relationship between and among shareholders themselves and the conflicts resulting from this relationship are critically important for closed corporations.[18] This relationship is primarily associated with opposing interests between *majority* and *minority shareholders*. In a closed corporation, minority shareholders often find themselves in a particularly vulnerable position because – as mentioned – there is no liquid market to value their shares and hence no place where the shares may be sold. Any share valuation must be undertaken outside an organised capital market on the basis of business valuation methods. It is well-known that these involve significant uncertainties. Hence, a simple exit from the corporation at a market price is impossible. Furthermore, the (majority) shareholder is not disciplined by otherwise applicable capital market regulations and – in an extreme case – by the threat of a public takeover of the corporation.[19]

As a result, conflicts between majority and minority shareholders particularly arise on the issues of open and hidden distributions (of profits) and other forms of remuneration. Typical examples are unbalanced business transactions which the corporation concludes with the majority shareholder (at the majority shareholder's own instigation), inflated directors' salaries which a majority shareholder "awards" him- or herself or the termination of a director's contract of employment with a minority shareholder.[20] Whilst the small number of share-

16 See *Easterbrook/Fischel* 38 Stan. L. Rev. 271, 278 (1986).

17 For more detail, see Chapter 4.

18 For more detail, see Chapter 3.

19 On the disciplinary effect of public takeovers, see *Manne* 73 J. Pol. Econ. 110 (1965); *Tirole* The Theory of Corporate Finance, 2006, p. 425 et seq.

20 For other forms/techniques of the exploitation of minority shareholders, see *McCahery/Vermeulen* supra (note 11), p. 46.

holders and the resulting (comparatively) low costs of negotiations between the participants promote the minority shareholders' possibilities of self-protection (e.g., in the form of contractually negotiated management or veto rights)[21] this self-protection remains inadequate for a number of reasons.[22] Future conflicts are frequently not anticipated at the time of formation or when shares are acquired. Often, risks are underestimated. Finally, in close personal (family) relationships, there can be a tendency not to proactively address and clarify potential points of dispute. Such clarification requires (financial) resources, which may not be sufficiently available in an individual case. Social codes of conduct, which operate more strongly in closed corporations than in public corporations, also do not offer reliable protection. For this reason, mandatory legal rules may be necessary as protective instruments and advisable in order to close gaps in both the private autonomous self-protection and the social convention structure. These mandatory rules include the important fiduciary duties developed in both continental European and certain Anglo-American legal systems.[23]

Even if possible "exploitation" of minority shareholders by majority shareholders represents the principal shareholder-shareholder problem in closed corporations, opportunistic conduct by a minority of shareholders also occurs and should be examined. For instance, a majority shareholder may have made considerable firm-specific investments, but a minority shareholder may be able to block necessary entrepreneurial decisions, for example, by exercising negotiated veto rights or majority requirements in the articles of association.[24] In this way, special advantages can be obtained. The fiduciary duties just mentioned therefore also constitute – and rightly so – a corrective in the opposite direction. Rights of dissolution or tender as instruments of minority protection should, in the absence of an explicit contractual regulation, be derived (if at all) only by way of exception through supplementary contractual interpretation.[25]

---

21 See *Easterbrook/Fischel* 38 Stan. L. Rev. 271, 279 (1986); *Bainbridge* supra (note 3), p. 806 et seq.

22 See *Fleischer* supra (note 3), Introduction GmbHG margin no. 203.

23 See *Bainbridge* supra (note 3), p. 816 et seq; *Fleischer* supra (note 3), Introduction GmbHG margin no. 139 et seq., 292. Even today the United Kingdom does not acknowledge intershareholder fiduciary duties as such, see *Northern Counties Securities, Ltd v Jackson & Steeple, Ltd* [1974] 1 W.L.R. 1133, 1144; *Davies* Introduction to Company Law, 2nd ed., 2010, p. 238. For a discussion on the capacity to contract out of corporate law fiduciary duties, see *Hellgardt* FS Hopt, 2010, p. 765 (opting out of fiduciary duties should not be considered invalid *per se*).

24 See *Fleischer* supra (note 3), Introduction GmbHG margin no. 276.

25 See *Bainbridge* supra (note 3), p. 825 et seq.; *Easterbrook/Fischel* 38 Stan. L. Rev. 271, 286 et seq. (1986); *McCahery/Vermeulen* supra (note 11), p. 52 et seq.

Deadlock situations between shareholders constitute distinct conflict risks specific to closed corporations. Such situations are particularly found in cases of equal representation (i.e., a 50 – 50 corporation) and frequently have a family background, which in itself creates conflict. From a legal point of view, the corporation's capacity to act must *prima facie* be ensured by supplementary provisions in case there is a lack of contractual regulations/mechanisms to resolve the situation.[26] On the other hand, it may well be a rational strategy for shareholders to make the resolution of deadlock situations more difficult in order to reduce the likelihood that a corresponding situation arises at all.[27] Legal intervention *ex post* then has undesirable *ex ante* effects for other cases.

III Shareholders – Third Parties (in particular Creditors)

A third field of conflict affecting closed corporations in the same way as open corporations – albeit with a different slant – exists between the shareholders of the corporation and third parties, particularly the corporation's creditors. In this context, the core problem is limited shareholders' liability. It results in misguided incentives for the shareholder(s) if they only (still) have a small amount of equity capital invested in the firm. These misguided incentives are a consequence of asymmetrical participation in profits and losses: the shareholders only bear losses up to the amount of the (remaining) equity capital, whereas they also benefit in full from the profits. Consequently, shareholders may make risky investments with negative net present value but with potentially high returns on the upside. In addition, shareholders may decline to make investments with a positive net present value (i.e., the problem of underinvestment) that would strengthen the equity capital position but which would nonetheless offer a less attractive upside compared to riskier investments.[28]

As the misguided incentives result from the shareholders' participation in a corporation's profits and losses under corporate law, the problem becomes particularly acute where the shareholders (can) strongly influence management, i.e., in case of closed corporations.[29] In public corporations, directors typically

26 See *Fleischer* supra (note 3), Introduction GmbHG margin no. 296.

27 See *Easterbrook/Fischel* 38 Stan. L. Rev. 271, 287 (1986).

28 *Jensen/Meckling* 3 J. Fin. Econ. 306, 335 et seq. (1976); *Myers* 5 J. Fin. Econ. 147 (1977). For more detail, see Chapter 5.

29 This incentive is mitigated in "good" times when the shareholders of a closed corporation have invested a large proportion of their assets in the corporation, and are likely to lose them in

are not the influential shareholders and usually have a greater degree of management independence secured by legal rules. Directors of public corporations only have a risk incentive to the extent that their interests coincide with those of the shareholders.[30]

The legal instruments used to counteract the risk-shifting incentive of shareholders of a closed corporation are varied. Primarily, creditors themselves are able to take corresponding precautions through covenants in loan contracts.[31] In addition, statutory or judge-made liability rules, particularly shareholder liability imposed by "piercing the corporate veil" in favour of certain creditors or groups of creditors,[32] may be put in place. This is especially sensible in the case of closed corporations for which the positive welfare effects of limited liability are significantly less compared with public corporations.[33] Director liability for management decisions harmful to creditors is also conceivable.[34] Ultimately, the initiation of insolvency proceedings usually leads to a loss of control over the corporation's assets and thus to the removal of the risk-shifting incentive for the shareholders/directors.[35]

Apart from the corporation's creditors, other third parties are also potential "conflict partners" of the shareholders of a closed corporation, or of the corporation itself. This especially applies to staff employed in the corporation. It is well-known that a controversial discussion has been waged with respect to public corporations regarding whether their primary aim is to increase the value of shareholders' assets or to improve the welfare of all parties affected by the corporation's activities.[36] In principle, the issue arises in a similar way in the case of closed corporations. However, it is usually mitigated in this context because the

---

"bad" times if and to the extent they are also personally liable for obligations of the corporation, e. g. because of guarantees.

30 On this problem, see *Davies* 7 Eur. Bus. Org. L. Rev. 301 (2006).

31 See *Tirole* supra (note 19), p. 103 et seq.; *Eidenmüller* Unternehmenssanierung zwischen Markt und Gesetz: Mechanismen der Unternehmensreorganisation und Kooperationspflichten im Reorganisationsrecht, 1999, p. 123 et seq.; *Servatius* Gläubigereinfluss durch Covenants: Hybride Finanzierungsinstrumente im Spannungsfeld von Fremd- und Eigenfinanzierung, 2008.

32 See *Hansmann/Kraakman* 100 Yale L. J. 1879 (1991); *Eidenmüller* JZ 2001, 1041, 1048 et seq.

33 See *McCahery* in: McCahery/Raaijmakers/Vermeulen, The Governance of Close Corporations and Partnerships: US and European Perspectives, 2004, p. 1, 4 et seq.; *Eidenmüller* JZ 2001, 1041, 1049.

34 See *Eidenmüller* ZIP 2007, 1729, 1732 et seq.

35 See *Eidenmüller* supra (note 31), p. 22 et seq.

36 See representatively *Romano* Foundations of Corporate Law, 1993, p. 179 et seq.; *Mayer* Firm Commitment: Why the corporation is failing us and how to restore trust in it, 2013, 27 et seq. et passim; *Mülbert* ZGR 1997, 129; *Eidenmüller* JZ 2001, 1041, 1043 et seq.

number of employees (per firm) is lower. Moreover, shareholders frequently invest a considerable proportion of their assets in the corporation and are more interested in the corporation in the broadest sense – including the avoidance of insolvency – compared to a shareholder with widely diversified investments focused exclusively on returns. If an employee is simultaneously a shareholder – where wages potentially fulfil the function of corporate return – the typical conflict also does not lie in the contrasting interests between work and capital, but rather between majority and minority shareholders. This regularly manifests itself in the director's termination of the employment relationship upon inducement by the majority shareholder.

C Goals, Contents and Forms of Regulation

If we wish to develop or propose rules for closed corporations, it is first necessary to determine the regulatory goals pursued. This then forms the basis for a discussion on the contents and forms of regulation with which to strive for these goals.

I Regulatory Goals

Regulatory goals seldom tend to be explicitly discussed in corporate law. If regulations are proposed, they are usually supported with arguments or evaluations that the proponent author intuitively considers plausible and persuasive. This, for instance, occurs when "protection of the individual", "protection of minorities" or "investor protection" are introduced as decisive "evaluation principles of corporate law" and taken as a basis for the analysis of individual regulatory issues.[37] Such evaluation principles are, however, very generic and therefore hardly selective. Without further specification or balancing against countervailing principles, they offer no guidance in an individual case. Finally, they presuppose what should be proven (e.g. why, under what preconditions and in which respect shall minorities be protected?). Succinctly put, the evaluation principles do not provide the normative justification required. The same applies to the use of "imperatives", which are occasionally applied to attempt to end the search for and discussion about the evaluative bases of private law regulation by means of

37 See *Wiedemann* Gesellschaftsrecht, Volume I, 1980, Chapter 3 (p. 355 et seq.).

a formula.[38] It is equally unconvincing, for instance, to concentrate solely on whether a certain rule is or will presumably be successful in regulatory competition. For national legislation, this success may be a relevant factor for consideration in order to avoid a loss in "market shares". Nevertheless, the mere reference to a situation that forces the lawmaker to act in a specific way does not provide a convincing argument or a sound basis for a particular regulation.

By contrast, it is more fruitful to answer normative questions in corporate law with a view towards the welfare economic consequences of certain legal regulations.[39] This yardstick has a clear – if admittedly not undisputed – philosophical basis (rule utilitarianism),[40] and in many cases – although by no means *all* cases – provides a comparatively distinctive analysis and evaluation of the consequences of different regulatory arrangements. The plausibility and convincing force of this yardstick originate from its universal approach, which does not favor any particular stakeholder group, from the *prima facie* attractive aim of increasing welfare or avoidance of waste and from the compatibility of this aim with the promotion of private contracting (see below). The "impartiality" of this approach to issues of distribution can be justified by the consideration that tax and social welfare law constitute a far more suitable mechanism for the creation of desired distribution patterns than private law.[41]

Focus on the welfare economic consequences of certain legal rules in no way means that, for instance, considerations of fairness must remain disregarded. Market participants are usually also – and sometimes quite especially – motivated by such considerations and therefore include them in their preferences and utility functions.[42] However, the contents of the respective conceptions of fairness usually differ considerably, and their motivational force is likewise specific to each individual.[43] This particularly applies to substantive criteria determining

---

38 *Grigoleit* Anforderungen des Privatrechts an die Rechtstheorie, in: Jestaedt/Lepsius, Rechtswissenschaftstheorie, 2008, p. 51, 53 et seq.

39 For an overview of the increased importance of the economic efficiency aim in corporate law and in corporate legal scholarship, see *Fleischer/Zimmer* in: Fleischer/Zimmer, Effizienz als Regelungsziel im Handels- und Wirtschaftsrecht, 2008, p. 9, 21 et seq., 28 et seq., 36 et seq., 41 et seq.

40 See *Eidenmüller* Effizienz als Rechtsprinzip: Möglichkeiten und Grenzen der ökonomischen Analyse des Rechts, 3rd ed., 2005, p. 173 et seq, 175 et seq, 213 et seq.

41 *Shavell* 71 Am. Econ. Rev. (Papers & Proc.) 414 (1982); *Kaplow/Shavell* 23 J. Legal Stud. 667 (1994).

42 From the extensive (economic) literature see, for instance, *Fehr/Klein/Schmidt* 75 Econometrica 121 (2007); *Fehr/Schmidt* 114 Q. J. Econ. 817 (1999); *Falk/Fehr/Fischbacher* 62 Games & Econ. Behav. 287 (2008).

43 See *Bühring-Uhle/Eidenmüller/Nelle* Verhandlungsmanagement, 2009, p. 33 et seq., 65 et seq.

fair distribution or a fair result.[44] Nevertheless, there are certain principles of almost universal acceptance. These include, for example, the maxim that results detrimental to one party are only legitimate if that party has had the chance to make its point in the decision-making process (i.e., the principle of "procedural fairness"). While evaluating different legal regulations, these principles or others like them can and should probably be taken into consideration because of their broad prevalence as best expressing the presumed intent of the parties. This is even more applicable if a participant in negotiations over corresponding rules has specifically referred to or emphasised a corresponding principle.

If we can agree on the goal that, for the conception of corporate law regulations, the primary consideration is their welfare economic consequences, this results in a series of recommendations, including how to address the aforementioned conflicts (of interest) in a closed corporation. Generally, a legal system should endeavour to limit the costs associated with such conflicts as much as possible. Such costs reduce the aggregate net welfare position of all participants. Likewise, it is also a sensible recommendation to keep the (transaction) costs associated with the formation of a corporation, its business activities and the transfer of shares as low as possible. These costs also reduce welfare. This policy recommendation, however, is particularly important due to the significance of transaction costs for negotiation and contracting processes of the market participants. We now discuss this in greater detail.

II Contents of Regulation

1 Promotion of Private Autonomous Arrangements

It has already been mentioned that, in the case of closed corporations, negotiations and agreements between the shareholders are generally easier to consummate due to the comparatively small group of shareholders. Such negotiations and agreements are very important for a welfare-increasing allocation of rights and duties, since private autonomous arrangements tend to result in an optimal allocation of resources (maximising welfare).[45] If a stakeholder originally has a legal position of lesser value to him than to another, the latter will purchase this position for a certain price, just as goods are traded on product markets.

---

44 See, for instance, *Brams/Taylor* Fair Division: From Cake-Cutting to Dispute Resolution, 1996; *Duve/Eidenmüller/Hacke* Mediation in der Wirtschaft: Wege zum professionellen Konfliktmanagement, 2nd ed., 2011, p. 213 et seq.

45 *Coase* 3 J.L. & Econ. 1 (1960).

This assessment presupposes that the participants behave rationally with the aim of maximising utility, i.e., that their actions fundamentally correspond to the general economic concept of *homo oeconomicus*.[46] Undoubtedly, this is not always the case. In particular, cognitive psychological research has identified numerous forms and phenomena of systematically irrational human behaviour, including in the business sphere.[47] Notwithstanding this, it is correct at the outset in precisely this context to follow the general concept of *homo oeconomicus*, i.e., the rational businessman, for two reasons: (1) the reality of this type of person (business people typically act in a predominantly rational way and "know what they are doing"), and (2) such a normative assumption also has desired economic effects in the long term, because it "encourages" rationality. However, the legal system must then react to systematic deficits in rationality if they are widespread and have grave consequences for the parties affected in any individual case. We will return to this later.[48]

As negotiation processes between the affected parties tend to result in economically sensible solutions, corporate law regulations should, in principle, not be mandatory, but optional (default rules).[49] Arrangements that correspondingly increase welfare are only possible if the participants can choose a regulation which differs from the statutory position. Mandatory corporate law regulations must therefore be the exception requiring specific justification (discussed in more detail below). In addition, the law should support the negotiation processes of participants by reducing their costs.[50] In this context, provisions on the formation of a corporation and on the structure of its articles of association, for example, are relevant alongside those provisions on the attribution of corporation-related conduct in legal transactions and on the transfer of shares. Potential benefits of cooperation can be canceled out by (excessive) transaction costs. The underlying rationale of the recommendation here is to reduce such costs. Not only

46 On this (critically), *Eidenmüller* supra (note 40), p. 28 et seq.

47 For an overview see *Kahneman* 150 J. Inst. Theor. Econ. (JITE) 18 (1994); monographically *Kahneman* Thinking, Fast and Slow, 2011; from the German literature see, for example, *Bühring-Uhle/Eidenmüller/Nelle* supra (note 43), p. 38 et seq.; *Eidenmüller* JZ 2005, 216, 218 et seq.; *Fleischer/Schmolke/Zimmer* in: Fleischer/Zimmer, Beitrag der Verhaltensökonomie (Behavioral Economics) zum Handels- und Wirtschaftsrecht, 2011, p. 9, 17 et seq.; *Altmann/Falk/Marklein* in: Fleischer/Zimmer, supra (note 39), p. 63 et seq.; *Eidenmüller* JZ 2011, 814, 816 et seq.

48 In this context, (mandatory) rules on severance settlement and termination rights particularly come into consideration as regulatory instruments.

49 *Easterbrook/Fischel* The Economic Structure of Corporate Law, 1991, p. 15 et seq., 22 et seq. For a historising analytical reconstruction of the "contractualisation" of corporate law, see *Hansmann/Kraakman* FS Hopt, 2010, p. 747.

50 See *Eidenmüller* supra (note 40), p. 64.

by their very nature do costs reduce welfare, they may also prevent the creation of useful party arrangements.[51]

2 Replication of Hypothetical Negotiation Solutions

In many constellations, such private arrangements will nevertheless be impossible to reach and will simply not arise due to prohibitively high anticipated transaction costs. An example would be potential agreements between the shareholders of a closed corporation and its creditors on the issue of whether – and, as the case may be, under what preconditions – the former should be personally liable for the corporation's debts by way of exception. In the case of public corporations, supplementary agreements between shareholders with diversified holdings can fail to be concluded due to high transaction costs. What should corporate law regulations look like in this case *as regards content?*

To start, the issue of the parties' "implicit will" will be raised in this context. It may have been only insufficiently expressed in the corporation's articles of association. Can a plan of regulation be explained that is at least rooted in a private autonomous decision by the parties? If this question must be answered in the negative, then in a second step it is helpful to consider a hypothetical negotiation solution: what would prudent parties have agreed to if they had been able to conclude an agreement?[52] This question reflects the normative general concept of *homo oeconomicus* (rational parties) referenced above, and which can – usually – be considered a reasonable assumption of behaviour for participants in business life or in the context of corporate law. However, the fewer the number of participants in a particular case whose behaviour corresponds to this general concept – for whatever reason –, the more important the hypothetical will of precisely *these* participants will be – and not that of the *homo oeconomicus.*[53] However, this is the exception and not the rule, as already discussed.

In order to answer the question about a hypothetical agreement of rational parties, a glance at usual corporate law problem solutions in similar cases can be helpful. For instance, a party agreement may be lacking in a "small" closed corporation, whereas it may be concluded in a "large" one where costs are compa-

51 However, these potential losses of allocation efficiency cannot be greater than the transaction costs themselves. The latter therefore caps the former.

52 *Eidenmüller* supra (note 40), p. 65 et seq.; *Eidenmüller* JZ 2001, 1041, 1043; *Easterbrook/Fischel* supra (note 49), p. 15; *Cheffins* supra (note 3), p. 264 et seq.

53 *Eidenmüller* supra (note 40), p. 456 et seq.

ratively less important.[54] The question then is: what can we learn from the practice of the latter for the former?

It is easy to see that the model of a "hypothetical contract" takes into consideration the regulatory goal of increasing welfare. At the same time, it must be emphasised that this only constitutes a statement about the *contents of regulation.* But it in no way constitutes a statement about the mandatory or optional character of a regulation. If private autonomous agreements, for example, fail as a result of prohibitively high transaction costs, this supports structuring legal rules in ways where the effect of a (hypothetical) agreement to promote welfare is achieved. However, this does not mean that the law should in principle make actual agreements completely impossible by mandatory regulation. Whether mandatory provisions are justified in an individual case is a separate issue from the content of these provisions and must be addressed separately.

III Forms of Regulation

1 Mandatory, Default and Enabling Rules

Analytically, it is initially helpful to distinguish between mandatory, default and enabling rules. If the object of the present investigation is the provisions for the closed corporation (in Europe), mandatory rules are those which automatically apply *when* the founders have decided in favour of the legal form created by these provisions. The relevant rules are therefore only mandatory within the framework of this legal form. Their choice as such, i.e., the formation of a corresponding corporation, is, by contrast, free. In this sense, we can say that mandatory corporate law is optional at a meta-level if and to the extent entrepreneurs can choose between different corporate forms to realize their entrepreneurial activities.[55] Non-negotiable issues on the primary level have optional character at the meta-level.

Default rules, by contrast, are rules which can be contracted away under private autonomy without further ado. Such rules inform about tried and tested patterns of regulation, relieve the parties of the necessity of having to contractually agree on every detail and fill gaps in such agreements.[56] The distinction from enabling rules is as yet unclear. The difference is frequently seen in default rules applying if and to the extent there has not been an opt-out, whereas enabling pro-

---

54 See *Cheffins* supra (note 3), p. 273 et seq.

55 See *Armour/Hansmann/Kraakman* in: Kraakman et al., supra (note 1), p. 22 et seq; *Bachmann* JZ 2008, 11, 13, 15 et seq.

56 See *Fleischer* ZHR 168 (2004), 673, 692.

visions require a conscious opt-in by the user.[57] Occasionally, this is also expressed in terminology where default rules are considered to have a "presumptive" character while enabling rules have a "permissive" character.[58] Substantively, the core of the issue is that enabling rules open up (new) structural possibilities for the participants which they would not otherwise have. If, for example, there is a rule under which several directors are entitled to represent the corporation together unless the articles of association provide otherwise, this would be a default provision in the sense just described. By contrast, a provision under which a corporation can establish a supervisory board and vest it with competences through the articles of association would have an enabling character.

Now we may ask whether, in substantive terms, both forms of rule should not, in any case, lead to the same results. In other words, is it not irrelevant whether the participants have to "opt in" or "opt out" of a particular rule? From what we have already discussed, it should be clear that the answer is "no". For one, (prohibitively high) transaction costs can lead to an original regulation remaining in place even if it does not maximise welfare. In addition, this result can also be the consequence of psychological effects. There is evidence that we value goods higher if we possess them than if we do not possess them (i. e., so-called endowment effects).[59] This can have the consequence that – using the aforementioned example – a supervisory board is not established if the rule is enabling, but it is established if provided for as a default rule. If the legislature must decide whether to make a provision a default or an enabling rule, these effects must be taken into account. If the correction of rules is unlikely due to high transaction costs, the decision between *opt in* and *opt out* should be made on the basis of considerations regarding a hypothetical negotiation solution. As the users of legal forms have different preferences, the decisive factor should sensibly be what the majority would (hypothetically) agree on.[60] If endowment effects are involved, this calculus cannot, however, be made. The regulatory aim of increasing welfare does not offer a clear solution here.[61]

High transaction costs are one reason for the content of rules to be orientated towards a hypothetical negotiation solution, but they do not justify mandatory provisions. It is therefore incorrect to say that external effects are not an argument for mandatory rules if the participants can negotiate about their contents at

---

57 See *Cheffins* supra (note 3), p. 218 et seq; *Bachmann* JZ 2008, 11, 14 et seq. ("soft option models").
58 See *Cheffins* supra (note 3), p. 218 et seq., 250 et seq., 257 et seq.
59 See *Eidenmüller* supra (note 40), p. 125 et seq. with further references.
60 See *Cheffins* supra (note 3), p. 253 et seq., 262.
61 See *Eidenmüller* JZ 2005, 216, 223 et seq.; *Eidenmüller* JZ 2011, 814, 820.

low transaction costs and that mandatory provisions are justified if this is not the case.[62] If the participants cannot negotiate on rule contents due to prohibitively high transaction costs, this is a good reason to formulate such contents in accordance with the hypothetical result of a hypothetical negotiation. However, this does not result in an argument for the mandatory character of such contents.

This raises the question under which circumstances and from which viewpoints mandatory provisions can be justified, if at all, in the corporate context.[63] In light of the regulatory aim formulated above, the following general guideline can be defined in this context: disruptions to private autonomous negotiation processes which lead to welfare-reducing arrangements can be a compelling reason for mandatory rules.[64] This affects the constellation in which a participant accepts or would accept solutions not in his or her interest due to information deficits, irrationality and/or negotiation weakness.[65] Information economics has shown that in certain circumstances, no information – or perhaps the "wrong" information – might be communicated, and this serves to justify mandatory duties of information.[66] Occasionally, however, negotiated contents are not optimal because participants are rationally uninformed (i.e., calculatingly or deliberately uninformed) and do not make their contractual decision dependent on quality characteristics.[67] Finally, as already discussed, (cognitive) psychological research has revealed numerous phenomena which lead to conclusions about limits to our rationality, or even systematically irrational behaviour under certain circumstances. For example, our capacity to forecast complex causal processes is limited, and we underestimate future risks.[68] This is one reason to take a critical view of corporate charter provisions that are relevant for the protection of minority shareholders (such as exclusion and settlement clauses) and, if necessary, to correct them by means of mandatory rules.[69]

---

62 See *Cheffins* supra (note 3), p. 245 et seq. Contradictory *Bainbridge* supra (note 3), p. 840 et seq. (mandatory rules justified where there are external effects – high transaction costs are an argument for default, not mandatory rules).

63 Monographically see *Haberer* Zwingendes Kapitalgesellschaftsrecht: Rechtfertigung und Grenzen, 2009.

64 See *Bachmann* JZ 2008, 11, 12 with further references.

65 *Bainbridge* supra (note 3), p. 840, in this context correctly states that one of the parties may be "... demonstrably unable to protect itself through bargaining ...".

66 See *Coffe* 70 Va. L. Rev. 717 (1984). For the contrary position, see *Easterbrook/Fischel* 70 Va. L. Rev. 669 (1984).

67 See *Akerlof* 84 Q. J. Econ. 488 (1970).

68 See *Fleischer* supra (note 3), Introduction GmbHG margin no. 279 et seq.

69 See *Eidenmüller* JZ 2005, 216, 223. On expulsion and valuation clauses see *Schmolke* ECFR 2012, 380.

Even if private autonomous negotiation processes are *not* disturbed, there will usually be (constitutional) regulations within a particular legal system that override corporate law and from which justifications for mandatory rules can be derived in an individual case. In this context, we see the relevance of the theory articulated in Chapter 1, namely, that the regulatory environment is important for the creation of rules for the closed corporation. Using a random case: whether the exclusion of a shareholder is validly stipulated in the articles of association when he reaches the age of 75 is always a function of the contingent, albeit overriding, framework conditions for the implementation of rules for a closed corporation in a particular legal system.

Just as mandatory rules may be optional at a meta-level if the parties have available alternative legal forms, forms that combine both enabling and mandatory rules are conceivable and practical. Consider the previous example of a provision permitting the establishment of a supervisory board for a closed corporation. If its competences are not subject to the structure of the articles of association, but are stipulated as binding, this is an enabling rule which has a mandatory content if the rule is chosen.[70]

2 Rules and Principles

A further analytical distinction is important: the distinction between rules and principles. Until now, we have only generally referred in non-technical terms to "rules" for closed corporations. Rules are provisions containing a clear stipulation of legal consequences, without exception, for a specific factual situation. In this sense, rules apply unconditionally and have an "all-or-nothing" character.[71] By contrast, principles are "precepts of optimisation": they impose an obligation to achieve a certain legal goal as far as possible, but must be balanced against countervailing principles.[72] Rule-like stipulations of legal consequences which apply without exception cannot be derived from a principle. Rules can be mandatory or default provisions. The same applies to principles. It would therefore be wrong to assume that rules always apply in a mandatory way and principles are always optional. The two forms of categorisation (mandatory/optional – rule/principle) are independent of one another.

The circumstances under which a legislator should choose a certain regulatory technique differ from case to case. The all-or-nothing character of rules ar-

70 See *Bachmann* JZ 2008, 11, 15 et seq., in this context discussing a "stricter option model".
71 See *Hart* The Concept of Law, 1961.
72 *Alexy* Begriff und Geltung des Rechts, 1992, p. 120.

gues in favour of only using this form – but then without exception – where clear, unconditional stipulations of legal consequences for a specific factual setting can be made and, importantly, where legal certainty and transparency play an important role. With principles, the necessary balancing of interests must, by contrast, be undertaken by the courts in case of dispute and is naturally less foreseeable. The amount of nominal capital to be raised by the closed corporation and the way in which it must be raised and maintained are exemplary questions that can and should be stipulated by clear rules. By contrast, the issues of whether, under what preconditions and in what manner a shareholder should participate in restructuring measures in an existential corporate crisis on the basis of fiduciary duties (towards the corporation or the other shareholders) are issues of specifying and balancing principles (fiduciary duties vs. risk mitigation and limitation of the shareholder's own [financial] commitment).[73]

Given the prominent role of the courts in the defining and balancing of principles, it is also relevant for the choice of a suitable regulatory strategy whether, and to what extent, a specific jurisdiction has a professional court system to handle such tasks. The legal system and culture more generally also play an important role: in many continental European legal systems, the role of the courts continues to be significantly different than in Anglo-Saxon legal systems. Continental European statutory law and Anglo-Saxon case-law and policy-making characterise the respective systems and the courts' understanding of their own role.[74]

3 Rules and Standards

A similar distinction as between rules and principles seems to exist with respect to rules and standards.[75] Standards would include, for example, provisions under which directors must apply the due care of a prudent businessman to their acts (or omissions). However, whereas principles primarily involve *the determination of legal consequences* in light of conflicting or competing principles,

73 However, the determination of fiduciary duties not only involves a weighing-up against countervailing principles on the level of legal consequences, but also the specification of an open and indefinite set of facts and circumstances at the factual level: fiduciary duties also have the character of standards, which will be discussed in the text below.

74 This naturally does not ignore the manifold convergent developments, including those under the influence of European law. However, judges in France or Germany continue to take a very different view of their role and task than do judges in the United Kingdom or in the United States.

75 See *Armour/Hansmann/Kraakman* in: Kraakman et al., supra (note 1), p. 35, 39 et seq.

standards instead concentrate on the *definition of facts and circumstances:* a comparatively open and indefinite set of relevant facts and circumstances must be applied to the elements of a specific individual case. However, this distinction in legal method should not cloud our view that specifying standards in detail, like the considered specification of principles, involves margins of discretion for those applying the law. In this context, too, the choice of the appropriate regulatory strategy is therefore, to some degree, a function of the relevant judicial system and, in particular, the professionalism and competence of the courts in formulating rules to develop the law.

Where the legislature or the parties wish to make stipulations concerning diverse future situations, there is, however, often no sensible alternative to codifying a standard. In addition to the aforementioned yardstick for directors' liability, consider, for example, a provision which forces the parties to renegotiate their commitment to the corporation in case of a fundamental change of circumstances. From a technical view of the law, legal certainty can always be increased by combining a (vague) standard with specific examples of rules that provide more detail. If a standard is made mandatory law – as may be the case with principles – a further advantage is that circumvention is more difficult than with a rule that is narrowly limited to certain facts and circumstances.[76]

Certain legal provisions possess a hybrid character: they can be vague and require further precision both as regards facts and circumstances, as well as legal consequences. This particularly applies to *fiduciary duties*, which are significant components of the law on closed corporations: fiduciary duties simultaneously constitute standards and principles. Subsumable statements can only be won on this basis after further precision regarding facts and circumstances and consideration of conflicting principles. The same is more or less true for the *corporate law principle of equal treatment.*

4 Instructions to Regulate

Finally, we discuss a special form of regulation which the European legislature recently used in connection with the project for a "European private company" mentioned at the outset. This involves so-called "instructions to regulate". In the specific case of the SPE project, the shareholders must regulate certain questions/issues in the articles of association (Art. 4 Draft SPE Regulation). However, it is unclear whether and in what respect the fulfilment of this obligation is a pre-

76 See *Fleischer* ZHR 168 (2004), 673, 699.

condition for registration according to the Commission's Draft Regulation (see Art. 10 Draft SPE Regulation).[77]

At first glance, the purpose of such instructions to regulate appears to be the promotion of party arrangements, as previously described. In the particular context of the SPE project, this has the additional advantage of elegantly solving – by reference to stipulations of a firm's founders – the difficult problem of reaching agreement on single rules for particular issues that are applicable throughout Europe. Very generally, this regulatory technique is fair to the diversity of factual situations which arise in corporate law settings and does not display a tendency to maintain the status quo characteristic of optional statutory law.[78] We have already seen that there can be bias towards the status quo due to endowment effects.

However, the parties' obligation to achieve private autonomous regulations triggers transaction costs and forces them to become active in agreeing to regulations where the benefit of private contracting is relatively slight compared to the costs involved. For closed corporations, too, a "complete offer" of regulating provisions by the state legislature for the legal relations between the parties is therefore preferable. Blanket instructions to regulate are in any case not recommended. They are only justified if sample articles of association are at the same time made available. Such articles of association can be agreed upon at little cost. It must be ensured that their stipulation can irrefutably be presumed to fulfil the instructions to regulate in a legally valid way. In this way, sample articles of association can therefore – as with optional law – apply as fall-back or catch-all regulations.

5 Sample Articles of Association

Such sample articles of association come into consideration as a form of regulation regardless of the context of the regulation instructions provided for in the SPE Draft Regulation. If they are intended to have the "validity guarantee" described above, then the authorisation of the relevant competent state legislature must be obtained.[79] Different variations may be made available and encourage

77 The Commission seems to take the view that such an obstacle to registration does not exist: "However national law has to set out the sanctions of such omission or other breach of the Regulation" (COM(2008) 396, final of 25 June 2008, p. 6).

78 *Fleischer* ZHR 168 (2004), 673, 696.

79 A good example of this are the sample articles of association considered by the Reflection Group on the Future of EU Company Law as an annex to a proposed Directive on the introduction of a simplified single-member form of corporation in national law in the Member States. This

the parties to at least decide in favour of one of the variations.[80] In addition to the state legislature, private persons are likewise possible originators and sources of explanation for sample articles of association. Whilst these lack the state seal of approval, they are usually characterized by the cumulative experience of proven specialists involved in relevant work in this sphere.

D Results

1. The closed corporation is the object of this investigation. The comparative functional concept of the *closed* corporation is initially characterised by the general features of the corporation: legal personality, limited liability, transferability of shares, possibility of delegated management and ownership by the equity capital providers. It is also characterised by shares that are not publicly traded and which can be subjected to further restrictions on transfer. The conception of rules for the closed corporation must begin by taking into consideration this defined object of investigation and the numerous uses of the closed corporation, ranging from start-ups through medium-sized firms to joint ventures and group holding structures. However, this investigation concentrates on the founders' perspective.
2. The specific characteristics and the use of the *closed* corporation are reflected by the shift in the respective relevance of the individual conflicts of interest in comparison to capital market-oriented (public) corporations:
   a. Conflicts between shareholders and directors are not as strong in the closed corporation. Firstly, the management is often undertaken by the shareholders themselves and not delegated to third parties. Secondly, coordination is easier amongst a limited number of shareholders than in a public corporation.
   b. By contrast, conflicts between shareholders are more serious in the closed corporation. The position of minority shareholders becomes precarious because they regularly do not have a good exit option due to the lack of liquid transferability of the shares. This means that they are particularly exposed to the danger of exploitation by the majority shareholders. Conversely, there is the threat of opportunistic obstruction by minority shareholders who instrumentalise veto rights or majority re-

Directive is an alternative to the introduction of an SPE by a European Regulation. See Report of the Reflection Group on the Future of EU Company Law, Brussels, 5 April 2011, p. 66.

80 On the mechanisms of such "liberal paternalism" see, for example, *Eidenmüller* JZ 2011, 814, 816 et seq., 818 et seq.

quirements in the articles of association for their own special interests. The risk of such blockades is particularly present if there is disagreement in corporations with two equally strong shareholders ("50/50 corporation"). Finally, conflicts among shareholders in the closed corporation are very frequently triggered or intensified by difficult family or personal relationships between the shareholders.

c. Conflicts between shareholders and third parties, in particular creditors, are also accentuated in the closed corporation. As the shareholders often have a strong influence on the management or are themselves directors, misguided incentives due to limited liability and asymmetric participation in the profits and losses are strengthened. In the closed corporation, there is therefore a stronger threat of risk shifts.

3. In this investigation, regulatory goals of the law on closed corporations are primarily addressed with regard to welfare economic considerations. For one thing, the aim is to limit the costs associated with the identified conflicts of interest. A second main aim is to minimise the transaction costs involved in the operation of a corporation or which arise upon its formation, in the course of its business activities or upon the transfer of shares.
4. Corporate law regulations should in principle be *default* rules and should encourage private autonomous arrangements, as these tend to produce an optimal allocation of resources (maximising welfare). This should also guide the content of the default rules: they should replicate hypothetical negotiation solutions. In choosing between default and *enabling* rules which open up structural opportunities for the participants without stipulating the structure to be used, legislation likewise can be guided by a hypothetical negotiation solution.
5. The economic general concept of *homo oeconomicus* is of limited use only where systematic rationality deficits arise and result in serious consequences for the parties affected in individual cases. *Mandatory* rules must be considered if disruptions to private autonomous negotiation processes lead to arrangements that reduce welfare. Mandatory rules can also be necessary in an individual case due to higher-ranking law.
6. It primarily depends on the relevant legal culture and the development of a legal system whether corporate law rules should technically stipulate a clear legal consequence for particular factual situations (*rule*) or impose an obligation to work towards a particular aim in the form of a *principle* and make the stipulation of the legal consequence dependent on a balancing with conflicting principles. On the facts and circumstances side, too, the application of the law in the form of *standards* can be made more flexible with open and indefinite provisions. Where the development of the legal

and judicial systems so allow, the use of principles and standards tends to permit (more) suitable solutions in an individual case. Foreseeability can be heightened by a hybrid structure, such as the enumeration of exemplary cases in a standard.

7. In view of the transaction costs involved, the lawmaker should avoid burdening the founders of corporations with *instructions to regulate* applying to particular issues in the articles of association. An offer of optional *sample articles of association* that cannot be challenged in court is preferable.

Chapter 3 Shareholder Conflicts in Closed Corporations*

Table of Contents

* The text is based on a draft by *Fleischer.*

A Problem Outline

I Internal Conflicts as the Cardinal Problem of Closed Corporations

Internal conflicts between majority and minority shareholders pose a cardinal problem for closed corporations. Their practical significance stems from the fact that the structural characteristics of a closed corporation leave minority shareholders particularly vulnerable to opportunistic behaviour by the majority shareholder.[1] These characteristics, the principle of capital majority for shareholders' resolutions and the almost ubiquitous appointment of the majority shareholder as director[2], put the minority shareholders' interests at risk of being overridden in favour of the majority [3]. The majority shareholder can use his extensive powers to enter into unbalanced transactions with the corporation, dismiss minority shareholders working in the firm, grant himself inflated directors' salaries and at the same time restrict the distribution of profits.[4] This often leaves minority shareholders only with the option of selling their shares to the majority shareholder at a significant discount.

While this chapter focuses on the opportunistic behaviour of the majority shareholder (see B. below), it also looks at the occasional use of exploitation strategies by a shareholder minority – *la tyrannie des faibles*[5]*:* minority shareholders may use their blocking minority or veto rights provided by the articles of association to obtain unjustified private benefits (see C. below). Finally, it also examines the conflict pattern created by deadlocks in closed corporations with equal shareholdings, which can lead to corporate organs being unable to fulfil their functions[6] (see D. below).[7]

---

1 See *Fleischer* Münchener Komm. z. GmbHG, 2010, Introduction, para. 276; comparing laws, *McCahery/Vermeulen* Corporate Governance of Non-listed Companies, 2008, p. 45 et seq.; extensively on the US viewpoint, *O'Neal/Thompson* Oppression of Minority Shareholders and LLC Members, 2nd ed., loose-leaf, April 2009; for a game theory approach *Mahoney* in: Mork, Concentrated Corporate Ownership, 2000, p. 177 under the heading "Trust and Opportunism in Close Corporations".

2 For the United States see *Illig* 56 Am. U. L. Rev. 275, 287 (2006): "Shareholders in close corporations typically serve simultaneously as both owners and managers."; for Great Britain *Davies* Introduction to Company Law, 2002, p. 217: "For this reason, we shall often refer to the majority shareholders in this chapter as 'controllers', so as to take account of the fact that the majority shareholders may express their powers either as shareholders or through the board."

3 For the French perspective see *Cozian/Viandier/Deboissy* Droit des sociétés, 25rd ed., 2012, para. 401: "Dans une société, comme dans une démocratie, les décisions se prennent à la majorité, devant laquelle la minorité doit s'incliner. [...] La minorité n'est pas pour autant livrée pieds et mains liés aux caprices de la majorité."

4 See *Fleischer* supra (note 1), Introduction GmbHG para. 291.

5 Taken from the vivid title of the Festschrift contribution by *Constantin* La tyrannie des faibles – De l'abus de minorité en droit des sociétés, Mélanges Y. Guyon, 2003, p. 313.

6 For further detail, see *Moll/Ragazzo* The Law of Closely Held Corporations, 2009, Chapter 7.02, 7–149 et seq.; for a pointed summary, *Wilcox v. Stiles*, 873 P.2d 1102, 1105 (Or. Ct. App. 1994): "[Deadlock] is the inaction which results when two equally powerful factions stake out opposing positions and refuse to budge."

7 For an overview of all three forms of conflict, see C*hampetier de Ribes-Justeau* Les abus de majorité, de minorité et d'égalité. Étude comparative des droits français et nord-américain des sociétés, 2010.

II Internal Conflicts as the Achilles' Heel of Closed Corporations

Internal conflicts between shareholders are the Achilles' heel of closed corporations.[8] Empirical evidence from both domestic and international sources suggests that a closed corporation is typically characterised by strong personal relationships: shareholders know each other well and are often related or close friends.[9] This is a considerable organisational advantage, because the greater cohesion and disciplining effect created by shared social norms reduces the costs of control and supervision.[10] In this context, sociologists point out that *relational governance* is an important element of *corporate governance.*[11] However, this advantage also has a dark side if the parties fall out: differences at a *personal* level can complicate *professional* interactions and may even endanger the corporation's existence. This has been demonstrated repeatedly in case law, where differences between feuding shareholders have resulted in disputes as bitter as between arguing spouses in an acrimonious divorce.[12]

---

8 Expressly *Neville* in: Krüger Andersen/Clausen/Skog, Shareholder Conflicts, 2006, p. 87, 91 under the subheading "Conflicts between shareholders – the Achilles heel of the SME"; most recently, *Wedemann* Gesellschafterkonflikte in geschlossenen Kapitalgesellschaften, 2013, p. 1 et seq.

9 See for instance *Bostock v. High Tech Elevator Indus.*, 616 A.2d 1314, 1320–21 (N.J. Super. Ct. App. Div. 1992): "A close corporation frequently originates in the context of personal relationship. Often such business entities are formed by family members or friends."

10 See *Mahoney* supra (note 1), p. 177: "The majority is constrained by the possibility of non-legal sanctions, including family or social disapproval and loss of reputation"; similarly *Neville* supra (note 8), p. 87, 89: "In family owned companies, the norms of equality, trust, altruism and loyalty normally guide the conduct of the owner-managers."; from a transaction cost analysis perspective, *Pollak* A Transaction Cost Approach to Families and Households, 23 J. Econ. Lit. 581, 591 et seq. (1985) under the subheading "Family Governance of Market-Oriented Work: Family Farms and Family-Managed Firms".

11 See for instance *Granovetter* Economic Action and Social Structure: The Problem of Embeddedness, 91 Am. J. Sociol. 481 (1985); *Nahapiet/Ghoshal* Social Capital, Intellectual Capital, and the Organizational Advantage, 23 Acad. Mgmt. Rev. 242 (1998); *Mustakallio/Autio/Zahra* Relational and Contractual Governance in Family Firms: Effects on Strategic Decision Making, 15 Fam. Bus. Rev. 205 (2002).

12 See *Gower/Davies* Principles of Modern Company Law, 9th ed., 2012, para. 20–11, p. 726: "Small companies emulate marriages in the frequency and bitterness of their breakdown."; for a more detailed comparison of family law and closed corporation law, see *Ertman* 36 Harv. C.R.-C.L. L. Rev. 79 (2001); also *Chiappinelli* 34 Ga. L. Rev. 699, 705 (2000): "I believe judges in these disputes use family law constructs to help them come to appropriate resolutions. The family law construct most analogous to many corporate law disputes is the issue of property distribution in marital dissolutions governed by statutes that typically direct the court to divide the property equitably [...]."

III Internal Conflicts: Gaps in Comparative Legal Research for Non-Listed Corporations

Internal conflicts between shareholders in *non-listed companies* have been neglected in comparative law research. In the past, comparativists have tended to focus mainly on *public companies*. This tendency is reflected, at least to some extent, in a ground-breaking collective work on the anatomy of corporate law compiled by an international research group.[13] Discussion on closed corporations focuses predominantly on creditor protection.[14] By contrast, the diverse layers of conflict between majority and minority shareholders are often only briefly touched upon.[15] However, given the different approaches to shareholder protection across jurisdictions, it is precisely this aspect of closed corporations that is the most difficult to structure in the comparative law context.[16] Taken together these difficulties have left closed corporations aptly characterised as "the orphan of corporate law"[17] in international debate.

---

13 See *Kraakman/Davies/Hansmann/Hertig/Hopt/Kanda/Rock* The Anatomy of Corporate Law, 2004; see the discussion in *Armour* 6 Eur. Bus. Org. L. Rev. 492 (2005); *Skeel* 113 Yale L.J. 1519 (2004); *Tröger* Die Aktiengesellschaft (AG) 2005, 627; *Wiedemann* ZGR 2006, 240; *Windbichler* FS Röhricht, 2005, p. 693; now *Kraakman/Armour/Davies/Enriques/Hansmann/Hertig/Hopt/Kanda/Rock* 2nd ed., 2009; see *Bachmann* ZHR 174 (2010), 486. Citations below refer to the 2nd ed.

14 For a valuable review, see the anthology of works collected by *Eidenmüller/Schön* The Law and Economics of Creditor Protection, 2008.

15 Early exceptions to this were provided by *Manne* 53 Va. L. Rev. 259 (1967); and *Easterbrook/Fischel* 38 Stan. L. Rev. 271 (1986); most recently in particular *McCahery/Vermeulen* Corporate Governance of Non-listed Companies, 2008; and *Neville/Sørensen* Company Law and SMEs, 2010.

16 See the introductory comments of the General Rapporteur P*erakis* Rights of Minority Shareholders, XVIth Congress of the International Academy of Comparative Law, 2002, p. 15: "In the matter of protection of shareholders the differences between the various legal systems are numerous. Whether they are also fundamental is open to debate. In any case, the whole issue is quite intricate, as there are no complete or coherent national "systems" of minority protection, and the relevant material is not easy to collect and to compare."

17 *Chayes* 73 Harv. L. Rev. 1532, 1533 (1959), drawing on US-American corporate law; once again taken up by *Wells* 5 Berkeley Bus. L.J. 263, 272 (2008).

B Protecting Minority Shareholders from Opportunistic Behaviour of the Majority Shareholder

I Structural Threats for Minority Shareholders

"Why minority rights?"[18] The answer to this question requires brief initial examination of the structural threats for minority shareholders in closed corporations that may arise either individually or in combination.[19]

1 Majority Principle for Shareholders' Resolutions

One of the key characteristics of corporate law is the principle of "*majority rule*" which merely requires a simple majority of votes for ordinary shareholders' resolutions. This principle is rooted in the capitalist tradition that resolutions are passed not by a headcount but rather according to the size of capital shares. The effect of the majority principle on internal power relationships is overwhelming: whoever possesses 51 % of the shares can make 100 % of the ordinary shareholders' resolutions.[20] It goes without saying that resolutions adopted under these conditions cannot guarantee the same level of fairness as a negotiated contract: "the majority shareholder does not pass a resolution but issues orders."[21] In light of this, the influential power of the shareholder majority requires legal limitations, for which very different legal concepts have developed in different jurisdictions.

2 Private Ordering for Internal Relationships

Internal relationships in closed corporations are characterised by considerable party autonomy. The primary source for their organisation is not statutory law,

---

18 Subheading in *Perakis* supra (note 16), p. 26.
19 See Chapter 2 B.II. above.
20 Similarly *Illig* 56 Am. U. L. Rev. 275, 289 (2006): "In a close corporation [...] the default allocation of power places near-complete control in the hands of any shareholders who hold more than fifty percent of the shares."; for further pointed comment bordering on cynical: *Humphrys v. Winous Co.*, 133 N.E.2d 780, 783 (Ohio 1956): "The old story, so often told, of a prominent Eastern newspaperman's reply to the question of what the shares in his corporation were worth, is very apt: 'There are 51 shares', said he, 'that are worth $ 250,000. There are 49 shares that are not worth a _'."
21 *Wiedemann* Gesellschaftsrecht, Volume I, 1980, p. 406.

but rather the articles of association.[22] This *wide-ranging autonomy of the articles of association* is in principle a welcome element of the closed corporation, and has also been promoted in the Draft SPE Regulation.[23] However, this expands the principle of majority rule under closed corporation law far beyond the majority rule principle for stock corporations:[24] Whereas small shareholders in a stock corporation are protected by mandatory law, at least in Germany according to § 23(5) Stock Corporation Act[25], no similar legislative safety net exists for GmbH-shareholders, giving the development of effective safeguards for minority shareholders even higher priority for GmbH law than stock corporation law.[26]

3 Stable Majority

Minority shareholders must also contend with the fact that the majority shareholder position rarely changes over time. For a listed corporation with a free float, "anybody is potentially a majority or a minority shareholder".[27] In a closed corporation, a similar change of roles is virtually unthinkable: legal power rests in the hands of homogenous majorities that remain stable even after the death of one or more shareholders, thanks to legal provisions allowing testamentary disposition of shareholdings. Restrictions on the transferability and rights of preemption eliminate the threat of take-over as a disciplinary instrument making a sudden or surprising change in command almost inconceivable.

---

22 Pointed out in *Langenfeld* FS Spiegelberger, 2009, p. 809, 812: "If someone unfamiliar with German corporate law wished to find the content of the GmbH [...] from reading the GmbH-Act, he would fail. He would only gain an impression of the complexity of the modern GmbH if he were to study examples of contracts or sample contracts in the Commercial Register or with the aid of the literature on drafting contracts."

23 See Proposal for a Council Regulation on the Statute for a European private company, COM (2008) 396, recital 3: "[...] and as many matters as possible should be left to the contractual freedom of shareholders." Likewise in the compromise version of the Swedish presidency of 23.05.2011.

24 See *Fleischer* supra (note 1), Introduction GmbHG para. 32; *Martens* FS the 100th Anniversary of the GmbH-Gesetz, 1992, p. 607, 616.

25 For a review of the particular strictness of German legislation by international comparison, see *Fleischer* AcP 204 (2004), 502, 517: "We know from comparative studies of company law that the rigid legislative strictures of § 23(5) Stock Corporation Act are internationally unique, albeit not treasured.", most recently *Kulss/Fleischer* AG 2013, 693.

26 Likewise *K. Schmidt* Gesellschaftsrecht, 4th ed., 2002, p. 467.

27 *Perakis* supra (note 16), p. 20.

4 No Liquid Secondary Market for Shares

Another key characteristic of the closed corporation is the lack of a liquid market for the sale of shares – the inability to trade on the public market is often seen as a defining attribute of closed corporations.[28] This lack of a market is not for lack of trying: some jurisdictions have attempted to establish a market to trade closed corporation shares; however demand has never been sufficient to initiate action.[29] Potential investors recognise the risks inherent in this form of investment: "Only a fool would purchase a minority interest in a closed corporation."[30] A minority shareholder wanting to divest shares is effectively *locked in* by the lack of a liquid market: there are no exit rights and the inefficacy of their voting rights under the majority principle means minority shareholders can achieve little in the corporation.[31] Their situation is particularly precarious in cases of oppression by the shareholder majority. By contrast, shareholders of listed companies may convert their shares to cash at any time, thanks to the *Wall Street Rule*,[32] enabling them to exert a certain level of pressure on management and majority shareholders.

5 No Reliable Valuation Instrument for Shares

The lack of liquid secondary markets also means that neither shareholders nor the courts have a reliable mechanism for establishing the value of shares, making the valuation of closed corporations particularly complicated and susceptible to error. Many fundamental principles of modern capital market theory cannot be applied to closed corporations.[33] Compounding this, the "correct" value of a corporation differs greatly depending on the purpose and function of the val-

---

28 See, for instance, s. 342(a)(3) Del. Gen. Corp. L.; also Chapter 2 A. above.

29 In more detail, *Michalski/Fleischer* Komm. z. GmbHG, 2nd ed., 2010, Systematic description 5: Finanzierung der GmbH, para. 110 et seq.; see also Chapter 6 C. below.

30 *Illig* 56 Am. U. L. Rev. 275, 320 (2006); similarly in the case law *Donahue v. Rodd Electrotype Co. of New England, Inc.*, 328 N.E.2d 505, 515 (Mass. 1975): "No outsider would knowingly assume the position of the disadvantaged minority. The outsider would have the same difficulties."

31 Fundamentally, on these two concepts: *Hirschman* Exit, Voice, and Loyalty: Responses to Decline in Firms, Organizations, and States, 1970.

32 See *Fischel* 35 Vand. L. Rev. 1259, 1278 (1982): "The ability freely to sell one's shares, therefore, the so-called "Wall Street Rule", is without question the single most important safeguard to all shareholders that managers will act in their best interests."

33 On the lack of diversification possibilities for shareholders of close corporations, see *Feldman* Principles of Private Firm Valuation, 2005, p. 80: "In estimating the cost of capital for a private firm, it is generally assumed that the owners cannot diversify away from the unique risk that the firm represents, and thus anybody desiring to purchase the firm would incorporate a premium to reflect this fact."

uation.[34] These numerous difficulties not only limit the recruitment of potential investors; they further complicate the final resolution of internal conflicts between majority and minority shareholders. The acceptance of privately agreed or statutory exit rights is wholly dependent on the financial conditions available: "What is needed is a right to exit at a "fair" price."[35] One important factor in determining this "price" is whether, and to what extent, discounts for both lack of control and lack of marketability are applied – a question answered differently according to the individual jurisdiction.[36]

6 Restricted Judicial Review of Business Policy

Minority shareholders also ultimately suffer from restricted judicial review of business policy issues.[37] The courts have been reluctant to intervene in the business decisions of corporations, granting directors and those in control broad discretion to act.[38] This judicial self-restraint is partly due to a lack of business acumen ("judges are not managers"), but is also fed by the conviction that the court should not seek to retrospectively replace business decisions with the its own discretionary considerations. There are indeed powerful arguments to support this approach, which have led to the introduction of the *business judgment*

34 See *Slee* Private Capital Markets: Valuation, Capitalization, and Transfer of Private Business Interests, 2004, p. 23: "Every private company, therefore, has a large number of different values at the same time, depending on the purpose *and* function of the valuation."

35 *Davies* supra (note 2), p. 228; see also *Fleischer/Strothotte* RIW 2012, 2.

36 For first comparative law discussions, *Fleischer/Strothotte* RIW 2012, 2, 4 et seq. (share valuation in English company law); *Fleischer* FS Hommelhoff, 2012, p. 223 (share valuation and valuation discounts in US closed corporation law); *Fleischer/Maugeri* RIW 2013, 24 (share valuation in Italian company law); *Fleischer/Jäger* RabelsZ 77 (2013), 694 (share valuation in French company law).

37 In detail *Moll* 40 Wake Forest L. Rev. 883, 908 et seq. (2005); more succinctly, *O'Neal/Thompson* supra (note 1), Section 3:3, 3–4: "This section discusses two basic precepts that make many squeeze-out activities possible: (1) the principles of majority control, and (2) the business judgment rule."

38 See for instance *Iwasaki v. Iwasaki Bros., Inc.*, 649 P.2d 598 (1982): "Courts will not interfere in legitimate business decisions of private corporations just to resolve dispute between majority and minority stockholders."; from the German perspective *Martens* FS for the 100th Anniversary of the GmbH-Gesetz, 1992, p. 607, 609: "In corporate law these kinds of conflicts are predominantly sparked by commercial decisions. As these decisions can only be judicially remedied to a certain extent, and usually carry a broad discretionary scope, the judge is not authorised to intervene in public decisions of this kind to benefit an opposing minority."

rule in many jurisdictions.[39] This judicial tradition of standing apart from business matters has nevertheless proved an enormous handicap for disadvantaged minority shareholders, because oppression strategies by the majority shareholder frequently come in the form of business policy decisions: the decision to retain all generated profits or to terminate a minority shareholder's employment can usually be attributed to business considerations.[40]

II Types of Abuse

To ensure that instruments designed to protect minority shareholders are as precise as possible, it is worth taking a look at the most important exploitation strategies employed by majority shareholders. This list is not intended to be exhaustive[41] and it must also be considered that an opportunistic majority shareholder often uses a combination of different "squeeze out techniques"[42] to force co-shareholders out of the company.

1 Unbalanced Third-Party Transactions with the Corporation

The majority shareholder can benefit himself by using the simple but very effective technique of entering into unfair transactions with his own corporation: purchasing corporate property for much less than market value, obtaining interest free loans from the corporation, leasing office space to the corporation at inflated rents, etc. To disguise the true nature of these "sweetheart deals" they are often conducted through members of the majority shareholder's family, rather than with the shareholder personally. An equally popular mechanism involves entering into contracts with people or companies controlled by the majority

---

39 In detail, *Fleischer* FS Wiedemann, 2002, p. 827 (on stock corporation law); on business judgment by the GmbH director and its limits specific to the GmbH, *Fleischer* NZG 2011, 521 with further comparative law references.

40 See *Chittur* 10 Harv. J.L. & Pub. Pol'y 129, 154 (1987): "So long as the controlling stockholder's conduct is not outrageous – that is, a plausible business reason can be articulated – his decisions are protected by the business judgment rule."; similarly *O'Neal/Thompson* supra (note 1), § 3:3, 3–12: "In general, courts will begin with the lax business judgment standard to review directors' decisions in selecting corporate officers and employees, fixing salaries, declaring or withholding dividends, authorizing contracts, or otherwise fixing business policies and determining the course of corporate affairs."

41 In more detail, *O'Neal/Thompson* supra (note 1), Sections 3:4–3:20, listing a catalogue of 17 oppression strategies; see also *Champetier de Ribes-Justeau* supra (note 7), p. 68 et seq., 109 et seq.

42 To use the chapter heading from *O'Neal/Thompson* supra (note 1), Chapter 3.

shareholder, known succinctly in accounting law as related-party transactions. In all these situations, the minority shareholder may have great difficulty obtaining information and a fair valuation.

2 Excessive Remuneration for Directors

The phenomenon of directors granting themselves excessive directors' salaries is widespread.[43] The decision to grant an inflated rate of remuneration may be partially motivated by tax considerations, as director's remuneration, unlike the payment of dividends, is tax-deductible.[44] For minority shareholders who are not directors, this practice presents a clear danger, as decisions regarding remuneration levels are regarded as business decisions and therefore only subject to a limited level of judicial review. In extreme cases the tax authorities, and their investigative powers, may prove to be a "natural ally"[45] providing a means for the minority shareholder to uncover hidden profit distribution.[46]

3 Appropriation of Business Opportunities and Corporate Resources

Majority shareholders who also are directors may repeatedly use their information advantages to redirect corporate business opportunities to themselves[47] or engage in impermissible competition with the corporation. In addition, there are many variations of "fringe benefits", which range from the reimbursement of private travel expenses, entertainment or representative expenses through impermissible use of a company car to the furnishing of a private home at the corporation's expense.[48] However, this is not a problem specific to closed corporations; it is also to be found in public corporations.

---

43 See BGHZ 111, 224; Cass. com., Rev. soc. 2012, 38; *Irvine v. Irvine* [2007] 1 B.C.L.C. 349; *Carlson v. Hallinan*, 925 A.2d 506 (Del. Ch. 2006).

44 *Moll* 40 Wake Forest L. Rev. 883, 890 – 891 (2005).

45 Wording similar to *Bank* 61 Wash. & Lee L. Rev. 1159, 1232 (2004): "Tax can be considered an ally of Corporate Governance."

46 For an example, OLG Frankfurt, GmbHR 2005, 550, 557 et seq.; conceptually *Fleischer/Hupka* Der Betrieb (DB) 2010, 601, 603.

47 Comparative law overview in *Fleischer* NZG 2003, 985; most recently, in the context of partnership law, *Fleischer* NZG 2013, 361.

48 Extensive case material in *Fleischer* Münchener Komm. z. GmbHG, 2012, § 43 para. 192.

4 Excessive Retention of Profits

Legal practice provides a rich source of cases involving a majority shareholder voting for full retention of profits in the shareholders' meeting over a period of years, while simultaneously awarding himself a generous director's salary.[49] The minority shareholder is thus placed on what the German jurisdiction has termed "starvation dividends" and faced with the difficulty of filing a claim against the decision to form reserves, which is a business decision not subject to full review by the courts.[50]

5 Dismissal of Minority Shareholders Employed in the Corporation

Termination of minority shareholder employment by the majority shareholder-director without good cause is a major problem in the United States and elsewhere.[51] For the minority shareholder, this frequently has drastic impact, as the money earned through this employment usually forms a major part of his yield on investment.[52] The closed corporation is clearly more than a collective of passive capital providers, instead providing a focus of active involvement for shareholders.[53] Where there are no express safeguards against dismissal,[54] the minority share-

49 Most recently, OLG Brandenburg, ZIP 2009, 1955: "Total retention of profits over seven years to a level of more than double the share capital burdens the minority shareholder alone, where there is no other means of obtaining an income from the GmbH, while the majority shareholder who holds the position of director benefits from hidden profit distributions."; in addition, OLG Nuremberg, DB 2008, 2415; Cass. com., Rev. soc. 2004, 337; *Re Mc Carthy Surfacing Ltd* [2009] 1 B.C.L.C. 622, 651 et seq. para. 67 et seq.; *Brodie v. Jordan*, 857 N.E.2d 1076 (Mass. 2006).

50 See *Ragazzo* 77 Wash. U. L. Q. 1099, 1125 n. 126 (1999): "The business judgment rule is seldom overcome on dividend questions."

51 For the American perspective, see the preparation of case material discussed in *Moll* 1999 U. Ill. L. Rev. 517; for an English perspective *Gower/Davies* supra (note 12), para. 20–7, p. 723: "It is now accepted that the interests of a member, at least in a small company, may be affected by his or her expulsion from the board, whether because it was expected that the return on investment would take the form of directors' fees or because a board position, even in a non-executive role, may be necessary to monitor and protect the member's investment."

52 See *Kleinberger* 16 Wm. Mitchell L. Rev. 1143, 1148 (1990): "Payout is frequently in the form of salary rather than dividends."; from case law practice *Balvik v. Sylvester*, 411 N.W. 2d 383, 388 (N.D. 1987): "Balvik was ultimately fired as an employee of the corporation, thus destroying the primary mode of return on his investment."; from the German perspective *Fleischer* NZG 2011, 521, 526 et seq.

53 In greater detail, *Fleischer* supra (note 1), Introduction GmbHG para. 37; along similar lines *Thompson* 48 Bus. Law. 699, 702 (1993), stating that within a close corporation "a more intimate and intense relationship exists between capital and labour."

54 See for instance *Utset* 2003 Utah L. Rev. 1329, 1343 (2003).

holder must prove that ongoing employment within the corporation was implicitly agreed upon at the time the articles of association were concluded.

6 Repurchase of Shares from the Majority Shareholder

Considerable international attention has also been devoted to cases featuring a company buyback of shares from the majority shareholder, without minority shareholders being given the same opportunity. The reason for treating a buy-back in this way is quite straightforward: where the purchase price is above the intrinsic value of the shares, it constitutes an unbalanced sweetheart deal and is therefore a transaction in breach of duty. In contrast, the question of whether the minority shareholder, on the basis of equal treatment principles, should also be granted the right to sell at a fair price has left many scratching their heads. Various courts in the United States have answered this question in the positive (so-called *Donahue doctrine*[55]), while others have favoured the subsequent *Nixon* doctrine, and spoken out against the formal adoption of an equal treatment principle.[56] This takes place against a background of fundamental questions of fairness and equal treatment in closed and public corporations.[57]

7 Exclusion of Minority Shareholders from Capital Increases

Another classic example of disadvantageous treatment of minority shareholders involves the exclusion of minority shareholders from potential capital increases. Particularly here, "greenfield" legislation must carefully consider the structure of a potential default rule: should there be an optional statutory provision of pre-emption rights, or should this be left to the provisions of the articles of association as agreed between the shareholders? The legal policy discussion on pre-emption rights in stock corporation law has provided valuable material for consideration in this context,[58] however, these rights do not always apply to closed

55 *Donahue v. Rodd Electrotype Co.*, 328 N.E.2d 505 (Mass. 1975).

56 *Nixon v. Blackwell*, 626 A.2d 1366 (Del. 1993).

57 For the most recent comprehensive legal comparison, see *de Luca* 34 Del. J. Corp. L. 853 (2009) with the following summary: "This article argues that a strong or rather mechanical equal treatment rule in share repurchases, distributions in kind, or capital reductions is not efficient. An economic analysis of the law shows that disparate treatments of shareholders may increase shareholders' welfare. Disparate treatment, however, should not result in the oppression of minorities. Rather, oppression of minorities should be prevented with the fairness standard."

58 For a legal comparison on the development in the United States, where the right of pre-emption is today structured optionally in the corporate statutes of the individual states (and generally as an *opt-in solution*), *Hirte* AG 1991, 166; *Kübler* ZBB 1993, 1.

corporations where shareholders have no opportunity to buy additional shares on the open market.

8 Non-Disclosure of Asset-Relevant Information

Finally, the majority shareholder-director may seek to gain an advantage over other shareholders by concealing important information. There is a long history of cases in which a majority shareholder has bought out a minority shareholder, without first disclosing potential share price increases stemming from commercial opportunities or more attractive offers from third parties.[59]

III Opportunities for and Limits of Self-Protection

Although these considerations suggest a strong need for rules to protect the minority shareholder, this does not mean that legislation is the only answer. A more appropriate solution calls for minority shareholders to first resort to existing "self-help" mechanisms[60] to protect themselves.[61] To this end, they should make themselves more familiar with the range of contractual safeguards against *ex-post* opportunism[62] by the majority shareholder.[63] These measures may include formalised warning notices, obligatory answering of questionnaires, initiatives for active self-help through statutory drafting requirements or a menu of various sample articles of association and the use of formalised contract conclusion procedures involving independent expert advisors (notaries, lawyers).[64]

---

59 See OLG Hamm, DB 1991, 799 (GmbH & Co. KG); comparative law perspective in *Fleischer* Informationsasymmetrie im Vertragsrecht, 2001, p. 528 et seq.; see also BGH NJW 2007, 917 para. 9.

60 To use the sub-heading from *Gower/Davies* supra (note 12), before paras. 19–43, p. 711.

61 For a British perspective, see *Davies* supra (note 2), p. 254: "The best protection for minority shareholders in this class of cases is careful negotiation of the terms on which the investment is made, plus careful monitoring of the majority's decisions."; for an American perspective, *McGinty* 46 Emory L.J. 163, 170 et seq. (1997).

62 For a list of the self-help measures available under Australian and British, law see *Boros* Minority Shareholders' Remedies, 1995, p. 104 et seq.

63 For the most recent review, see *Molitor* 14 Fordham J. Corp. & Fin. L. 491 (2009) under the heading "Eat Your Vegetables (Or at Least Understand Why You Should): Can Better Warning and Education of Prospective Minority Owners Reduce Oppression in Closely Held Businesses?".

64 See, for instance, *Molitor* 14 Fordham J. Corp. & Fin. L. 491 (2009); *Sneirson* 2008 Wis. L. Rev. 899; for an extensive discussion of menu options and debiasing strategies for founder-shareholders, *Schmolke* Grenzen der Selbstbindung im Vertragsrecht, § 8, 2013 under 2.3.2.

1 Self-Protection through Contractual or Statutory Veto Positions

In the original 1892 drafting of the German GmbH legislation, shareholders were effectively left to provide sufficient protective measures for themselves.[65] This still makes sense as a small group of founder-shareholders is able to conduct contractual negotiations cheaply, usually without the collective action problems of large public corporations. [66] This offers a degree of negotiating power for those minority shareholders, who as the "last capital provider", bring the remaining funds necessary to found the corporation.[67] However, minority shareholders generally tend to shy away from hard negotiations for fear of compromising their commercial and private interests.[68]

a) Statutory Veto Rights and Shareholder Agreements

Minority shareholders have an initial opportunity to negotiate a *right of veto* into the articles of association for particular measures. This right may require an express declaration of consent or in a weaker form, merely a lack of objection.[69] It sets aside the majority principle when dealing with extraordinary business matters.[70] Recognising its potential, the Swiss legislature gave the right of veto an increased prominence by enshrining it in GmbH law in 2008.[71] Article 807(1) Swiss Code of Obligations (*Obligationenrecht* – OR) now explicitly provides

---

65 See Begründung zum GmbH-Gesetz, 1892, p. 45, which argues there is no reason to create binding provisions due to the lack of participation of the "general public" and because the persons participating in a GmbH are in a position to protect their interests themselves.

66 See also *Bainbridge* Corporation Law and Economics, 2002, p. 798: "Unlike a large public corporation, where collective action problems preclude shareholders from bargaining with one another, the small group of investors in a close corporation permits them to bargain at a comparatively low cost. Investors would be foolish to agree to invest in the business but leave planning the details about the firm until the future." See also Chapter 2 B.II. above.

67 See the corresponding reference in *Oesterle* 66 U. Colo. L. Rev. 881, 893 with note 54 (1995): "In many small corporations, attracting the last investor necessary to capitalize the business can be very difficult. The last investor, even if a minority investor, has hold-up power; without him there is no firm. Such a minority investor has bargaining power at formation that exceeds the proportion represented by his equity investment." Similarly *Moll* 42 B.C. L. Rev. 989, 1074–75 (2001).

68 As described in *Moll* 40 Wake Forest L. Rev. 883, 916 (2005).

69 On both variations, *Wiedemann* Gesellschaftsrecht, Volume II, 2004, p. 213.

70 See from the US perspective *Moll* 40 Wake Forest L. Rev. 883, 906 (2005): "One way for a minority shareholder to avoid the norm of majority rule is to contract around it."

71 Explicitly stated in the Botschaft zur Revision des Obligationenrechts of 13.12.2001, Bundesblatt (BBl.) 2002, 3148, 3203 ("fulfilment of a considerable need"); monographically addressed in *Nater* Die Willensbildung in der GmbH, 2010.

that the articles of association may include a *right of veto* for specific resolutions by the shareholders' meeting.[72] The matters subject to veto rights must be listed in the articles of association and these rights cannot be transferred according to Article 807(3) Swiss Code of Obligations (OR). In other jurisdictions, private ordering also allows the inclusion of veto rights in the articles of association.[73] Public policy objections in the US claiming that a right of veto would make amending the articles of association potentially impossible[74] have not prevailed.[75]

Separate from the articles of association, shareholders can create a *voting agreement* that requires voting rights be used in a specific way. The legal permissibility of these shareholder agreements was cast in doubt on the other side of the Atlantic by a series of landmark decisions handed down by the New York Court of Appeals (the "Big Four").[76] However, the US legislature rushed to permit shareholder agreements as they met a practical need.[77] Today this kind of agreement in closed corporations is recognised in all jurisdictions[78] and protects the interests of minority shareholders during important changes in the life of the corporation.[79]

72 In more detail, *Truffer/Dubs* in: Honsell/Vogt/Watter, Basler Kommentar, Obligationenrecht II, 4th ed., 2012, Art. 807 para. 3 et seq.

73 See for Germany *Seibt* in: Römermann, Münchener Anwaltshandbuch GmbH-Recht, 2nd ed., 2009, § 12 para. 147: "The determination of majority requirements for specific managerial or administrative measures is one of the most crucial points in managing the balance of interests between majority and minority shareholders. They must determine in their articles of association [...] which measures will be granted a right of veto, and to which shareholder."

74 On the invalidity of far-reaching unanimity requirements, see the *New York Court of Appeals* in *Benintendi v. Kenton Hotel*, 60 N.E.2d 829 (1945).

75 See current §§ 616 and 709 N.Y. Bus. Corp. L.; also, *Sutton v. Sutton*, 637 N.E.2d 260 (1994).

76 See in detail *Bauman/Palmiter/Partnoy* Corporations – Law and Policy, 6th ed., 2007, p. 354 et seq.

77 See s. 620 N.Y. Bus. Corp. L.

78 For comparative law analysis see *Fleischer* in: Schmidt/Lutter, AktG, 2nd ed., 2010, § 54 para. 17.

79 See *Gower/Davies* supra (note 12), para. 19–53, p. 716: "The shareholders' agreement does play an important role in establishing the requirement for minority shareholder consent to important changes in the company's financial or constitutional arrangements in situations such as management buy-outs, venture capital investments and joint ventures."

b) Qualified Statutory Majority Requirements

Minority shareholder rights[80] can also arise from qualified statutory requirements for specific matters for resolution. In many jurisdictions, an increased quorum is customary for changes to the articles of association. However, the size of the quorum and the matters for resolution to which it applies, vary across national legislatures: under French limited liability corporation law, different extraordinary resolutions require different quora, ranging from unanimity for extraordinary resolutions *(décisions extraordinaires)* (e.g. change of seat of the corporation, Article L. 223–30(1) CCom) to a majority of three quarters of the shares (changing the articles of association, Article L. 223–30(2) CCom) to a double voting and capital majority (e.g. sale of shares to third parties, Article L. 223–14(1) Ccom).[81] For SARLs founded after 3 August 2005, legislative reforms reduced the required majority vote count for changes to the articles of association to two thirds of the shares of the shareholders present or represented (Article L. 223–30(3) CCom), although quorum regulations for shareholder resolutions were introduced at the same time. For European legislation, Article 27(2) of the Draft SPE Regulation requires a qualified majority of not less than two thirds of the total voting rights for specific resolutions.

In legal literature, the option of amending the articles of association by means of a qualified majority of the votes[82] has met with criticism on various occasions, alleging it is simply inappropriate for the typical closed corporation consisting of only a few members who usually have some level of personal relationship. For these shareholders, the argument continues, it is preferable for matters related to the articles of association to be resolved on the basis of unanimity, to provide all members of the closed corporation with equal say in the decision.[83] For very similar reasons, some jurisdictions in the United States made unanimity a statutory requirement for amendments to the articles of association for the limited liability corporation.[84] This approach finds support in the much-touted similarity between closed corporations and incorporated partner-

---

80 See the classification by *Davies* supra (note 2), p. 217; concurring *Enriques/Hansmann/Kraakman* in: Kraakman et al., supra (note 13), p. 92 et seq.: "Minority shareholder decisions rights".

81 See *Merle* Sociétés commerciales, 16th ed., 2012, para. 216.

82 *K. Schmidt* argues this point is particularly worth noting, supra (note 26), Chapter 16 II 1, p. 453.

83 In this regard, see *Martens* FS for the 100th Anniversary of the GmbH-Gesetz, p. 607, 614.

84 In more detail, *Miller* 38 Harv. J. on Legisl. 413, 456 (2001): "Some states provide a default rule requiring unanimity for amending the operating agreement [...] The capacity to amend the operating agreement [...] by majority vote [...] has been regarded as a potential weapon in the hands of a majority owner."

ships.[85] However, it must be considered that the principle of unanimity may make necessary changes to the articles of association more difficult[86] and may also invite an abuse of veto rights. These difficulties argue in favour of retaining the qualified majority as a *default rule* for amending the articles of association, with the duty of loyalty serving to prevent minority shareholders from vetoing necessary changes, as is done in German law.[87] In cases of fundamental changes appraisal rights may also be considered for minority shareholders who suffer disadvantage as a result of specific fundamental changes to the articles. This approach was first put forward in a leading judgement in 1859, in which the Pennsylvania Supreme Court broke with the traditional doctrine that a unanimous vote was necessary for changes to the articles. Outvoted shareholders were granted a right to full compensation as a *quid pro quo* for restricting the unanimity requirement, known as an *appraisal* or a *dissenter's remedy.*[88]

Alternatively, one could question the persuasive power[89] of the prevailing approach in Germany – that minority rights should be protected by a statutory three-quarters majority requirement for changes to the articles of association[90]. Its reference to an *argumentum e contrario* to § 53(2) sentence 2 GmbHG is not convincing *de lege ferenda*. The 13th recital of the proposed Draft SPE Regulation imposes a quorum of two thirds in Article 28(2) but only makes oblique reference to minority protection. Ultimately, there appears to be agreement that statutory qualified majority requirements do not solve the problem of minority protection entirely: "Any majority requirement short of unanimity carries the potential to leave some minority shareholders exposed."[91]

---

85 Generally, *Fleischer* supra (note 1), Introduction GmbHG para. 37 et seq.; *Bauman/Palmiter/Partnoy* supra (note 76), p. 339 et seq.; *Mayson/French/Ryan* Company Law, 27th ed., 2010, p. 71: "Quasi partnership companies".

86 See *Lauman v. Lebanon Valley R.R. Co.*, 30 Pa. 42 (1858).

87 See BGHZ 183, 1 para. 23.

88 For more information on the development of *shareholder decision rules* in the United States, see *King* 21 Del. J. Corp. L. 895, 897 et seq. (1996); for a comparative law analysis, see *Fleischer* ZGR 1997, 368, 394 et seq.

89 In favour, *Zöllner* FS for the 100th Anniversary of the GmbH-Gesetz, p. 85, 90: "There must be versions that are undisputed – even though they *could* be."

90 See *Hüffer* in: Ulmer/Habersack/Winter, Komm. z. GmbHG, 2006, § 47 para. 22.

91 *Davies* supra (note 2), p. 223.

2 Supplementary Minority Protection by Statutory and Case Law

Where the minority shareholder fails to take adequate precautions *ex ante*, legislators and courts must examine whether and in which cases relief should be extended *ex post* by recognising a duty of loyalty or granting exit rights.

a) Parallels to Minority Protection in Politics?

Some jurisdictions, particularly Delaware, refuse outright to provide protection for minority shareholders in closed corporations: "It would be inappropriate judicial legislation for this Court to fashion a special judicially created rule for minority investors [...] when there are no negotiated special provisions in the certificate of incorporation, bylaws, or stockholder agreements."[92] However, the overwhelming majority of the American states,[93] in particular Massachusetts,[94] and most European States do perceive a need for additional minority rights protection mechanisms. The principle of minority protection has spilled over from politics[95] and become enshrined as one of the most recognised principles of closed corporation law and is even explicitly recognised as a regulatory aim in the Draft SPE Regulation.[96] However, the parallels often drawn between constitutional law and corporate law [97] should not be overemphasised:[98] Firstly, the minority investor voluntarily enters into his position, while ethnic or other mi-

---

92 *Nixon v. Blackwell*, 626 A.2d 1366 (Del. 1993).

93 See the explanation by *Ragazzo* 77 Wash. U. L. Q. 1099, 1100 – 1101 (1999): "There is, however, one area in which Delaware corporate law is starkly at odds with the rest of the nation. This area, now almost a quarter-century old, involves the special rights and obligations of shareholders in closely held corporations. [...] If *Nixon* is to be read literally, much of what the rest of the country accepts as illegal conduct in the close corporation sphere has no remedy in Delaware."

94 Fundamentally, *Donahue v. Rodd Electrotype Co.*, 328 N.E.2d 505 (Mass. 1975).

95 See also *Cozian/Viandier/Deboissy* supra (note 3), para. 401: "À l'instar des régimes politiques, le droit de sociétés est confronté au redoutable problème de la protection de minorités."

96 See the 13th recital which states that "unfair treatment" of minority shareholders by the majority must be prevented.

97 In detail *Wiedemann* supra (note 21), p. 405, who introduces his comments on minority protections with "In constitutional law, the protection of minorities is a necessary legal and ethical extension of the majority principle."; from the US perspective *Chander* 113 Yale L.J. 119 (2003), providing intellectually highly interesting, but also very far-reaching preliminary considerations for a "grand unifying theory of corporate and constitutional law".

98 Also cautious: *Martens* FS for the 100th Anniversary of the GmbH-Gesetz, p. 607, 608 who reminds the reader that corporate law is, in the end, about capital interests.

nority groups do not.[99] Secondly, while constitutional law generally guarantees minority rights by prohibiting discrimination based on readily discernible characteristics,[100] corporate law demands exactly the opposite by requiring minority status to be factored into the decision-making process.[101] Minority protection in closed corporations amounts to more than mere *non-discrimination*, becoming in part a form of *affirmative action*.

b) Economic Grounds

The main arguments in favour of supplementary minority protection come from economic considerations.

aa) Initial Conclusion of the Contract

One initial argument is that smaller corporations often have limited financial resources for seeking legal advice.[102] For minority shareholders, a rational cost-benefit calculation frequently does not justify the engagement of competent consultants to draft the articles of association: "One can simply not expect a two-person dry-cleaning operation to run with the same level of attorney supervision as a Fortune 500 company."[103] There is at least a basic level of protection in legal systems where articles of association must be notarised (see for instance § 2(1) GmbHG), as the notary has an advisory duty (see § 17 Notarisation Act).[104]

Even if this transaction-cost argument may be addressed through default rules or model articles of association,[105] there are arguments from behavioural

---

99 See references to this in *Illig* 56 Am. U. L. Rev. 275, 309 (2006): "Being a minority investor is quite different from being a racial or ethnic minority, however. Presumably, one is born with certain largely immutable physical characteristics that determine one's race or ethnicity."

100 See Art. 3(3) German Constitution: "No person shall be favoured or disadvantaged because of sex, parentage, race, language, homeland and origin, faith, or religious or political opinions. No person shall be disadvantaged because of disability."

101 Likewise *Chander* 113 Yale L.J. 119, 120 (2003): "Constitutional law believes that equality requires blinding oneself to minority status. Corporate law, to the contrary, believes that equal treatment can only be assured by taking minority status in account. For corporate law, equality is not sameness".

102 See *Cheffins* Company Law. Theory, Structure and Operation, 1997, p. 273, very similarly *Gower/Davies* supra (note 12), para. 20–11, p. 725 et seq.

103 *Ragazzo* 77 Wash. U. L. Q. 1099, 1130 (1999).

104 For the German perspective, see *Mayer* Münchener Komm. z. GmbHG, 2010, § 2 para. 21 et seq.; see above Chapter 2 C.III.1.

105 See particularly *Oesterle* 66 U. Colo. L. Rev. 881, 920 (1995): "The traditional transaction costs rationale is not satisfying for three reasons. First [...] Second, the costs of drafting a

economics in favour of a minimum mandatory standard of protection.[106] This is due in part to the problem posed by the 'embeddedness', or the social relationship between the parties mentioned above:[107] personal knowledge and mutual trust usually combine to prevent parties from raising potentially critical issues during negotiations[108] for fear this demonstrated lack of faith may endanger the conclusion of the contract.[109] They instead trust that their existing relationship will lead to subsequent differences of opinion being informally resolved.[110] This is closely linked to overoptimism[111] – empirical evidence shows that parties entering into long-term contractual agreements often underestimate the potential for future tensions.[112] Finally, the long-term nature of articles of association makes it virtually impossible for the founder-shareholders to precisely define the important elements of their agreement in advance: they cannot foresee every conceivable eventuality and due to these inadequate telescopic capacities[113] are often not in the position to objectively compare present and future condi-

customized organizational document seem minimal. Forms for special clauses abound in libraries and lawyers' files, and the major risks assumed by the minority equity-holder are familiar and predictable. And third, a transaction cost-based theory does not justify non-waivable rules. At issue is only what the default rules ought to be."

106 See *Fleischer* ZGR 2001, 1, 6 et seq.

107 For more on this concept, see *Granovetter* 91 Am. J. Sociol. 481 (1985): "How behaviour and institutions are affected by social relations is one of the classic questions of social theory. The paper concerns the extent to which economic action is embedded in structures of social relations [...]."

108 See *Bauman/Palmiter/Partnoy* supra (note 76), p. 337: "There is also a danger of dissension if the parties discuss hypothetical problems that may never arise."

109 See *Cheffins* supra (note 102), p. 273: "Investors in smaller businesses will usually prefer to avoid bringing up potentially contentious matters since doing so might engender feelings of mistrust and thereby jeopardize the survival of the business relationship."; *Heatherington/Dooley* 63 Va. L. Rev. 1, 36 (1977): "The minority investor may be hesitant to raise too many reservations for fear of demonstrating too little confidence in the majority and thereby queering the deal. Introducing the subject of future dissension may produce present discontent and prevent the firm from being organized."

110 See *Blair/Stout* 149 U. Pa. L. Rev. 1735, 1805 (2001).

111 Generally, *Weinstein* 39 J. Personality & Soc. Psychol. 806 (1980); in a corporate law context *Eisenberg* 47 Stan. L. Rev. 211, 251 (1995): "Furthermore, at the time the contract is made, each party is likely to be unduly optimistic about the relationship's long-term prospects and the willingness of the other party to avoid opportunistic behaviour or unfair manipulation of the relevant contractual rules as the relationship unfolds."

112 See *Meiselman v. Meiselman*, 307 P.E.2d 551, 558 (1983): "Close corporations are often formed by friends or family members who simply may not believe that disagreements could ever arise."

113 The concept is already cited by *Pigou* The Economics of Welfare, 4th ed., 1960, p. 25: "Our telescopic faculty is defective [...]."

tions.[114] Given all these considerations, the founders of closed corporations frequently act under 'bounded rationality' or the influence of systematically distorted perceptions of reality.[115]

bb) Subsequent Alterations to the Articles of Association

In addition, the argument for private ordering loses its persuasive powers where subsequent alterations to the articles of association or fundamental changes are concerned:[116] with each alteration, the articles of association risk becoming further removed from the initial agreement between founding shareholders. Even sworn adherents of freedom of contract argue in favour of some protective measures when dealing with "midstream changes".[117] This applies not only to public companies with their collective action problems[118] but also (especially) to closed corporations where *ex-post* opportunism by the majority shareholder is not restrained by market forces, and where no liquid secondary market is available to minority shareholders.[119] Qualified majority requirements in cases of alterations to the articles of association and appraisal rights in cases of fundamental changes may alleviate the problem, but will not completely solve it.

---

114 Fundamentally *Ulen* 12 Hamline L. Rev. 385, 386 (1989); developed in detail for contract law by *Eisenberg* 47 Stan. L. Rev. 211 (1995).

115 In a similar vein see *Carney* 65 Wash. U. L. Q. 1, 59–60 (1987): "Investors in closely held enterprises are likely to be subject to conditions of bounded rationality, under which they either fail to perceive the complete set of problems that may occur later, or underestimate the probability of their occurrence."; for a general behavioural economic perspective and its application in business law, *Fleischer/Schmolke/Zimmer* in: Fleischer/Zimmer, Der Beitrag der Verhaltensökonomie (Behavioral Economics) zum Handels- und Wirtschaftsrecht, ZHR Supplement no. 75, 2011, 1 et seq.

116 See *Fleischer* supra (note 1), Introduction GmbHG para. 280.

117 As argued in *Easterbrook/Fischel* 89 Colum. L. Rev. 1416, 1443 (1989): "The difference between governance provisions established at the beginning and provisions added later suggests some caution in treating the two categories alike. Some of the harder questions in corporate law concern arrangements that are adopted or changed after the firm is under way and the capital has been raised."; see the contrary view in *Butler/Ribstein* The Corporation and the Constitution, 1995, p. 16 et seq.: "Courts and legislators do not have a larger arsenal of weapons against opportunistic amendments than have the parties themselves."

118 Tailored to this is the argumentation in *Bebchuk* 102 Harv. L. Rev. 1820, 1828 et seq. (1989).

119 See *Fleischer* supra (note 1), Introduction GmbHG para. 280.

3 Inalienable Member Rights and Mandatory Standards of Conduct

More difficult issues arise where a minority shareholder waives the membership rights or protection standards available to him from the outset.[120] In Germany, this is often discussed in relation to partnerships under the key term inalienable self-protection.[121] In closed corporation law, it is permissible to waive voting and dividend rights.[122] That being said, a shareholder can never *completely* waive his membership rights, and must retain the opportunity to challenge illegal shareholders' resolutions.[123] Moreover, a shareholder is not permitted to pre-emptively waive his rights to information or the right to participate in shareholders' meetings. However, some guidance as to the application of those rights may be included in the articles.

Internationally, lively academic debate has sprung up over whether the members' duty of loyalty, which we will investigate in detail later,[124] can be waived by the parties.[125] The so-called *contractarians*, who conceptually view corporations as a nexus of contracts, tend also to consider *fiduciary duties* of shareholders and directors as capable of being contracted away.[126] They point out that there may be a need for an "opting out" of fiduciary duties, for example, in venture capital contracts. It is also conceivable that minority shareholders have already been compensated for the high risk of opportunistic behaviour, either through a reduced purchase price or through a higher share of the profits

---

120 Recently from the US perspective *Sneirson* 2008 Wis. L. Rev. 899, 932: "A much harder case presents itself where [...] the jurisdiction normally affords oppressed minority shareholders relief, and the parties have the soft-paternalistic nudge and opted out of such protection."

121 Fundamentally *Wiedemann* supra (note 21), p. 365 et seq.: "Der unverzichtbare Selbstschutz"; for the most recent review of the core elements, see *Ulmer/Schäfer* Gesellschaft bürgerlichen Rechts und Partnerschaftsgesellschaft, 5th ed., 2009, § 709 para. 90 et seq.

122 For Germany, see BGHZ 14, 264, 269 et seq.; for Delaware § 18–302(a) Del. Limited Liability Corporation Act: "[...] A limited liability company agreement may provide that any member or class or group of members shall have no voting rights."

123 See BGHZ 14, 264, 273; *Scholz/Westermann* Komm. z. GmbHG, 10th ed., 2006, Introduction para. 79.

124 See B.IV.1.a).

125 For an overview of fiduciary duties of organs, see *Fleischer* ZHR 168 (2004), 673, 685 et seq.; most recently *Hellgardt* FS Hopt, 2010, p. 765.

126 For specific reference to the fiduciary duties of members in close corporations, see *Illig* 56 Am. U. L. Rev. 275, 324, 328 (2006): "Mandatory legal protections for minority investors in close corporations appear both overly rigid and likely to misconstrue the relative equities of many cases. [...] Thus, conceiving of minority protections as default norms makes it possible to permit investors the freedom of waiver, as is generally advocated by the contractarians, while retaining a concern for the adequacy of the status and sophistication of the investor."; likewise *Oesterle* 66 U. Colo. L. Rev. 881, 885 et seq. (1995); generally *Butler/Ribstein* 65 Wash. L. Rev. 1 (1990).

than they would otherwise be entitled to. By contrast, the so-called *anticontractarians* view this notion of stock corporation law as a contractual nexus to be fundamentally flawed. They perceive fiduciary duties as a non-negotiable, predetermined set of rules.[127] Giving parties the ability to do away with fiduciary duties may strip these duties of their ethical weight[128] and could lead to unforeseen effects on general operating morals.[129] Finally, there have also been preliminary attempts to use the general concept of *libertarian paternalism*[130] for resolving problems in closed corporations.[131]

Although this question is rarely discussed in Germany, one promising compromise solution has emerged:[132] while a *general* waiver of fiduciary duties is not considered valid, it is possible for shareholders to pre-emptively waive their fiduciary rights for a specific individual case or for a specific class of activities.[133] This also draws on behavioural economics: minority shareholders may underestimate the costs and risks associated with a full waiver of all fiduciary duties due to systematic errors in decision making,[134] whereas a case specific waiver implies

127 See *DeMott* 48 Ariz. L. Rev. 925, 926 (2006); *Laby* 56 Buff. L. Rev. 99, 129 et seq. (2008).
128 In this sense *Leslie* 95 Geo. L.J. 67, 70 (2005): "Labelling fiduciary duties 'default rules' threatens to strip fiduciary rules of their moral content."
129 See *Moore Dickerson* 26 J. Corp. L. 1001, 1015 et seq. (2001).
130 Fundamentally *Sunstein/Thaler* 70 U. Chi. L. Rev. 1159 (2003); *Thaler/Sunstein* 93 Am. Econ. Rev. 175 (2003); most recently, *Sunstein* 122 Yale L.J. 1826 (2013): "The Storrs Lectures: Behavioural Economics and Paternalism".
131 See *Sneirson*, 2008 Wis. L. Rev. 899, 932 et seq., who views the negotiation of minority protection rules, with some exceptions, as valid; critical in part, *Means* 79 Fordham L. Rev. 1161, 1184 et seq. (2010): "Third, it might be objected that even useful default settings cannot substitute for mandatory rules, and that the Sunstein and Thaler model could undermine existing shareholder protections. [...] Unless some level of protection is mandatory, trusting and optimistic shareholders may be induced to abandon it at the outset of the venture"; previously already in *Black* 84 Nw. U. L. Rev. 542, 572 (1990): "Giving close corporations the power to dispense with the duty of loyalty would be troublesome."
132 For a recent examination of the problem, as part of a larger contribution on "Grenzen der Vertragsfreiheit im Innenverhältnis von GmbH und O(H)G" *Koppensteiner* GesRZ 2009, 197, 199: "In truth, things are more complicated. Restraints on competition affecting the shareholders of a commercial law partnership (§ 112 Corporate Code/Commercial Code) is generally perceived as a legal expression of the fiduciary bond. This rule can nevertheless be contracted away [...] However, there must be a mandatory core of fiduciary duties. The contrary cannot be assumed because the joint interest characteristic of associations could then evaporate altogether."
133 For an examination of shareholder fiduciary duties, see *Fleischer* supra (note 78), § 53a Stock Corporation Act para. 60; similarly *M. Winter* Mitgliedschaftliche Treuebindungen im GmbH-Recht, 1988, p. 215 et seq.
134 For a general context *Tversky/Kahneman* Judgment under Uncertainty: Heuristics and Biases, 1982, p. 23 et seq. and passim.

a greater probability they have considered the risks in advance. The prevailing doctrine in German civil law applies a similar concept, stating that fundamental principles of loyalty and trust as such cannot be done away with, but at the same time consenting to contractual partners agreeing to "reduced" service or duty standards for specific activities.[135] Internationally, this differentiation is also found in the newly introduced Article 803(3) of the Swiss Code of Obligations, which according to leading interpretation only provides for situational and specific exceptions to the fiduciary duties of GmbH shareholders, without providing for a general elimination of these duties.[136] In the US, the Revised Uniform Partnership Act is even clearer on the rule-exception relationship in s. 103(b)(3), stating that fiduciary duties may not be negotiated, but that in the corporation's articles of association "the partners by agreement may determine the standards by which the performance of the obligation is to be measured, if the standards are not manifestly unreasonable".[137] US case law has arrived at similar conclusions for closed corporations.[138]

IV Standards of Conduct in Statutory and Case Law

To prevent judges presiding over a case from relying solely on their personal preconceptions and ideas of fairness in the resolution of majority/minority conflicts,[139] overarching standards must be developed as a guide to resolution in each case. From a theoretical viewpoint, the standards for majority shareholders

135 See *Roth* Münchener Komm. z. BGB, 5th ed., 2007, § 242 para. 76 with further references.
136 See *Amstutz/Chappuis* in: Honsell/Vogt/Watter, Basler Kommentar, Obligationenrecht II, 4th ed., 2012, Art. 803 para. 11.
137 Further clarification is provided by the (official) Comment under 4: "RUPA attempts to provide a standard that parties can rely upon in drafting exculpatory agreements. It is not necessary that the agreement be restricted to a particular transaction. That would require bargaining over every transaction or opportunity which would be excessively burdensome. The agreement may be drafted in terms of types or categories of activities or transactions, but it should be reasonably specific."
138 See *Neubauer v. Goldfarb*, 108 Cal. App. 4th 47 (2d Dist. 2003).
139 Frequently, the self-perception of the presiding judge is critical to intervention for the benefit of the minority shareholder, *Oesterle* 66 U. Colo. L. Rev. 881, 914 (1995): "To make the point graphically, at the expense of a bit of crassness, consider a judge's retirement banquet. Which of the following accolades would a judge prefer: 'He used his power to help the oppressed and victimized (overriding formality, precedent and convention)'; or 'He predictably enforced contracts (giving voice to the private-ordering power and autonomy of individuals)?' I would guess that, currently, the legal profession and thus its judges prefer the former."

and directors must be strictly separated, even when these roles are played by the same person.

1 Standards of Conduct for Majority Shareholders

a) Shareholders' Fiduciary Duties

aa) International Acceptance

Many jurisdictions use the concept of fiduciary duty as the basis of their standards of conduct for majority shareholders. Two decisions handed down independently, but at almost the same time by the highest courts of the United States and Germany promoted the idea of fiduciary duty between shareholders, finding that shareholders in a closed corporation owe a fiduciary duty to each other, as well as to the corporation. In a landmark decision that still holds today, the Massachusetts Supreme Judicial Court ruled: "We hold that stockholders in the close corporation owe one another substantially the same fiduciary duty in the operation of the enterprise that partners owe to one another."[140] Five weeks later, the German Federal Court of Justice ruled that "the corporate law fiduciary duty governs not only the relationship between shareholders and the GmbH, but also the relationship between shareholders themselves".[141] Swiss legislation recently codified the fiduciary duty between GmbH shareholders in Article 809(2) Swiss Code of Obligations (OR).[142] Several US states have recently taken the same course in their limited liability corporation statutes.[143]

Using slightly different terminology, but with similar effect, French case law and doctrine draws on the concept of *abus de majorité*, which although tied in with general civil law thinking on abuse of power, has gradually become an in-

140 *Donahue v. Rodd Electrotype Co.*, 328 N.E.2d 505, 515 (Mass. 1975).

141 BGHZ 65, 15, 18 – ITT.

142 Art. 803(2) Swiss Code of Obligations (OR) states: "They (the shareholders) must refrain from all activities which may negatively affect the interests of the corporation. Particularly, they must not engage in business activities which provide them with a significant advantage while negatively impacting on the corporation. Articles of association can provide that shareholders must refrain from engaging in competing business activities."

143 See for instance Cal. Corp. Code § 17153: "The fiduciary duties a manager owes to a limited liability company and to its members are those of a partner to a partnership and to the partners of the partnership."; see also *Moll* 40 Wake Forest L. Rev. 883, 965 (2005): "Significantly, many of the statutes explicitly indicate that fiduciary duties run to the individual members as well as to the LLC entity."

dependent concept.[144] In Scandinavia, although there is no general provision, codification has included provisions addressing an abuse of voting rights in the legislation.[145] In Great Britain, the legislature and courts seem hesitant to recognise a general fiduciary duty of the majority[146] towards the minority shareholder.[147] However, the British version of the remedy for oppression – unfair prejudice –provided in ss. 994–999 Companies Act 2006 [148] relies on very similar considerations of fairness. Generally, when speaking of fiduciary duties and oppression remedies, the fiduciary duties of the majority and the exit rights of minority shareholders, are often two sides of the same coin.[149]

The conclusion drawn from this is that a general approach, either in the form of fiduciary duty or *abus de majorité,* has been almost universally incorporated into the unwritten law of closed corporations. Incorporating a similar provision into a model statute for closed corporations is therefore also highly recommendable.

---

144 See *Cozian/Viandier/Deboissy* supra (note. 3), para. 402: "Qu'est-ce que'un abus de majorité? C'est la transposition en droit des sociétés de la théorie civiliste de l'abus de droit ou du détournement du pouvoir"; recent monograph in *Champetier de Ribes-Justeau* supra (note 7)
145 For example, §§ 5–21 Norwegian Private Limited Companies Act (English version): "Abuse of the authority of the general meeting. The general meeting of the company cannot adopt any resolution which may give certain shareholders or other parties an unreasonable advantage at the expense of other shareholders of the company."; see *Truyen* in: Krüger Andersen/Clausen/Skog, supra (note 8), p. 131, 135: "The Norwegian general clause on shareholders' abuse of authority, and the supporting unwritten principles, can be seen as a specific mutual duty of loyalty between shareholders. In small and medium-sized companies different variations of the duty of loyalty are known, among others, from the German *Treuepflicht* and the American 'fiduciary duties'. The general clause in the Norwegian Private Limited Companies Act, §§ 5–21 does not constitute a common duty of loyalty between shareholders, but rather a specific duty which comes into play when shareholders use the authority derived form the right to vote in the general meeting."
146 As opposed to the fiduciary duties of directors – see *Gower/Davies* supra (note 12), para. 30–6, p. 1132 et seq.
147 See *Davies* supra (note 2), p. 231: "The common law does not perceive the controlling shareholders to be in a fiduciary position towards non-controlling shareholders, so that basis for the individual shareholder to restrain the power of the majority as it reveals itself in shareholder decision-making is not available."
148 See C.III. below.
149 Similarly from the US perspective *Moll* 40 Wake Forest L. Rev. 883, 895 (2005): "In the close corporation context, therefore, it is sensible to view the parallel development of the statutory action [of oppression] and the fiduciary duty action as two sides of the same coin."; before that, *Thompson* 48 Bus. Law. 699, 700 (1993): "It makes sense to think of them as two manifestations of a minority shareholder's cause of action for oppression."

bb) Economic Function

Some theorists see an ontological basis to the loyalty element of fiduciary duty between shareholders of a closed corporation: loyalty, they claim, is an inherent element of every association as a corollary of the trust relationship between its partners.[150] Others interpret fiduciary duty as a necessary counterpart (primarily) to the decision-making power held by the majority shareholder.[151] From an economic perspective, the development of this duty is a reaction to the long-term horizon of articles of association. This indefinite time frame does not allow founding partners to fully identify, negotiate and provide for all eventualities contractually. In other words, the articles of association constitute *incomplete or relational contracts.*[152] This incompleteness exposes shareholders, particularly in closed corporations, to a heightened danger of *ex-post* opportunistic dealings: a minority shareholder cannot rule out that the majority shareholder will act to the minority's disadvantage at some time in the future just as majority shareholders must protect themselves against possible minority shareholder rejection of future necessary or desirable changes to the articles of association. These unknown future problems can only be resolved practically through the establishment of a general principle, broad enough to incorporate the expectations of all shareholders, *ex ante*, of how the corporation will react to unexpected situations *ex post*. Fiduciary duty lends itself to interpretation as a *focal or guiding principle* for the development of decision-making rules for as yet unforeseen conflicts.[153] In other words, it is *not an absolute rule for conflict resolution,* but rather one that needs to be specified on case-by-case basis.[154]

cc) Practical Application

The fiduciary duty of members under German case-law demands that the majority shareholder consider the interests of the corporation and membership interests of co-shareholders.[155] This applies to the exercise and actual influence of rights and other entitlements within the closed corporation, but without completely prohib-

---

150 See *A. Hueck* Der Treuegedanke im modernen Privatrecht, 1947, p. 12 et seq.

151 See *Zöllner* Die Schranken mitgliedschaftlicher Stimmrechtsmacht bei den privatrechtlichen Personenverbänden, 1963, p. 342 et seq.

152 See *Fleischer* ZGR 2001, 1, 4 et seq.; also very clear *Moll* 86 Minn. L. Rev. 717, 754 (2002): "The investment bargains entered into by close corporation shareholders reflect the characteristics of relational contracts."

153 In this sense *Fleischer* ZGR 2001, 1, 5.

154 See *Amstutz/Chappuis* supra (note 136), Art. 803 Swiss Code of Obligations (OR), para. 7.

155 See BGHZ 65, 15, 18 et seq. – ITT.

iting the consideration of personal interests.[156] Functionally comparable safeguards are provided in English law in ss. 994–999 Companies Act 2006, which protect shareholder interests against unfair prejudice.[157] Unfair prejudice is defined as a breach of good faith: "Unfairness for the purposes of [s. 994] is not to be judged by reference to subjective notions of fairness, but rather by testing whether, applying equitable principles, the majority has acted, or is proposing to act, in a manner which equity would regard as contrary to good faith."[158] In France the classical definition of *abus de majorité* is provided in the *arrêt Piquard c. Schumann* from 1961: a decision constitutes abuse when it is made "contrary to the general interests of the corporation and with the sole purpose of benefiting the members of the majority to the detriment of the minority."[159]

b) Pros and Cons of Protecting Justified Expectations

The most difficult question in practice is the extent to which implied agreements between shareholders and unspoken expectations are protected by fiduciary duties.[160] This is closely linked to the tensions between self-protection and external protection discussed earlier.[161]

aa) Current Approaches in Case Law and Jurisprudence

Scholars of economic analysis differ greatly on the need to protect reasonable shareholder expectations. One widely held opinion proposes that courts should limit themselves to enforcing the contractual arrangements specifically agreed by the parties.[162] Failure to do so may reduce shareholder motivation to formalise the desired mixture of minority protection and entrepreneurial flexibility in the articles of association.[163] Other equally influential opinions however seek to broaden the court's considerations to include informal agreements, previous contractual practice and the reasonable expectations of minority sharehol-

---

156 *Fastrich* in: Baumbach/Hueck, Komm. z. GmbHG, 20th ed., 2013, § 13 para. 21.
157 See *Mayson/French/Ryan* supra (note 85), p. 571 et seq.
158 *Re Guidezone Ltd* [2000] 2 B.C.L.C. 321, 355.
159 Cass. com. 18.4.1961, D. 1961, 661.
160 See *Fleischer* supra (note 1), Introduction GmbHG para. 293.
161 See B.III. above.
162 See *Easterbrook/Fischel* The Economic Structure of Corporate Law, 1991, p. 27.
163 In this sense: *O'Kelley* 87 Nw. U. L. Rev. 216, 247 (1992).

ders.[164] One of their main arguments is that this will encourage minority investors to invest further in the corporation.[165]

Case law is equally split on the matter. In the United States, courts are divided into pro-majority and pro-minority camps,[166] with the pro-minority adherents further divided between competing views: (1) The majority perspective focuses primarily on the majority shareholder and then asks whether his/her behaviour serves a legitimate business purpose.[167] (2) In contrast, the minority perspective first looks at the effects on minority shareholders,[168] i. e. not the conduct, but its effect.[169] In measuring these effects, there are differing views as to whether the original or subsequent expectations should be used as a yardstick.[170] In Great Britain, the courts sided with the pro-minority standard of protection within the framework of the legal remedy of unfair prejudice: s. 994 Companies Act 2006 accordingly protects those "legitimate expectations" or "equitable considerations"[171] that formed the basis of the shareholders' association, even where not explicitly included in the contract.[172]

164 See *Johnston* 70 Wash. U. L. Q. 291, 295 et seq., 333 et seq. (1992); similarly *Charny* 89 Mich. L. Rev. 1815, 1870 et seq. (1991); in detail also *Eisenberg* 89 Colum. L. Rev. 1461, 1465 et seq. (1989).

165 In this sense *Johnston* 70 Wash. U. L. Q. 291, 333 et seq. (1992).

166 In further detail, *Bauman/Palmiter/Partnoy* supra (note 76), p. 385 et seq.

167 See *Wilkes v. Springside Nursing Home, Inc.*, 353 N.E.2d 657, 663 (Mass. 1976): "When minority stockholders in a close corporation bring suit against the majority alleging a breach of the strict good faith duty owed to them by the majority, we must carefully analyze the action taken by the controlling stockholders in the individual case. It must be asked whether the controlling group can demonstrate a legitimate business purpose for its action."

168 See *In re Kemp & Beatley, Inc.*, 473 N.E.2d 1173, 1179 (N.Y. 1984): "Oppression should be deemed to arise [...] when the majority conduct substantially defeats expectations that, objectively viewed, were both reasonable under the circumstances and were central to the petitioner's decision to join the venture."

169 In this sense *Moll* 53 Vand. L. Rev. 749, 765 (2000): "Whereas the majority perspective focuses primarily on the *conduct* of the majority shareholder, the minority perspective focuses primarily on the *effect* of that conduct on the minority shareholder."

170 See the case law references in *Bauman/Palmiter/Partnoy* supra (note 76), p. 415.

171 See *Gower/Davies* supra (note 12), para. 20 – 11, p. 725 with references to case law practices.

172 See *Saul D. Harrison & Sons Plc, Re* [1995] 1 B.C.L.C. 14, 19: "[...] arise out of a fundamental understanding between the shareholders forming the basis of their association but was not put into contractual form".

bb) Advantages of Considering Implied Agreements

There are good reasons to consider implied agreements between majority and minority shareholders. Firstly, they account for the fact that for a range of reasons, shareholders in closed corporations often fail to include contractual provisions for potential future events when forming their articles of association.[173] Gently pushing for agreements of this kind is a difficult and often counterproductive proposition that may lead to an erosion, or "crowding out" of mutual trust between the parties.[174] Secondly, recourse taken to "informal arrangements among the members"[175] is not an encroachment on private ordering, but actually holds shareholders to their own – albeit vaguely formulated – contractual expectations.[176] In this, there is an obvious conceptual similarity to the remedies offered by contract law (implied contract, frustration, interference with the basis of the transaction).[177] Thirdly, reference to shareholders' initial mutual understandings and expectations prevents the courts from retrospectively imposing their own understanding of "fairness". Finally, British authors also suggest that the massive increase in the amount of litigation triggered by s. 994 CA 2006 (previously s. 459 CA 1985) suggests that there was a substantial unmet need for minority protection in these companies before the introduction of this remedy.[178]

---

173 See in detail *Moll* 40 Wake Forest L. Rev. 883, 911 et seq. (2005) under the heading of "The Absence of Advance Planning"; more succinctly *Gower/Davies* supra (note 12), para. 20 – 11, p. 725 et seq.

174 See *Blair/Stout* 149 U. Pa. L. Rev. 1735, 1806 – 1807 (2001): "Participants in closely held corporations accordingly may often decline to negotiate complex formal contracts because doing so would destroy the filtering value of mutual vulnerability as a means of excluding the intrinsically untrustworthy. [...] Worse, attempts to use contracts in relationships in which trust plays a central role can prove counterproductive and promote exactly the sort of opportunistic behaviour they were intended to discourage."

175 A subheading in *Gower/Davies* supra (note 12), before para. 20 – 11.

176 Likewise *Gower/Davies* supra (note 12), para. 20 – 16, p. 729: "The courts can claim to be, and indeed are, using as the criteria for judging unfairness the standards laid down, albeit informally, by the members themselves, and the judges can thus avoid the more challenging task of developing their own criteria."; examined in more detail with a view to the US perspective by *Means* 79 Fordham L. Rev. 1161, 1194 et seq. (2010).

177 From the American perspective in detail *Moll* 42 B.C. L. Rev. 989 (2001): "Oppression law is effectively stepping in for contract law and is accomplishing what contract law itself should be doing"; and reflected from the British perspective in *Gower/Davies* supra (note 12), para. 20 – 13, p. 727 et. seq.

178 See *Davies* supra (note 2), p. 253; very similarly *Gower/Davies* supra (note 12), para. 20 – 20, p. 731 et seq.: "At least in small companies, the articles systematically fail to capture the full agreement between the members, the development of this case law has brought company law into much greater touch with corporate reality and, as the amount of litigation shows, has addressed a previously unmet legal need."

This is not to say that protection of minority shareholders should extend to safeguarding vague hopes and one-sided expectations: "Majority conduct should not be deemed oppressive simply because the petitioner's subjective hopes and desires in joining the venture are not fulfilled."[179] Instead, minority shareholders must be able to provide credible evidence that informal agreements were intended to supplement the articles of association.[180]

cc) The Problem of Procedural Costs

The potential enormous increase in the number of claims provides a final, more serious impediment to using informal agreements as a means of protecting reasonable expectations.[181] This approach requires the entire history of the relationship between the majority and minority shareholders be considered, thus significantly increasing procedural costs.[182] To prevent this, adherents of *modern economic formalism* in contract law have suggested that it would appear to better serve the interests of the parties were the court to only enforce written agreements.[183] However, this proposal tends to favour *ex-post* opportunism,[184] does not address the problem of filling contractual gaps[185] and assumes that the parties are risk-neutral which is precisely not the case in this situation: (minority) shareholders of closed corporations have frequently invested a significant part of their personal assets in the corporation[186] and tend therefore to be highly

---

179 *In re Kemp & Beatley, Inc.*, 473 N.E.2d 1173, 1179 (N.Y. 1984).

180 See the cases reported in *Gower/Davies* supra (note 12), para. 20 – 16, p. 729.

181 See *Mayson/French/Ryan* supra (note 85), p. 569: "Unfortunately, lawyers presenting a case on unfair prejudice in a company often deal with the whole history of the company in detail, so as to build up an overall picture of prejudice, and this is countered by equally extensive evidence and cross-examination from the other side."

182 For the British perspective see *Gower/Davies* supra (note 12), para. 20 – 33, p. 739 et seq. with the addition: "All this will typically occur in relation to small companies, whose net value may not be large."

183 See for instance *Schwartz/Scott* 113 Yale L.J. 541, 572 – 73 (2003), who talk about a "minimum evidentiary base": most recently, *Schwartz/Watson* 42 J. Leg. Studies 1 (2013).

184 See *Kostritsky* 96 Ky. L.J. 43 (2007); for a general critique also *Badawi* 6 Berkeley Bus. L. J. 1 (2009); *Burton* 88 Indiana L. J. 339 (2013).

185 See *Bayern* 97 Cal. L. Rev. 943, 956 et seq. (2009).

186 For further detail, see *Ragazzo* 77 Wash. U. L. Q. 1099, 1109 (2001): "Many investors in small businesses invest a significant portion of their life savings in the business. This practice defeats their ability to diversify their investment portfolios and exposes them to company- and industry-specific risk."

risk-averse. For these reasons, referring shareholders to contractual means of self-protection is not a valid response.[187]

Alternative legislative solutions could encourage mediation as a means of conflict resolution for disputes between shareholders[188] or introduce an arbitration scheme, as has been discussed in Britain[189] and which has already been introduced in Italy.[190] In the English courts, Lord Hoffman attempted to resolve the situation by suggesting parties could not claim *unfair* conduct where a minority shareholder had rejected an offer to purchase shares at a fair price without minority discounts.[191] Various states in the US provide the majority shareholder with the ability to end proceedings early by purchasing the shares held by the claimant minority shareholder.[192]

2 Standards of Conduct for Directors

a) Duty of Care and Duty of Loyalty

With regard to directors' duties, the international dichotomy between duty of care and duty of loyalty has become the accepted taxonomy.[193] In Germany, directors' standards of conduct have been divided into a *Sorgfaltspflicht* and a

---

187 For more detail about underinsurance against *ex-post* opportunism on the basis of rationality deficits and distortions of perception, see B.III.2.b)aa) above.

188 For an overview of the opportunities in Germany see *Dendorfer/Krebs* MittBayNot 2008, 85; comprehensively *Duve/Eidenmüller/Hacke* Mediation in der Wirtschaft, 2nd ed., 2011; in further detail in B.VII.

189 See note in *Gower/Davies* supra (note 12), para. 20–33, p. 739.

190 For further information, see *Spada* in: Abbadessa/Portale, Il Nuovo Diritto Delle Società, Liber amicorum Gian Franco Campobasso, 2006, p. 257.

191 See *O'Neill v. Phillipps* [1999] 2 B.C.L.C. 1, 16–17.

192 For more on similar regulations in Oregon, Illinois, Florida and other US states see *Art* 28 J. Corp. L. 371, 414 (2003): "When a shareholder brings a proceeding seeking judicial relief, the corporation and the other shareholders receive an option to bring the action to an early conclusion by purchasing the shares of the plaintiff. Unlike the compulsory buyout remedy discussed above, this decision to purchase is made by the corporation or shareholders, not by the court, and does not entail a full trial or a judicial determination of liability."

193 See *Enriques/Hansmann/Kraakman* in: Kraakman et al., supra (note 13), p. 78; specific to closed corporations *Moll/Ragazzo* supra (note 6), Chapter 6.01, 6–6: "In the corporations context, fiduciary duties primarily take two forms: a duty to exercise care in the management and operation of the corporation, and a duty to exercise loyalty by putting the corporation's interests before personal interests."; see also Chapter 4 B.II.

Treuepflicht;[194] in France, a distinction is made between a *devoir de diligence* and a *devoir de loyauté*.[195] The business judgment rule has also come to be widely recognised.[196]

b) Specific Restrictions on Directors' Discretion

There has been little discussion on whether the broad discretionary powers held by directors of listed companies can simply be transferred to directors of closed corporations, or whether specific limitations are required.[197] There is strong argument for stricter controls, as the usual market control mechanisms in listed companies, ranging from variable remuneration elements, labour and product markets and financial market discipline[198] either do not apply or have limited application in closed corporations. The standard argument in favour of the business judgment rule, that diversified and therefore risk-neutral shareholders are interested in encouraging risk-averse directors to undertake business risks, does not apply here either: typically shareholders of closed corporations have contributed a large proportion of their assets into the corporation and are therefore risk averse.[199] Finally, some directors' decisions in closed corporations have a more dramatic long-term effect on shareholders than in public corporations, a classic example being the dismissal of a shareholder employee.[200] Depending on

---

194 As regards members of the management board in stock corporations, see *Fleischer* in: Spindler/Stilz, AktG, 2nd ed., 2010, § 93 para. 8 and 200; for GmbH directors, *Fleischer* supra (note 48), § 43 GmbHG para. 4.

195 In detail : *Redenius-Hoevermann* La responsabilité des dirigeants dans les sociétés anonymes en droit français et droit allemand, 2010, p. 29 et seq.

196 See *Fleischer* supra (note 194), § 93 AktG para. 9 with further references.

197 See *Fleischer* NZG 2011, 521, 524 et seq.; *Moll/Ragazzo* supra (note 6), Chapter 6.02[C], 6–42; see also Chapter 4.B.II.1.a).

198 See *Richter/Furubotn* Neue Institutionenökonomik, 3rd ed., 2003, p. 429 et seq.

199 Convincingly, *Jungmann* FS K. Schmidt, 2009, p. 831, 842 et seq.; *Moll/Ragazzo* supra (note 6), § 6.02 [C], 6–42: "It should be noted that some of the justifications for the business judgment rule are poor fits in the close corporation setting. With respect to the risk-return trade-off, for example, shareholders in closely held corporations often invest a considerable amount of their savings into the enterprise, which tends to leave them undiversified."

200 See *Easterbrook/Fischel* supra (note 162), p. 244 et seq.: "For example, the decision to terminate an employee in a publicly held corporation is a classic example of the exercise of business judgment that a court would not second-guess. In a closely held corporation, by contrast, termination of an employee can be a way to appropriate a disproportionate share of the firm's earnings. It makes sense, therefore, to have greater judicial review of termination of managerial (or investing) employees in closely held corporations than would be consistent with

the type of business decision being made, individual cases may call for greater levels of judicial review.[201]

3 Standards of Conduct for the Corporation and its Organs

Finally, the corporation shall ensure equal treatment for all shareholders who are in the same position. This principle, set out in Art. 42 of the Second Company Law Directive for public companies, also applies to closed corporations even without explicit codification.[202] In legal practice, however, it is frequently not accorded independent significance, but is instead regarded as part of the doctrine of fiduciary duties.[203]

4 Control Mechanisms for Conflicts of Interest

Finally, many legal systems have developed special control mechanisms for conflicts of interest. These apply in particular to related party transactions between a (majority) shareholder and his company that harbour patent risks for the pecuniary interests of other shareholders.[204] Under German law, the second sentence of § 47(4) GmbHG disqualifies the contracting shareholder from voting. In French law, Art. L. 223–19 C.com. provides a special control procedure for such "self-dealing" on the basis of a report by the director or the *commissaire aux compte:* the shareholders' meeting must consent to the transaction while the shareholder participating in the transaction must abstain from voting on this decision. English law has a comparable control procedure in ss. 190 et seq. Companies Act 2006, albeit restricted to contracts between a *director* and the corporation, thus only offering minority shareholder protection if the *director* is at the same time a (majority) shareholder. In addition, s. 239(4) Companies Act 2006 – comparable to § 47(4) sentence 1 GmbHG – prohibits directors' votes from being counted in a resolution to ratify their own actions.

The level of protection this provides is disputed in Germany and abroad. According to German case law and legal doctrine, corporate acts (*Sozial- oder Ver-*

---

the business judgment rule"; explained in further detail in *Moll* 53 Vand. L. Rev. 749, 822–825 (2000); on German law, *Fleischer* NZG 2011, 521, 526 et seq.

201 See for US law *O'Neal/Thompson* supra (note 1), Chapter 10:4, p. 13 et seq.; for German law *Fleischer* NZG 2011, 521, 525 et seq.; *Jungmann* FS K. Schmidt, p. 831 et seq., goes too far in seeing no room for directors' discretion in the GmbH.

202 See for German law BGHZ 116, 359, 372 et seq.

203 In more detail, *Fleischer* supra (note 78), § 53a AktG para. 11 with further references.

204 See II.1 above; for related party transactions of *directors*, see also Chapter 4 B.II.5.

bandsakt) are not encompassed by § 47(4) sentence 2 GmbHG. Specifically, these include the appointment of a shareholder as director, and the determination of his executive compensation.[205] Instead, case law uses the principle of equal treatment and the fiduciary duty between shareholders as control instruments: the compensation paid to the shareholder acting as director must therefore be reasonable and proportionate with the payment a non-shareholder director would have received for the same work.[206] The French *Cour de Cassation* recently also dealt with the same problem: in a leading decision in May 2010, it found that the involvement of a majority shareholder-director in determining his own remuneration was not subject to the control procedure pursuant to Art. L. 223–19 C.com.[207] A follow-up decision in October 2011 overturned an appellate court decision that had declared null and void the resolution of a shareholders' meeting on the amount of the shareholder-director's remuneration as illegal without detailed grounds by reason of *abus de majorité*.[208] In England, case law has considered inflated salaries of a shareholder-director in a closed corporation to be a prohibited repayment of contribution: in the initial decision *Re Halt Garage* in 1982, the defendant failed to work for the corporation again after a period of illness, but continued to receive her director's salary. *Oliver J.* stated in his decision that the payments were "so out of proportion to any possible value to her holding of office that the court is entitled to treat them as not being genuine payments of remuneration."[209]

V Legal Remedies for Minority Shareholders

1 Minority Protection through the Right to File an Action

a) Actions Challenging the Validity of Shareholders' Resolutions

In most continental European legal systems, outvoted minority shareholders may bring an action to set aside a resolution of the shareholders' meeting that violate the law or the articles of association.[210] This issue is regulated differently

205 See II.2 above; from case law BGHZ 18, 205, 210; 51, 209, 125 et seq.
206 See BGHZ 111, 224.
207 See Cass. com., Rev. soc. 2010, 222 with annotation *Couret*.
208 See Cass. com., Rev. soc. 2012, 38 with annotation *D. Schmidt*.
209 *Re Halt Garage* (1965) Ltd. [1982] 3 All ER 1016, 1042; see also *MacPherson v. European Strategic Bureau*, [2000] B.C.L.C. 683, 701–704; for a comprehensive analysis, see *Fleischer* in: Lutter, Das Kapital der Aktiengesellschaft in Europa, 2006, p. 121 et seq.
210 For a comprehensive analysis, see *Fleischer* GmbHR 2013 (forthcoming).

from jurisdiction to jurisdiction. The German GmbH Act does not contain specific provisions to deal with unlawful shareholder resolutions; to fill this gap, courts draw on §§ 241 et seq. Stock Corporation Act by analogy.[211] The Swiss Code of Obligations states in Art. 808c that the provisions for setting aside shareholder resolutions in stock corporations also apply *mutatis mutandis* to closed corporations. Other jurisdictions, for example Austria (§§ 41–44 Austrian Act on Limited Liability Companies (öGmbHG)) or Italy (Art. 2479-*ter Codice Civile*), have an independent regime for actions against shareholder resolutions in a closed corporation. Yet other jurisdictions, namely France (Art. L. 235–1 C.com), provide a single set of rules for an *action en nullité* across all forms of commercial companies. By contrast, in English law the concept of a general shareholders' right of review for majority decisions is completely unknown. Litigation is only available for resolutions pertaining to the transformation of a public company into a private company, for variations in share capital and the purchase of a company's own shares (ss. 98, 633, 721 Companies Act 2006). For all other matters, the minority shareholder only has recourse to general legal principles and remedies, such as an unfair prejudice petition (s. 994 Companies Act 2006). The Draft SPE Regulation provides in Art. 28(4) sentence 2 that the shareholders' right to challenge shareholders' resolutions is determined according to the law of the individual state. To ensure legal protection against illegal shareholders' resolutions, a model statute for closed corporations should provide for a special action to set aside such resolutions.

b) Claims for Compensation

Minority shareholders' claims for compensation are divided into direct actions (*personal action, action directe*) and derivative shareholder actions (*actio pro socio, action sociale ut singuli*).

aa) Direct Action

Grounds for a direct action arise under German law when a GmbH-shareholder suffers individual, direct loss over and above indirect losses suffered due to damage to the corporation's assets.[212] In the United Kingdom, a shareholder whose rights have been affected by the company can seek to have these rights enforced

211 Established case law since the case reported in Entscheidungssammlungen der Entscheidungen des Reichgerichts in Zivilsachen (RGZ) 85, 311, 313 et seq.

212 See BGHZ 95, 330, 340; *Merkt* Münchener Komm. z. GmbHG, 2010, § 13 para. 310.

by a personal action;[213] however, the no reflective loss principle ensures that indirect losses cannot be recovered.[214] In France, Art. L. 223–22 C.com allows shareholders of a SARL to file an action for the compensation of personal losses distinct from losses suffered by the corporation resulting from a breach of duty by corporation directors; however, such an *action directe* is often extremely difficult to enforce in practice. For a model statute, the inclusion of direct actions is recommended in order to protect minority shareholders from individual losses.

bb) Derivative Shareholder Actions

In Germany, derivative shareholder actions are also recognised in GmbH law[215] as an extension of the *actio pro socio*[216] found in the law of partnerships, although they are not codified. They permit individual shareholders to bring an action against other shareholders on behalf of the corporation, to the extent that the corporation does not pursue this action itself. In England, this approach has been codified in s. 260 et seq. Companies Act 2006, adopted from the famous decision in *Foss v. Harbottle* [217] allowing a shareholder to pursue a derivative action against directors of the corporation for actions that breach their fiduciary duty as illegal or ultra vires.[218] The shareholder must apply to the court for leave to pursue this action, which must then pass a two-stage test to ensure the application is being made in good faith and to prevent frivolous actions against the corporation. However, the derivative action, despite being extended to include actions for simple negligence, continues to operate only on the legal periphery, as its practical application is extensively overshadowed by the remedy for unfair prejudice.[219] Shareholders of a SARL in France can use the actions for compensation (*action sociale ut singuli*) afforded by Art. L. 223–22 (3) C.com. if a director has breached his duty causing loss or damage to the corporation. In Italy, Art. 2476 (3) *Codice civile* provides that any shareholder may file an action against the corporation's director. In the light of the almost universal recognition of derivative actions in Europe, it is surprising that it has not been

213 See *Gower/Davies* supra (note 12), para. 17–27.
214 See *Prudential Assurance Co Ltd. v. Newman Industries Ltd.* (No 2) [1982] Ch. 204; *Johnson v. Gore, Wood and Co.* [2002] 2 A.C. 1.
215 See Federal Court of Justice (BGH) in NJW 1990, 2627, 2628.
216 See Entscheidungssammlungen der Entscheidungen des Reichsgerichts in Zivilsachen (RGZ) 70, 32, 34; BGHZ 25, 47, 49.
217 2 Hare 461.
218 See *Gower/Davies* supra (note 12), para. 17–12, p. 652; for a comparative law perspective see *Braun/Strothotte* RIW 2010, 424.
219 See *Reisberg* 6 Eur. Co. & Fin. L. Rev. 219 (2009).

put forward as an instrument for protecting minority rights in the Draft SPE Regulation.[220] A model statute for closed corporations should provide for a derivative shareholder action, because it facilitates the enforcement of compensation claims.

Drawing a line between direct actions and derivative actions can lead to greater problems for closed corporations than for stock corporations.[221] Some jurisdictions in the United States therefore tend to allow direct actions in all cases of breach of fiduciary duties to the detriment of minority shareholders,[222] while others do not differentiate between direct and derivative actions.[223] The Principles of Corporate Governance of the American Law Institute provide a compromise in this respect.[224]

2 Minority Protection through Exit Rights

Shareholder rights to exit for good cause are generally recognised in Germany even without specific regulation in the articles of association.[225] However, they are only used as a last resort when less drastic measures, namely the sale of shares, are unreasonable. Attempts to create a statutory exit right at will have not been successful; however, the articles of association may include an ordinary right of exit from the corporation. In Switzerland, Art. 822 (1) Swiss Code of Obligations provides that a shareholder can seek a court's permission to exit a corporation for good cause; while Art. 822 (2) Swiss Code of Obligations states that the articles of association may provide a right to exit that is contingent on specific circumstances.

---

220 However, there is some criticism of the suitability of derivative actions for closed corporations in *McCahery/Vermeulen* in: Neville/Sørensen, supra (note 15), p. 207, 234 et seq.: "Arguably, the remedy is unlikely to provide a good fit for closely held companies where shareholders serve as management. Not only is there doctrinal incoherence, but there is some question as to whether this technique is too costly, given the other legal remedies available to private companies."; also *Ribstein* 64 Bus. Law. 739 (2009).

221 See *Moll/Ragazzo* supra (note 6), Chapter 9.02 under the heading "Derivative Suits in Closely Held Corporations"; for the German perspective see BGHZ 65, 15 (ITT).

222 See *Crosby v. Beam*, 548 N.E.2d 217 (Ohio 1989).

223 See *Bagdon v. Bridgestone/Firestone, Inc.*, 916 F.2d 379, 384 (7th Cir. 1990): "The author of the leading treatise treats *Abelow* as establishing the proposition that the closely held nature of the corporation [is] irrelevant to the distinction between direct and derivative action. [...] *Abelow* is the law of Delaware today."

224 See ALI, Principles of Corporate Governance, 1994, Chapter 7.01(d).

225 See BGHZ 9, 162 et seq.; 116, 359, 369.

The *Codice civile* provides a more detailed solution in Art. 2473. According to Art. 2473 (1), the initial articles of association determine when a shareholder may exit a corporation, as well as the relevant conditions. In any case, shareholders are entitled to a right of exit if they have not agreed with a resolution of the shareholders' meeting that proposes to change the purpose or legal form of a corporation, to merge or split-up the corporation, to revoke liquidation, to transfer the seat of the corporation abroad, to remove one or more of the exit grounds provided for in the articles of association, and the conduct of such transactions involves a significant alteration of the purpose of the enterprise specified in the articles of association or a significant alteration of the shareholder's rights. According to Art. 2473(2), the right of exit can be exercised by the shareholder of a corporation created for an indefinite period at any time with a notice period of at least 180 days. The articles of association can provide for a longer period of notice, but not longer than one year.

The Draft SPE Regulation proposed by the Commission views the exit right contained in Art 18 (1) primarily as an instrument to protect minority rights: it affords the shareholder the right to exit from the SPE when commercial operations are being, or are about to be, conducted in a way that would severely damage their interests in the corporation, for example when: (a) a significant amount of corporate capital is removed from the SPE; (b) the registered office of the SPE is relocated to another member state of the EU; (c) the commercial areas in which the SPE operates are significantly altered; (d) there have been no distributions of dividends for at least three years, even though the SPE had the financial capacity to do so.[226] In the compromise version put forward under the Swedish presidency, this provision was deleted.

Statutory exit rights in closed corporations have always been judged differently from a legal policy and an economic perspective. Those in favour of exit rights emphasise the similarities between closed corporations and partnerships, which already have exit rights.[227] They highlight that minority shareholders can use their exit rights to put pressure on directors to manage business efficiently[228]

---

226 For more on this and the significant changes suggested by the European Parliament, see *van den Braak* 6 Utrecht L. Rev. 1, 11 et seq. (2010).

227 From a US perspective, see *Hetherington/Dooley* 63 Va. L. Rev. 1 (1977); see also *O'Neal* 33 Bus. Law. 873, 883 (1977).

228 See *Neville* in: Neville/Sørensen, supra (note 15), p. 247, 288: "Moreover, the whole idea of an exit right is to give the minority some bargaining power, so that it can put pressure on the majority to manage the company effectively"; also *de Kluiver* 8 Eur. Bus. Org. L. Rev. 103 (2007); *van den Braak* 6 Utrecht L. Rev. 1, 21 (2010): "My conclusion is therefore that the shareholder should not be allowed to embark on the SPE adventure unless he is equipped with an adequate

and point out that minority shareholders often do not make sufficient use of the opportunity to include a right of exit in the articles of association for various reasons, some of which were discussed above.[229] Opponents of a statutory right of exit point to financing and liquidity problems for the corporation which may result from buying out shareholders wishing to exit,[230] and stress the increased danger of minority shareholders engaging in opportunistic behaviour.[231] They also point out that liberal exit rights can lead to problems of under-investment, as shareholders are less compelled to commit to higher levels of investment in the corporation.[232] This would also lead to disadvantages for the corporation's creditors.[233] Taken overall, there are significant grounds against generous statutory exit rights.

VI Minority Shareholders' Rights of Information and Inspection

Successful enforcement of minority protection remedies often stands or falls on the availability of adequate information. For this reason, rights of information and inspection for minority shareholders take on tremendous significance. In Germany, § 51a (1) GmbHG guarantees individual shareholders the right to information on the affairs of the company and the right to inspect the books and records. This individual right is distinct from the comprehensive auditing rights of the shareholders as a whole (§ 46 no. 6 GmbHG), which allow for an independent special audit of the corporation to be undertaken on a simple majority resolution of the shareholders' meeting.[234] There are no grounds *de lege lata* for an individual or minority right to institute a special audit in a GmbH similar to that provided in § 142 (2) AktG; however, it is worth considering *de lege ferenda*.[235] In France, the SARL shareholders have far-reaching rights of information: they have a per-

buy-out remedy."; see also *Andersson* in: Neville/Sørensen, supra (note 15), p. 191, 204 et seq.; and *Mahoney* supra (note 1), p. 177, 180 et seq.

229 See *Neville* in: Neville/Sørensen, supra (note 15), p. 247, 280 et seq.

230 See *Davies* supra (note 2), p. 228: "A unilateral exit right might undermine the company's business activities by requiring it to pay out cash from the business (to the minority shareholders) at an inappropriate time, for example when it was needed to expand the company's business."

231 See *Easterbrook/Fischel* supra (note 162), p. 238 et seq.

232 See *Rock/Wachter* 24 J. Corp. L. 913 (1999).

233 See *Davies* supra (note 2), p. 228; *Easterbrook/Fischel* supra (note 162), p. 242.

234 See *Bayer* in: Lutter/Hommelhoff, Komm. z. GmbHG, 18th ed., 2012, § 46 para. 30.

235 See *Fleischer* GmbHR 2001, 45, 48 et seq.

manent right to disclosure of documents (Art. L. 223–26 (4) C.com. and R. 223–15 C.com.), a specific right to information at shareholders' meetings (Art. L 223–26 (2) C.com. and R. 223–18 C.com.; Art. R. 223–19 C.com.), and the right of every shareholder to submit written questions to the director of a SARL (Art. L. 223–26 (3) C.com., Art. L. 223–36 C.com.). Shareholders who together represent at least one-tenth of corporation capital can seek to have an *expert de gestion* appointed by the court, to report on one or more of the acts by the management (Art. L. 223–37 C.com.). Finally, they may, as part of a pre-trial procedure, enforce an *expertise 'ad futurum'* (Art. 145 CPC). In the UK, information rights for minority shareholders are, by contrast, less developed:[236] In addition to the right to receive a copy of the annual accounts and reports contained in s. 423(1)(a) Companies Act 2006, minority shareholders merely have the right to request and receive copies of specific documents (s. 229(1) or s. 358(4) Companies Act 2006). However, in practice, case law grants inspection rights for corporate documentation for small private companies, particularly in conjunction with pending unfair prejudice cases.[237] The Draft SPE Regulation proposed by the Commission provides shareholders with the right to ask questions of and receive information from corporation directors (Art. 29(1)). The right to an independent special audit originally contained in the Commission Draft has been deleted after sharp criticism from legal scholars.[238] However, the provisions granting minority shareholders the right to propose a resolution (Art. 30(1), quorum: 5 %) and to call a shareholders' meeting (Art. 30 (2), quorum: 10 %) remain unaltered.

VII Out-of-Court Settlements

The potential for extrajudicial solutions becomes particularly worth examining in the case of closed corporations.

1 Arbitration

In Germany, the Federal Court of Justice gave an enormous impetus to arbitration when it recognised that, under certain conditions, disputes related to shareholder

---

236 See *Hannigan* Company Law, 3rd ed., 2012,, para. 17–6.

237 See *Re Hydrosan Ltd* [1991] B.C.C. 19; *Arrow Trading & Investment Est 1920 v Edwardian Group Ltd* [2005] 1 B.C.L.C. 696; see also *CAS (Nominees) Ltd v Nottingham Forest FC plc* [2002] 1 B.C.L.C. 613.

238 For example, criticism made by the Arbeitskreis Europäisches Unternehmensrecht, NZG 2008, 897, 901.

resolutions in closed corporation law could be settled by alternative dispute resolution.[239] Elsewhere on the continent, for example in Italy and Spain, this was already underway. In Great Britain, following preparations for the most recent company law reform, carefully prepared proposals for an arbitration scheme for shareholder conflicts were presented.[240] The British government, however, has not yet made a decision on its implementation, although tentative promises were made to conduct a comprehensive cost-benefit analysis.[241] In the United States, arbitration clauses are common in articles of association for closed corporations; these contracts however, must comply with the provisions of the individual state where the corporation is registered.[242] In its legislative decision on the Draft SPE Regulation, the European Parliament encouraged the Commission to add a further article allowing closed corporations to include an arbitration clause in the articles of association for settling conflicts between shareholders.

2 Mediation

Mediation has also recently been gaining in importance as a means of dispute resolution. The advantages are particularly apparent for shareholder disputes in closed corporations: As mentioned at the beginning of this chapter,[243] internal conflicts tend to involve an interwoven mesh of personal and commercial interests that is almost impossible to unravel. To view conflicts through the magnifying glass of a court or arbitral settlement that isolates the conflict and reduces the case to its bare legal bones hardly contributes to a long-term solution for these conflicts.[244] Mediation is a worthwhile alternative, providing a more comprehensive case-by-case approach, capable of reviewing the whole "relationship history". Moreover, it can be provided for merely by including a mediation clause

239 See BGHZ 180, 221; overruling the previous decision: BGHZ 132, 278.

240 See Modern Company Law for a Competitive Economy: Developing the Framework, 2000, para. 7.44 – 7.69; Modern Company Law for a Competitive Economy, Final Report, 2001, para. 4.10 – 4.12.

241 See White Paper, Modernising Company Law, 2002, Cm 5553-I, Part II, para. 2.36.

242 See *Cox/Hazen* supra (note 138), § 14.14, p. 866 et seq.: "Before deciding to use arbitration in a close corporation, the lawyer should carefully search the statutes and judicial decisions of the state of incorporation for corporate norms that would either invalidate arbitration agreements in the particular business situation involved or would otherwise nullify their effectiveness."

243 See A.II. above.

244 For a convincing discussion, see *Dendorfer/Krebs* MittBayNot 2008, 85, 88.

in the articles of association.[245] The legislature, for its part, can provide an opportunity for mediation to play a more significant role in closed corporation law by implementing the Cross-Border Mediation Directive[246].

C Protecting the Majority Shareholder from Opportunistic Behaviour by Minority Shareholders

I The Problem of Ex-Post Opportunism by Minority Shareholders

A majority shareholder, in principle, does not need special protective measures, as his voting power usually allows him to remedy any disadvantageous situations himself.[247] There are, however, situations in which he is dependant on the cooperation of minority shareholders.[248] This is often the case where legislation imposes a unanimous vote requirement for specific resolutions or where shareholders have a statutory right of veto.[249] A similar situation arises where the majority shareholder does not possess a sufficient qualified majority to make changes to the articles of association. In these cases, a minority shareholder may abuse his veto rights in order to further his own position. Just as the types of abuse by the majority can be listed,[250] one can present a "*typologie des abus de minorité*"[251].[252] Conceptually, one can separate abuse through positive conduct (*abus positif*), for example through deliberate exploitation of an individual or mi-

245 See *Casper/Risse* ZIP 2000, 437; *Heckschen* in: Heckschen/Heidinger, Die GmbH in der Gestaltungs- und Beratungspraxis, 2nd ed., 2009, § 4 para. 387 et seq.; for a comprehensive view, *Eidenmüller* Vertrags- und Verfahrensrecht der Wirtschaftsmediation, 2001.
246 Directive 2008/52/EC of the European Parliament and of the Council of 21 May 2008 on certain aspects of mediation in civil and commercial cases, OJ L, 24.5.2008, p. 3–8; on the German perspective in closed corporation law, *Wedemann* (note 8), p. 510 et seq., 553 et seq.
247 See, in the context of unfair prejudice remedies *Gower/Davies* supra (note 12), para. 20–2, p. 720: "Controlling shareholders are not in terms excluded from using the section but normally any prejudice they are subject to will be remediable through the use of the ordinary powers they possess by virtue of their controlling position."
248 See *Smith v. Atlantic Properties, Inc.*, 422 N.E.2d 798, 801 (Mass. App. Ct. 1981): "Cases may arise in which, in a close corporation, majority stockholders may ask [for] protection from a minority stockholder."
249 See *Moll/Ragazzo* supra (note 6), Chapter 7.01[D][e], 7–104.
250 See B.II. above.
251 *Merle* supra (note 81), in note 2 (p. 730).
252 See *Le Cannu* Bull. Joly 1986, 429.

nority right, and negative abuse (*abus négatif*), for example an unfounded refusal to agree on urgently needed shareholders' resolutions.[253]

II Statutory or Case Law Remedies

Remedies against opportunistic minority behaviour have developed in almost all jurisdictions. German courts use the concept of the member's duty of loyalty, which not only applies to the majority shareholder, but also to the minority shareholder with blocking power. In France, the majority shareholder has increasingly called upon the court-based remedy of *abus de minorité*[254] in recent years.[255] In the UK, the remedy of unfair prejudice is also available to a majority shareholder, under certain conditions.[256] In the United States the courts apply the provisions on "oppressive actions" contained in individual state regulations.[257]

1 Standards of Behaviour for Minority Shareholders

Substantively, the members' duty of loyalty as developed in German case law requires minority shareholders to consider the commercial interests of other shareholders in the exercise of their membership rights, particularly co-administrative and supervision rights.[258] Very similarly, the French *Cour de Cassation* has described abuse by minority shareholders as "conduct contrary to the general interest of the corporation, in which [the minority] prevents the implementation of an essential operation, with the sole purpose of advancing their own interests to the detriment of other shareholders."[259]

2 Appropriate Sanctions for Abuse of Voting Rights

For a range of reasons, some jurisdictions have difficulty with the provision of effective legal consequences for the abuse of voting rights by minority sharehold-

253 See *Merle* supra (note 81), para. 581.

254 See *Champetier de Ribes-Justeau* supra (note 7), p. 182 et seq.

255 See *Merle* supra (note 81), para. 581: "Depuis quelques années, il est de plus en plus fréquemment invoqué."

256 See, for example, *Parkinson v. Eurofinance Group Ltd* [2001] B.C.C. 551.

257 In further detail, *Moll/Ragazzo* supra (note 6), Chapter 7.101[D][e] under the heading "Oppression of the Majority by the Minority".

258 See BGHZ 129, 136 – Girmes (AG); for the GmbH *Merkt* supra (note 213), § 13 GmbHG para. 91.

259 Cass. com. 15.7.1992, D. 1993, 279.

ers: "the most delicate problem is that involving sanctions for abuse by the minority".[260] These difficulties arise because compensation claims by majority shareholders do not lead to a valid shareholders' resolution. The French courts, for example, hesitate to consider a shareholders' resolution valid[261] if it has been rejected by the minority shareholders in abuse of their rights by recourse to the concept of *jugement valant acte*[262] because they do not wish to interfere with the corporation's internal affairs. In Germany, these difficulties are overcome by considering votes cast in a way inconsistent with the duty of loyalty as void[263] or allowing a combination of an action for rescission and an action for a positive declaratory judgment that the regulation has been adopted.[264]

III Exclusion of Minority Shareholders

One particularly draconian measure against abusive conduct by minority shareholders is to exclude "trouble-makers" from the corporation.

1 Exclusion for Good Cause

In Germany, case law[265] and legal literature[266] recognise a right of exclusion for good cause when a GmbH shareholder's conduct becomes unbearable for the corporation. This is based on the shareholders' duty of loyalty [267] and the general principle that longer-term legal relationships encroaching significantly on the daily lives of their members should be prematurely dissolved on demonstration of good cause.[268] In the UK, despite the lack of statutory regulation the courts

260 *Merle* supra (note 81), para. 581.
261 For a compromise solution, see Cass. com., 9.3.1993, JCPE 1993, II, 448 – *arrêt Flandin*, in accordance with which a judge cannot hand down a decision but can appoint a *mandataire ad hoc* who is instructed to vote in place of and in the name of the minority shareholder acting abusively; critically *Cozian/Viandier/Deboissy* supra (note 3), para. 383: "La jurisprudence de la Cour ne manque pas d'hypocrisie."
262 See *Couret*, in: Mélanges Spitéri, 2008, p. 411; *Champetier de Ribes-Justeau* supra (note 7), p. 366 et seq.
263 See *Zöllner* in: Baumbach/Hueck, Komm. z. GmbHG, 20th ed., 2012, § 47 para. 108.
264 See *Zöllner* supra (note 263), Anh. § 47 GmbHG para. 191 with further references.
265 See BGHZ 9, 157, 159 et seq.; 16, 317, 322 et seq.; 32, 17, 22 et seq.; 80, 346, 348 et seq.; BGH NJW 1999, 3779.
266 See etwa *Strohn* Münchener Komm. z. GmbHG, 2010, § 34 para. 3 with further references.
267 See BGHZ 9, 157, 163; 80, 346, 349.
268 See BGHZ 9, 157, 161; 80, 346, 349 et seq.; see now also § 314 BGB.

have recognised the need for a right to exclude a minority shareholder for good cause.[269] The measure must be provided for in the articles of association, and must stand up to judicial review.[270] In addition, exclusion for good cause is also conceivable in individual cases, as part of the court's broad discretion for claims of unfair prejudice under s. 996(1) Companies Act 2006. This remedy is only granted to majority shareholders when all other remedies have been exhausted.[271] The *Cour de Cassation* in France elevated the prohibition on the exclusion of shareholders to a legal principle in 1996:[272] a judge is not permitted to rule that an individual shareholder should be excluded from a corporation, although legislation does provide specific exceptions. Additionally, French legislation has explicitly acknowledged on more than one occasion that clauses for the exclusion of a shareholder may be included in the articles of association, although not for the SARL. Case law has likewise confirmed the validity of such clauses[273], although thus far only for the *société en nom collectif.* It should be noted, however, that these provisions are subject to judicial review. Codified exclusion clauses for good cause exist in Italy (Art. 2473 Codice Civile) and Switzerland (Art. 823 Swiss Code of Obligations). The Commission's Draft SPE Regulation provided in Art. 17(1) that the competent court can, upon application by the SPE, order the exclusion of a shareholder if that individual has severely damaged the interests of the corporation or the continued involvement of that individual as a shareholder may prove detrimental to the operation of the corporation. In the compromise version put forward under the Swedish Council presidency, this provision was deleted without replacement.

2 Squeeze-Out Regulation

Most corporate law systems recognise some form of squeeze-out regulation with which a majority shareholder, upon reaching a threshold of 90 % or 95 %, can simply exclude a minority shareholder from the corporation.[274] The legislature

269 See *Sidebottom v Kershaw, Leese & Co Ltd,* [1920] 1 Ch. 154; *Gower/Davies* supra (note 12), para. 19 – 11.

270 See *Citco Banking Corp N V v Pusser's Ltd* [2007] 2 B.C.L.C. 483; *Shuttleworth v Cox Bros & Co Ltd* [1927] 2 K.B. 9; *Allen v Gold Reefs of West Africa Ltd* [1900] 1 Ch. 656.

271 See *Re Legal Costs Negotiators* [1999] 2 B.C.L.C. 171, 199, 201; *Gower/Davies* supra (note 12), para. 20 – 2; *Hannigan* supra (note 237), para. 17– 20.

272 Cass. com., Rev. soc. 1996, p. 554.

273 Cass. com., D. 2005, p. 839, obs. *Lienhard*; JCPE 2005, 1046, no.° 9, obs. *Caussain/Deboissy/Wicker.*

274 For a comparative overview see *Fleischer* in: Hopt/Wiedemann, Großkomm. z. AktG, 4th ed., 2007, before § 327a para. 60 et seq.

has justified this general right of exclusion by referring to the potential for these minimal shareholdings to obstruct corporate operations and force the majority to make financial concessions.[275] Leading opinion in Germany has continued to resist attempting to apply the relevant stock corporation provisions in §§ 327a AktG et seq. directly into the GmbH by analogy, as GmbH investors, even those with a very small holding, do not want to be reduced to mere capital investors.[276] Austrian legislation took an alternative route in the Shareholder Exclusion Act (GesAusG) of 2006: according to § 1 (1) GesAusG, the main shareholder in a GmbH has the right to exclude other shareholders once he has reached a control threshold of 90 %.[277] However, the regulation is optional: according to § 1 (4) GesAusG, the articles of association can rule out the exclusion of shareholders or require the majority shareholder to hold more than 90 % of the shares.

D Resolution of Shareholder Deadlocks

I The Problem of Deadlock

Shareholder conflicts in closed corporations can also arise for reasons other than opportunistic behaviour by majority or minority shareholders. These involve deadlocks at the shareholder and the director level, for which neither or both[278] parties may be responsible, but which make continuing commercial operation difficult or even call into question the capacity of the corporation's organs to act.[279] Known as deadlocks in Anglo-Saxon legal literature, these situations have yet to be given a catchy title in German.[280] In France, they are called *abus d'égalité*.[281]

275 See grounds of the Government Draft of the Wertpapiererwerbs- und Übernahmegesetz (WpÜG), Bundestagsdrucksache 14/7034, p. 31.
276 In more detail, *Fleischer* supra (note 275), § 327a AktG para. 8 with further references; dissenting, *Harrer* FS Sonnenberger, 2004, p. 235, 237 et seq., 244 et seq.
277 See *Gall/Potyka/Winner* Squeeze Out. Der Gesellschafterausschluss bei AG und GmbHG, 2006, para. 35; *Kalss/Zollner* Squeeze out, 2007, § 1 GesAusG, para. 22.
278 See *Knies* GmbHR 2005, 1386, 1389: "It will often not be possible to identify the clear culprit."
279 See *Fleischer* supra (note 1), Introduction GmbHG para. 276; for a comparative perspective, *Wolfram* US-amerikanischer Deadlock und Selbstblockade der GmbH-Organe, 1999; for the Australian perspective the description in *O'Donovan/Grady* (1982) 1 Comp. & Sec. L.J. 67: "an impasse in the corporate decision-making process".
280 See from the British perspective *Mayson/French/Ryan* supra (note 85), p. 585; from the US perspective *Moll/Ragazzo* supra (note 6), Chapter 7.02.

Legal practice shows that these deadlock situations most frequently arise in two-member corporations,[282] a particularly common structure in Germany and abroad:[283] according to a recent study conducted across different German regions, 37 % of all GmbHs are two-member corporations,[284] and according to an older study, even up to 51 %.[285] The spectrum ranges from the ordinary GmbH with two shareholders to GmbHs formed between married spouses to joint ventures between two stock corporations. Often, the two shareholders each possess one half of the GmbH, and the same time, serve as directors of the corporation. This structure effectively results in a need for unanimous voting, creating a continuous need for the partners to reach agreement. This is particularly problematic in cases of dispute, as the shareholders may seek to block each other's resolutions, with the conflict often escalating to attempted reciprocal removal from office as a director and exclusions as a shareholder.[286]

II Private Autonomy Precautions

As the two-member corporation is considered particularly prone to conflict for the reasons set forth above, the inclusion of appropriate safeguards against any disputes in the articles of association or in contractual side agreements become particularly relevant.[287] Well-prepared proposals to this effect have been

---

281 See *Champetier de Ribes-Justeau* supra (note 7), p. 21, where the *abus d'égalité*, at least from a systemic legal perspective, is portrayed as a subcategory of *abus de minorité*.

282 Monographically *Knies* Das Patt zwischen den Gesellschaftern der zweigliedrigen GmbH, 2005; for the Swiss perspective, *von der Crone* Schweizerische Juristen-Zeitung (SJZ) 89 (1993), 39.

283 See *Champetier de Ribes-Justeau* supra (note 7), p. 21: "Finally, the *abus d'égalité* is able to take its place in 50/50 corporations. In these corporations, according to egalitarians, no decision can be made without the agreement of both shareholders. Both shareholders therefore possess a veto right for every proposed resolution."

284 See *Kornblum/Hampf/Naß* GmbHR 2000, 1240, 1245.

285 See *Limbach* Theorie und Wirklichkeit der Gesellschaft mit beschränkter Haftung, 1966, p. 42.

286 From the US perspective *Cox/Hazen* supra (note 138), Chapter 14.11, p. 852: "Deadlocks among the shareholders and in the directorates of closely held corporations may occur because of the way voting shares and positions on the board are distributed. Shares are sometimes divided equally among two or more shareholders or groups of shareholders. And it is not unusual for a close corporation to have an even number of directors; thus a deadlock of directors is likely to occur."

287 From a German perspective *Fleischer* supra (note 1), § 1 GmbHG para. 79; from the US perspective *Cox/Hazen* supra (note 138), Chapter 14.11, p. 853: "Therefore, during the organization of a close corporation, counsel must anticipate such problems and may need to provide

helpfully provided by legal practice[288] and have become part of the standard procedure for forming joint venture contracts.[289] For the resolution of *voting deadlocks on specific resolutions,* provisions may be made that (a) one member, for example, the (rotating) Chairperson of the general shareholders' meeting, holds the casting vote, (b) the resolution is referred to another corporate body, particularly the supervisory board or advisory board, or (c) the decision should be made by an arbitrator. In case of *permanent deadlock*, the articles of association can make provision for (a) a right of exit for good cause, (b) a duty to transfer shares to the partner, similar to a double sealed bid process, or (c) a right to sell shares in the corporation to third parties, despite restrictive provisions in the articles of association.

From a corporate law perspective, these individual safeguards only raise individual issues: A first question is whether the articles of association can also provide for a casting vote to be made by a third party outside the corporation. In German literature, this is often answered in the negative, under the doctrine of corporate sovereignty (*Verbandssouveränität*).[290] In contrast, the Supreme Court of the German Reich (*Reichsgericht*) considered it permissible for the casting vote to be vested with the corporation's general counsel, even where this person was not a shareholder of the GmbH.[291]

The solution to internal deadlocks in companies with two shareholders developed by Anglo-American contractual practice, known as shoot-out clauses, is increasingly the subject of discussion.[292] These clauses can help one of the two shareholders to purchase all the shares in the corporation as part of a strictly for-

special contractual arrangements to resolve them. These arrangements usually are set up in the corporation's charter or bylaws or in a shareholders' agreement. They typically take one or more of the following forms: (a) provisions for the buyout of the interests of aggrieved shareholders, (b) the creation of special dissolution rights and procedures, or (c) undertakings to arbitrate disputes."

288 See, for example, *Natterer* in: Hamann/Sigle, Vertragsbuch Gesellschaftsrecht, 2008, Chapter 5 para. 220 et seq.

289 See for example *Fett/Spiering* in: Handbuch Joint Venture, 2010, Chapter 7, para. 524 et seq.

290 Rejecting this position: *Michalski/Römermann* Komm. z. GmbHG, 2nd ed., 2010, § 47 para. 575; *Zöllner* supra (note 264), § 47 GmbHG para. 23.

291 See Entscheidungssammlungen der Entscheidungen des Reichsgerichts in Zivilsachen (RGZ) 49, 141, 147: "The law does not state that the decision in question cannot be transferred to a third party outside of the corporation. Given the nature of the situation, it seems preferable that the decision be made by an impartial third party, who is capable of objective judgement and unfettered discretion instead of one of the shareholders involved or the company director."; see also *Zutt* ZHR 155 (1991), 213, 214 et seq.

292 In greater detail, *Fleischer/Schneider* DB 2010, 2713; also *Fleischer/Schnelder* ECFR 2012, 35 et seq.

malised price-setting process. Shoot-out procedures, due to their consistency with the 'cake cutting rule' ("I cut, you choose"), promise a process fair to both parties. However, game theory research has revealed that these procedures can be inefficient *ex post*.[293] Instead, the research recommends auction-bidding processes to establish a price, thereby ensuring that the corporation's shares end up in the hands of the party that most values them. From a corporate law perspective, the validity of shoot-out clauses is an open question. A first indication has come from a ruling given by the Court of Appeal in Vienna that accepted such clauses in a corporation's articles of association. This judgment was based on the fact that shoot-out clauses contained sufficient "checks and balances" to prevent any disadvantage to dissenting shareholders.[294] The Paris Court of Appeal has likewise approved such a clause, because it does not have a sanctioning character and therefore does not constitute an invalid exclusion clause, but instead only contains a voluntary exit procedure agreed between the parties.[295] However, there may be a reason for judicial intervention in individual cases to protect one of the two shareholders where that shareholder cannot finance a purchase offer from the outset, making a shoot-out procedure potentially disadvantageous and something to be avoided.[296]

III Conflict Resolution through Statutory or Case Law

Where voluntary mechanisms are lacking, the contractual Gordian knot may only be severed through recourse to legislation or case law. This external intervention is justified by the fact that valuable resources would otherwise lie idle.[297] Most jurisdictions consider the *ultima ratio* to be compulsory dissolution of the corporation upon application to the court by one of the members. In Germany, case law has confirmed that irreconcilable differences between the members of a two-member GmbH or a deadlock at a shareholders' meeting constitute good cause as defined in § 61 (1)

293 See *McAfee* 56 J. Econ. Theory 266, 284 (1992).

294 See Vienna Court of Appeal, 20.4.2009, 28 R 53/09 h, GesRZ 2009, 376.

295 See CA Paris, Rev. trim. dr. comm. 2007, 169, 170 annotated by *Le Cannu*.

296 See *Fleischer/Schneider* Der Betrieb (DB) 2010, 2113, 2117 et seq.; see also *Fleischer/Schneider* ECFR 2012, 35 et seq.

297 See also *Moll/Ragazzo* supra (note 6), Chapter 7.02, 7–149 – 7–150: "The conventional explanation for the harm of deadlock is that socially useful assets are unable to be productively deployed when disagreements between the corporation's decision-makers paralyse the company from taking action."

GmbHG.[298] For these situations in Great Britain, the court has usually resorted to a winding up of the corporation in accordance with s. 124 Insolvency Act 1986.[299] In France, the courts have spoken in favour of exceptional dissolution for disputes between shareholders in a corporation.[300] In the United States, s. 14.30(2) of the Revised Model Business Corporation Act provides a compulsory mechanism for dissolution for deadlock situations, which has been adopted in different forms in the corporate law legislation of various states;[301] in Kansas, for example, only corporations with two members may be dissolved.[302]

As compulsory dissolution often reduces the value of otherwise prosperous corporations to nothing, there is scope for courts and legislature to consider less drastic conflict resolution measures. This could include setting a higher duty to cooperate for both shareholders on the basis of the duty of loyalty[303] or the replacement of a disputed resolution by a court decision.[304] This seems to have

298 See BGHZ 80, 346, 348; BGH NJW 1985, 1301; Munich Court of Appeal GmbHR 2005, 428; in the literature *Knies* GmbHR 2005, 1386.

299 See *Mayson/French/Ryan* supra (note 85), p. 583 and 585; an early example from case law in *Ng Eng Hiam v. Ng Kee Wei* (1964) 31 MLJ 238, 240: "The principle is clear that if the court is satisfied that complete deadlock exists in the management of a company the jurisdiction [to wind up a company if the court thinks it just and equitable to do so] will be exercised. [...] It may be that the jurisdiction will be more readily exercised where [...] although the business is carried on by means of a private limited company, the case is not unlike one of a partnership."

300 See Cass. com., Rev. soc. 1982, 804; Montpellier, 18.6.2002, Revue de Jurisprudence de Droit des affaires (RJDA) 2004, p. 893, no. 981; in the literature *Merle* supra (note 81), para. 580: " In exceptional circumstances, a corporation may be declared dissolved due to an inability between shareholders to come to agreement."

301 For a good overview see *Cox/Hazen* supra (note 138), Chapter 14.12, p. 853 et seq.

302 See Kans. Stat. Ann. § 17–6804(d): "If the stockholders of a corporation having only two stockholders, each of which owns 50 % of the stock therein, are unable to agree upon the desirability of dissolving the corporation and disposing of the corporate assets, either stockholder may file with the district court a petition stating that it desires to dissolve the corporation and to dispose of the assets thereof in accordance with a plan to be agreed upon by both stockholders."

303 Considerations in this direction in *Schneider* FS Kellermann, 1991, p. 403, 412 et seq.: "In these kinds of companies, structural reality produces a pressure to cooperate and agree, that means a particularly extensive duty to actively participate in managerial shareholder resolutions, such as passing resolutions selecting authorised signatories, the adoption of annual financial statements, etc."; critically, however, *Knies* GmbHR 2005, 1386, 1389: "Even mutual bonds of loyalty cannot form the basis of a compromise against the clearly stated position of a shareholder."

304 Initial attempt in *Zöllner* ZGR 1988, 392, 416 et seq., who suggested using the provisions of §§ 15 et seq. German Civil Code to permit judges to substitute a resolution in deadlocks over the adoption of the annual financial statement and allocation of profits according to § 894 German Code of Civil Procedure.

been intended in Swiss legislation with the recently amended third sentence to Art. 821 (1) Swiss Code of Obligations, which states that the court is in a position to identify potential solutions that are appropriate and reasonable for the participants, rather than dissolving the corporation. This is particularly relevant with regard to providing compensation that truly reflects the value of the shares owned by the claimant shareholders. This opportunity to provide a judgment that deviates from the petitions filed by the claimant or the defendant is considered just as revolutionary as it is problematic in legal literature[305] and exceeds the mandate of corporate law judges in some countries.[306]

In the overall interests of the corporation's ability to operate, legislative solutions to deadlock situations should be considered. Legal literature has repeatedly called for various special statutory rules to govern two-member corporations.[307] § 69(5) sentence 3 Government Draft of the GmbHG 1973 contained a special provision for withdrawal of the power of management and representation in a two-member GmbH,[308] but German – and Swiss[309] – legislation has not yet followed up on these reform considerations. However, German case law has established a range of special rules to reflect the special interests of a two-member GmbH.[310] Key issues addressed include the exclusion or expulsion of members, removal from office of a shareholder-director, dissolution of the corporation and assertion of rights of compensation against co-shareholders.[311] In addition to these features of substantive law, numerous civil procedure questions have also arisen.[312]

---

305 For regulation similar to Art. 736 no. 4 Swiss Code of Obligations (OR) for stock corporations, *Böckli* Schweizer Aktienrecht, 4th ed., 2009, Chapter 16 para. 195.

306 Generally from the French perspective *Jeantin* Le rôle du juge en droit des sociétés, in: Mélanges Perrot, 1995, p. 149; *Mestre*, Réflexions sur les pouvoirs du juge dans la vie des sociétés, Rev. juris. com. 1985, 81.

307 Already in favour, *Mayer-Wegelin* Die Willensbildung in der paritätischen Zweimann-Gesellschaft bei Uneinigkeit der Gesellschafter, 1968, p. 103 et seq.

308 See Bundestagsdrucksachen 7/253, p. 19 (wording) and p. 123 (grounds).

309 Rejecting this position in advance, *Böckli/Forstmoser/Rapp* Reform des GmbH-Gesetzes, 1997, p. 112.

310 For a summary, see *Fleischer* supra (note 1), § 1 GmbHG para. 74 et seq.

311 Monographically *Reher* Die Zweipersonen-GmbH – Notwendigkeit eines Sonderrechts? 2003.

312 In more detail, *Wolf* ZGR 1998, 92, 96 et seq.

E Results

1. Internal conflicts between shareholders are the Achilles' heel of closed corporations. Three different patterns of conflict are typically found: exploitation of the minority shareholders by the majority shareholder (oppression of the minority), opportunistic behaviour by minority shareholders (*tyrannie des faibles*) and deadlock situations in corporations with equal shareholdings (deadlock).
2. In closed corporations, minority shareholders are particularly at risk due to the interaction of various factors. These factors include the majority principle for shareholders' resolutions, private ordering for internal relationships, a stable majority, the lack of a liquid secondary market, no reliable mechanism for determining the value of the shares and restricted judicial review of business policy decisions.
3. Initially, each (minority) shareholder is responsible for ensuring adequate self-protection through provisions in the articles of association or by contractual side agreements. However, due to potential overoptimism and the often close personal relationships between founder-shareholders, they are particularly susceptible to rationality deficits and distortions of perception which lead to underinsurance against opportunistic behaviour. This results in the necessity of supplementary minority protection by statutory or case law.
4. Various instruments have been developed in Germany and abroad for the solution of majority-minority conflicts, which should be incorporated into a model statute. In particular, these include a general clause, limiting the influential power of the majority shareholder (shareholders' fiduciary duties, *mitgliedschaftliche Treuepflicht*, *abus de majorité*). To protect the minority from harmful director behaviour, strict standards of conduct for directors (duty of care, duty of loyalty) should be put in place. Finally, special control procedures and/or statutory voting prohibitions are advisable for dealing with conflicts of interest, such as in related party transactions between shareholders and their company.
5. Rights of action and exit rights for minority shareholders serve to enforce minority protection. Rights to information and other auxiliary mechanisms make the effective enforcement of action and exit rights easier. The action to challenge the validity of shareholder resolutions, an instrument deeply rooted in the legal tradition of continental Europe, is useful to guarantee legal protection against resolutions in violation of the law or the articles of association. There should also be the opportunity to claim compensation, either as an individual claim (direct action, *action directe*) or as a shareholders' derivative action (*actio pro socio*, derivative action, *action sociale ut sin-*

guli). By contrast, generous statutory exit rights are not recommended, because they can lead to massive under-investment and liquidity problems.

6. Irrespective of this, special attention should be given to the development of out-of-court dispute settlement in legislation and case law. In addition to dispute resolution by arbitration, mediation offers a promising alternative to fully address and smooth out the complicated and often intertwined business and personal differences that frequently form the basis of shareholder disputes in closed corporations.
7. Suitable instruments should be available to fight ex-post opportunism by minority shareholders. As a mirror image of the majority shareholder's fiduciary duty, recourse to a general clause is recommended here (*abus de minorité*, oppression remedy). Exclusion of the troublemaker from the corporation should also be possible as a last resort.
8. Private autonomous safeguards in the articles of association or shareholders' agreement are recommended for the resolution of deadlocks, which are particularly problematic in two-member corporations. Where contractual mechanisms are lacking, conflict resolution through statutory or case law is indispensable in order to prevent socially valuable resources lying idle. In this context, compulsory dissolution of the corporation, is only a last resort; discussion of less drastic conflict resolution mechanisms, such as through a more active role of the judge, is as yet little developed in Germany and abroad.

Chapter 4 The Board of Directors*

Table of Contents

* The text is based on a draft by *Engert*.

While closed corporations typically have few shareholders, most jurisdictions nonetheless provide for a mandatory board of directors as a further organ in addition to the shareholders' meeting, and the remaining jurisdictions at least permit it.[1] The law thus allows to entrust persons other than the shareholders with managing the corporation. Even if most closed corporations are run by the shareholders themselves, delegated management offers an additional organisational option and extends how the closed corporation as a legal form can be used in practice.[2] It enables a division of labour between active entrepreneurs and passive – or at least less active – owners. Whether and to which degree delegated management offers an advantage depends on the corporate law regulation of the management organ(s).

The management of the closed corporation raises two overlapping regulatory challenges: if not all shareholders serve as directors, there is – firstly – the task of controlling the agency conflict between capital providers and directors in order to enable the desired division of labour. Compared to public corporations, this line of conflict figures less prominently in closed corporations:[3] with few shareholders, monitoring the directors is easier than in a public corporation. But even though the "separation of ownership and control" is less pronounced, it still needs effective legal precautions. At the same time, the stronger influence of the shareholders (or a majority of the shareholders) puts more emphasis on the agency conflict between the majority and the minority as well as between shareholders and third parties.[4] Therefore, the second regulatory challenge is to define the role of the management in relation to these conflicting interests. As we will see, it is at this point that a separate management body confers the greatest potential benefits, which justifies the existence of an additional organ in the first place.

This Chapter starts out by outlining the general role of management in the closed corporation. This includes the issue of why there is a need for an additional organ in the corporate constitution alongside the shareholders' meeting (Section A.). Subsequently, the important issues in regulating the management of a closed corporation will be considered: the management's role in the corporate

1 Examples from US-American corporate law below in notes 25 and 28.

2 By contrast, some legal systems stipulate that in the law on partnerships, non-delegated management is mandatory, such as in Germany and Great Britain, see Sec. 5 Partnership Act 1890 and Sec. 6(1) Limited Liability Partnerships Act 2000. France differs here, see Art. L221–3 Abs. 1 C.com.

3 See Chapter 2 B.I.

4 See Chapter 2 as well as Chapter 3 and Chapter 5.

constitution, the control of director behaviour and the sanctions applicable to directors (Section B.). The last Section C. summarises the most important results.

Instead of a single management body, larger closed corporations sometimes have a supervisory board or an advisory board as an additional organ for appointing, monitoring and advising the managing directors.[5] For the sake of simplicity, it will be assumed in the following that there is only a board of directors (or "directors" for short) as the only corporate organ in addition to the shareholders' meeting.

A The Role of the Board of Directors

To understand and regulate the management in the closed corporation, we should first be sure which functions it must fulfil. This raises the fundamental question of why closed corporations need an additional organ alongside the shareholders' meeting.

I Acting Organ

The existence of a board of directors is sometimes justified by the fact that the corporation itself is not capable of acting and, therefore, is in need of an "organ" as primary actor.[6] This argument has some merit. However, it fails to explain why the shareholders' meeting should not be sufficient to make the corporation capable of acting.[7] In principle at least, a single corporate organ would suffice. The shareholders' meeting may be an unwieldy place to manage the corporation's daily business in practical terms, but the corporation's ability to act

---

5 In a random sample of German corporations with 100 – 499 employees (without distinction as to legal form), 41 % had a supervisory board or advisory board, *Woywode/Keese/Tänzler/Hauer* Betriebswirtschaftliche Forschung und Praxis (BFuP) 63 (2011), 628, 633.
6 For instance *Flume* Allgemeiner Teil des Bürgerlichen Rechts I/2, 1983, p. 379; *K. Schmidt* Gesellschaftsrecht, 4th ed., 2002, p. 248; *Merle* Droit commercial, Sociétés commerciales, 12th ed. 2008, p. 126; on the ability to act on behalf of the corporation as a rationale for any corporate organs, see *Guyon* Droit des affaires I, 12th ed., 2003, p. 198 et seq.; *Wiedemann* Gesellschaftsrecht, Volume I, 1980, p. 212. For the US perspective, see *Aviram* Officers Fiduciary Duties and the Distinction Between Corporate Agents and Corporate Organs, U. Ill. L. Rev. 2013, forthcoming.
7 Even for the shareholders' meeting, there has to be a legal provision, whether explicit or implicit, to the effect that a resolution of the shareholders' meeting is attributed to the corporation as its own "act", see *Savigny* System des heutigen römischen Rechts, Second Volume, 1840, p. 283 ("Even if all individuals, without exception, act together, this is not to be seen as if the ideal body which we call a legal person, had acted", translation by the authors).

would in any case be assured. The corporation could employ agents on a contractual basis and have their legal acts (likewise knowledge and possession) attributed to it in accordance with the general law of agency and representation. The legal transactions needed to hire agents could be undertaken by the shareholders' meeting. The corporation's capacity to act therefore does not necessitate a board of directors as an additional organ of the corporation. However, if the closed corporation has a board – for reasons to be discussed below – there is a forceful argument that the board, rather than the shareholders' meeting, should be the sole or primary acting organ.

II Delegation

The board as an additional corporate organ enables the shareholders to delegate decision-making or the implementation of decisions to other persons, the directors.[8] Delegation confers the advantages of a division of labour: many matters are not important enough to warrant the involvement of all shareholders. In addition, a need for specialisation can arise even in a closed corporation. The paradigmatic case is the division of labour between the entrepreneur or a professional corporate director on the one side and the mere capital provider on the other side. In the closed corporation context, this differentiation of tasks can be found in young firms with venture capital providers or in certain family firms where only some family members participate in the management, or none at all. Likewise, corporations belonging to a larger group may be managed more or less independently. In addition to specialisation, the board can have an institutional advantage: if the corporation has more than one shareholder, collective decision-making by majority is required. This often costs more time and attention than decisions to be made by individual directors. Delegation also reduces the risk from shareholder deadlock or shareholder passivity.

However, delegation as such would not have to be dealt with under corporate law. There is a ubiquitous need to entrust agents with far-reaching decision-making power in business life, not just in corporations. Delegation could easily be accomplished under the general law of agency and representation. In fact, French corporate law for a long time considered directors to be authorised agents of the corporation (*mandataires*).[9]

8 See generally *Fleckner* Antike Kapitalvereinigungen, 2010, p. 47 et seq. (in the context of a "theory of capital associations").
9 See *Vidal* Droit des sociétés, 7th ed., 2010, p. 204 et seq., 517 et seq.

Meanwhile, the French theory has turned away from this position and today considers the board a corporate organ.[10] An advantage of the organ view (as opposed to an agency approach) may be that an organ can be vested with an exclusive competence whereas in agency law, a principal may not be able to divest the right to act for himself/herself.[11] If the shareholders' meeting were the only corporate organ, it could instruct representatives, but could not waive its power to act on behalf of the corporation. By contrast, the board as an organ exercises its own powers under the corporate constitution. There could be a legitimate interest in precluding short-term interference from shareholders (for example, to prevent careless decision-making leading to random majorities).

III The Board as Guardian of Minority and Third Party Interests

Lastly, the board can serve as a mediator for the conflicting interests of the various stakeholders involved in the firm. There are diverging interests both *amongst the shareholders* (in particular with a stable majority) and *between shareholders and third parties* (business partners, employees, involuntary creditors, the general public, etc.). If the board is to mediate and balance the interests of different stakeholders, it can easily find itself taking decisions against the will of the (majority of) shareholders. In this role, directors are not just agents of shareholders. We now have a compelling reason for the institutionalisation of the board as a separate organ of the corporation: in its sphere of competence, it acts "for the corporation" in the same, immediate way as does the shareholders' meeting.

Whether and to which extent the board must represent the interests of third parties against the shareholders, and of minority shareholders against the majority, is of great import for the corporate constitution. There is, of course, an extensive discussion of the matter with regard to the stock corporation. Key issues include defining the "corporate objective function", the existence of a "corporate

10 *Vidal* supra (note 9), p. 205; *Merle* supra (note 6), p. 126. In Germany, the same view has been adopted much earlier. While there is a dispute on the nature of the board's power of representation between the "representation theory" (*Vertretertheorie*) and the "organ theory" (*Organtheorie*), even the former attributes the board's power to a specific problem of corporate law, namely the corporation's natural incapacity to act, see *Flume* supra (note 6), p. 377. On the US perspective, see Restatement (Third) of Agency, Sec. 1.01, note (f)(2) (no agency relationship between the directors and the corporation or its shareholders); *Aviram* Officers' Fiduciary Duties and the Distinction Between Corporate Agents and Corporate Organs, U. Ill. L. Rev. forthcoming 2013.

11 This argument has been made for German law by *Reuter* AcP 207 (2007), 673, 694 et seq.; *Reuter* FS Steindorff, 1990, p. 229, 233 et seq. (in each case as justification for the principle of non-delegated management in partnerships).

interest" distinct from that of the shareholders, the alleged primacy of shareholders' interests or, more recently, the debate on corporate social responsibility.[12] Instead of pursuing this debate in the abstract, the following discussion focuses on two modes of regulation. A distinction is made between the duties requiring a specific course of action (Section 1.) and the indirect regulation of discretionary decision-making which is not fully determined by legal duties (Section 2.).

1 Specific-Conduct Duties

It is generally agreed that, in certain settings, directors should be required to take specific actions (or abstain from them) in the interests of minority shareholders, creditors and other stakeholders. Such duties prescribing a specific course of action will, in the following, be referred to as "specific-conduct duties". Specific-conduct duties can be imposed in the statute or derived from the general duty of care owed to the corporation. In any event, the required conduct must be sufficiently clear and predictable if the law is to impose liability for violations of the duty.

> There are numerous examples of specific-conduct duties in favour of minority shareholders and third parties: the directors can have an obligation – in the interests of minority shareholders – to maintain a shareholders record, to keep the books of the corporation, to grant individual shareholders a right of inspection and to treat the shareholders equally. On behalf of the creditors, the directors may have to resist distributions of corporate assets to shareholders, or they may be required to initiate insolvency proceedings if necessary. In addition, the directors have duties under tort law towards third parties.[13]

The directors thus act as the guardians of third-party interests against the corporation's owners.[14] What has been noticed little to date is that the imposition of duties on the directors is mirrored in a corresponding relief for the shareholders: with the board as a corporate organ, the law has created a new locus of legal obligations. Placing duties on the corporate directors is a precondition for releasing the shareholders from certain legal requirements and sanctions that, otherwise, would have to be imposed on them as owners of the corporation. This greatly enhances the potential for division of labour between active directors and passive shareholders: not only are the shareholders not liable for the corpo-

---

12 In summary, *Keay* The Corporate Objective, 2011, p. 40 et seq.; *Keay* 71 Modern L. Rev. 663, 667 et seq. (2008); *Klöhn* ZGR 2008, 110; *Birke* Formalziel der Aktiengesellschaft, 2005.
13 See B.II.1 for more detail.
14 If a director is not at the same time a shareholder, this regulatory approach resembles the "gatekeeper" strategy. On this regulatory strategy, see seminally *Kraakman* 2 J.L. Econ. & Org. 53 (1986).

rate debt;[15] they are also released from the threat of sanctions for violating duties in managing the corporation. Limited liability would remain imperfect without the latter element.[16] Conferring the shareholders' duties on the board of directors extends the range of available organisational forms.[17] In this sense, shareholders themselves benefit when the board is called to account for the interests of third parties.

2 Beyond Specific-Conduct Duties

Specific-conduct duties can only go so far in determining how the corporation's business is conducted:[18] Directors can be ordered to keep the books and how to do so, under what circumstances to initiate insolvency proceedings or when it is permissible to distribute corporate assets to the shareholders, etc. Apart from rare cases, however, it is hardly possible to regulate the corporation's choice of supplier from amongst several alternatives, the business opportunities to pursue or abandon or the amount of risk to take in a transaction. A court cannot discern, and the law cannot require, the optimal business decision in a given setting. Inevitably, directors enjoy a considerable margin of judgement in which the law cannot directly determine behaviour.[19]

The legal framework nonetheless remains important. It can influence how the board exercises its discretion. Corporate law can guide the directors by granting other persons a right of instruction or other supervision rights (for instance on the removal from office or on remuneration), by regulating remuneration or by controlling conflicts of interest. In devising the legal incentive structure, one has to define the proper role of the board in applying its business judgement. If the board is conceived as an independent guardian of the interests of

---

15 It has long been realised that limited liability promotes the division of labour between capital providers and active directors, see *Easterbrook/Fischel* 52 U. Chi. L. Rev. 89, 94 et seq. (1985) (for public corporations); on the advantages of limited liability in corporate groups, see *Couwenberg* 4 Rev. L. & Econ. 621 (2008).

16 The ECJ has emphasised this cecently in Case C-81/09 *Idrima Tipou AE v Ipourgos Tipou kai Meson Mazikis Enimerosis* [2010] ECR I-10161. There, the Court found that imposing fines for infringements of broadcasting regulations by a media company on shareholders, rather than on directors or employees, violated the fundamental freedoms of establishment and free movement of capital even if liability was restricted to shareholdings of more than 2.5 %.

17 See also Chapter 5.

18 For public corporations, see *Roe* 31 J. Legal Stud. 233, 234 et seq., 242 et seq. (2002).

19 For further detail, see B.II.1. below.

minority shareholders or third parties,[20] one might want to restrict the power of shareholders (or the shareholder majority) over directors in order to ensure unbiased decision-making.

Again, it may benefit the shareholders themselves if the board were to safeguard the interests of third parties and the minority: in relation to its business partners, employees and creditors, the closed corporation would offer an institutional guarantee that their interests will not be sacrificed for short-term profits. This can foster business relationships that rely on trust. It can also encourage minority shareholders to join or remain in the corporation.[21] In addition, different shareholder groups could mitigate potential conflicts if they agreed on impartial third parties as directors and accepted their decisions as binding.

In spite of these advantages, the better reasons militate against conceiving the board as a mediator between the shareholders and third parties or between the majority and the minority. Closed corporations usually have a single dominant shareholder or a stable shareholder majority. In addition, the business is typically much smaller than that of a public corporation. Thus, majority shareholders in a closed corporation can easily act as directors themselves. Under these conditions, it is not a promising regulatory strategy to pitch the board as an independent guardian against the shareholders or the majority by, for instance, denying the shareholders a right to instruct the board or otherwise restricting shareholder influence.[22] Such an attempt would lead to majority shareholders being less willing to delegate management to qualified outsiders.[23] They would prefer to serve as directors themselves or to elect their confidants, in spite of lesser qualifications, in order to better enforce their own interests. For instance, the dominant branch in a family corporation would hardly agree to appoint an external director if this would significantly reduce its influence. In the closed corporation, a legislative policy of vesting the board with independence would severely distort the choice between delegated and non-delegated management.

---

20 See *Blair/Stout* 85 Va. L. Rev. 247, 271 et seq. (1999) (management of the corporation as a mediating hierarch of all stakeholders).

21 On this notion of (majority) shareholder self-commitment, see *Stout* 152 U. Pa. L. Rev. 667, 677 et seq. (2003); *Blair/Stout* 85 Va. L. Rev. 247, 273 et seq. (1999); *Blair/Stout* 7 Eur. Bus. Org. L. Rev. 473, 488 et seq. (2006).

22 Similarly *Kroeze/Wezeman* Reform of Dutch Private Company Law, in: McCahery/Timmerman/Vermeulen, Private Company Law Reform, 2010, p. 181, 188 et seq.; for a contrary view, *Schwarz* in: Zaman/Schwarz/Lennarts/de Kluiver/Dorresteijn, The European Private Company (SPE), 2009, p. 110 et seq.

23 The conclusion would only be different if the law deprived shareholders of the right to elect the board. Not even labour codetermination in Germany goes as far as this.

Of course, nothing should preclude the shareholders themselves to turn the board into an impartial mediator.[24] The shareholders could commit to appoint only outsiders as directors, or to elect representatives of all shareholder groups. Such an agreement indicates that, in the particular corporation, the benefits of a neutral intermediary outweigh the possible disadvantages. This can, for example, be the case in joint ventures or in family corporations with shareholder factions of equal weight. Likewise, shareholders should be able to structure the board (or establish an additional supervisory or advisory board) with a view to balancing the interests of shareholders and third parties, such as through representation of employees or important business partners.

IV The Role of the Board: Preliminary Conclusion

The board of directors, being a separate organ of the closed corporation, fulfils three functions: it permits, firstly, to delegate the management of the business to qualified individuals, who may or may not be shareholders. Secondly, as a corollary of the management function, the board serves as the primary acting organ of the corporation. Thirdly, the board of directors, rather than the shareholders, is the primary locus of specific legal duties on behalf of the minority and other stakeholders. Beyond such duties in the realm of business judgment, corporate law should not attempt to institute the board as an impartial mediator between the conflicting interests of the majority and the minority or between the shareholders and other stakeholders. By contrast, the shareholders themselves should be able to provide for an independent role of the board through the articles of association.

B Regulating the Board of Directors

Having outlined the proper role of the board, we now consider particular policy issues. To begin with, one needs to clarify the board's position in the corporate constitution (Section I.). The greatest regulatory challenge consists of ensuring that directors act as faithful stewards of the interests entrusted to them (Section II.). Sanctions for breaches of duty are treated separately (Section III.).

24 This could be a means of breaking an existing deadlock between the shareholders, see Chapter 3.

I The Board in the Corporate Constitution

1 The Board as a Mandatory Organ

As found above, a closed corporation could in principle operate with the shareholders' meeting as its only organ.[25] However, little would be won if shareholders had the option to dispense with the board of directors.[26] Shareholders can appoint themselves as directors if they wish to manage the corporation; one could even imagine a statutory default rule to this effect.[27] Even without a separate board of directors, the corporate constitution would have to distinguish between the management of the corporation and certain fundamental decisions, which might, for instance, require a formal resolution of the shareholders or stricter majority requirements.[28] While there is little to be gained from an optional board, mandating it simplifies the structure of corporate law. If every closed corporation has a board of directors, there is a clear locus to which duties and power of representation can attach. The latter is of particular relevance for third parties dealing with the corporation. With a mandatory board of directors in place, the corporation is able to act and can be approached at all times.[29]

2 Allocation of Competences between Board and Shareholders

Allocating decision-making powers between the board and the shareholders determines the organisation structure of the closed corporation. The law should provide a set of default rules (Section a)) but the shareholders should be allowed to modify them in the articles of association. This raises the question as to the legal limits on amending the default allocation of competences. We will investi-

---

25 Under Delaware law, a closed corporation can be managed directly by its shareholders, Sec. 351 Del. Gen. Corp. L.

26 Likewise on the reform in the Netherlands, *De Kluiver* 3 Eur. Co. & Fin. L. Rev. 45, 56 et seq. (2006).

27 As is the case in Switzerland, Art. 809(1) sent. 1 Swiss Code of Obligations.

28 German partnership law distinguishes between fundamental transactions, decisions in the course of ordinary management and extraordinary management decisions (for the latter, see Sec. 116(2) German Commercial Code). Sec. 407(b)(3)–(5) ULLCA 2006 contains the corresponding distinction for the member-managed limited liability company in the US.

29 In European corporate law, the principle that a corporation is represented by its directors is anchored in Art. 9 First Council Directive 68/151/EEC. By contrast, according to the US model statute, a limited liability company can freely grant or restrict power of representation, which may, but does not have to, be disclosed to the public, Sec. 302 ULLCA 2006. Service can always be made to the registered office of the corporation, Sec. 113 et seq. ULLCA 2006.

gate this separately for inalienable decision-making powers of the board (Section b)) and the shareholders' meeting (Section c)).

a) Default Allocation of Competences

The law can allocate decision-making powers using a general standard or by rules on clearly defined subject matters.[30] The second approach conduces to legal certainty. Since the board is to serve as the corporation's primary representative, the statute should enumerate conclusively the competences of the shareholders' meeting and refer the remaining decisions in a catch-all provision to the board.[31]

Competences in relation to a particular subject-matter need not be allocated to a single organ; they can be split up, notably through competing competences, rights of instruction or approval requirements. For the sake of clarity, both within the corporation and towards third parties, competing competences should be avoided. By contrast, a right of instruction of the shareholders' meeting in relation to the board deserves further thought.[32] As discussed above,[33] the shareholders should usually be able to assert their own interests in the management of the corporation as long as this does not violate the directors' specific-conduct duties. A right of instruction by the shareholders' meeting as statutory default would reflect this consideration.

30 Sec. 116(1) German Commercial Code offers an example of a standard by defining "management" as comprising "all actions in the ordinary course of conducting the business of the company".

31 Art. 26(1)c of the Draft SPE Regulation provides for such a catch-all competence of the board. The Regulation is cited here and below in the version of the Hungarian presidency, dated 23 May 2011, available under http://www.europeanprivatecompany.eu/legal_texts/download/Hungarian-presidency-Mai2011.pdf.

32 A right of instruction is provided in Germany by Sec. 37(1) GmbHG, in Spain by Art. 161 Ley de Sociedades de Capital and in Great Britain (with a three-quarter majority) by Sec. 70 Table A of the Companies (Tables A to F) Regulations 1985. In the Italian s.r.l., shareholders can force a decision of the shareholders' meeting with one third of the issued share capital, Art. 2479 Abs. 1 Codice Civile. On Netherlands and Swiss law, see note 36.

33 A.III.1.

b) Mandatory Competences of the Board

In comparative perspective, there is widespread agreement that shareholders are permitted to tailor the allocation of competences to their needs.[34] To ascertain the limits of such freedom, we first consider the competences that must be reserved to the board. If the law requires the existence of a board of directors alongside the shareholders' meeting, it should also secure a minimum set of powers.

As a tribute to transparency and legal certainty, the board should be the sole representative of the corporation in relation to third parties.[35] However, this does not preclude the shareholders from imposing internal bounds on the decision-making powers of the board and subjecting it to tight shareholder control. Restrictions on the shareholders' freedom can only be justified by the interests of minority shareholders or other stakeholders. We have already considered the main argument for granting the shareholders broad autonomy in framing the corporate constitution: there is little promise in attempting to shield the directors against shareholder influence in the hope of protecting minority shareholders or third parties. The law can do no better than to require a certain conduct on behalf of these stakeholders, to the extent that such duties can be specified and enforced. It follows from this approach that, in its internal dealings with the shareholders, the board must only retain the right to discharge the specific legal duties imposed on it in the interest of the minority and other stakeholders. Apart from this, the articles of association may freely restrict the internal powers of the board.[36] Since the board is responsible for external acts in relation to third parties, this must take place through approval requirements or rights of instruction.

c) Mandatory Competences of the Shareholders' Meeting

We can also ask about mandatory competences in the opposite direction: which decisions must remain reserved to the shareholders' meeting and therefore can-

---

34 See Sec. 37(1) GmbHG; Art. L223–18(4) C.com.; Art. 2475 (5), Art. 2479(1) Codice Civile; Art. 804(2) No. 18, Art. 810(1) OR.

35 See note 29 above.

36 By contrast, Swiss closed corporation law is much stricter: it secures for the directors the right to determine the overall management of the corporation and its business organisation, Art. 810(2) No. 1, 2 OR. Similarly, Dutch law used to allow only "general instructions" by the shareholders. After the reform of 2012, the articles of association can provide that the board must follow the instructions of another corporate organ, see the new Art. 2:239(4) Burgerlijk Wetboek.

not be transferred to the board? As shareholders themselves write and amend the articles of association of the closed corporation, the core issue is whether and to what extent shareholders can deprive themselves of power. Shareholders may wish to delegate decision-making to lower the corporation's transaction costs. Yet this only justifies a revocable transfer of competences. Typically, the shareholders will want to retain a right of instruction.

As has been said above, however, it may be in the interests of shareholders to relinquish even a right of instruction and to vest the directors with greater independence. In this way, the shareholders can instate the board as a neutral arbiter between the interests of the various stakeholders. A waiver of power can be worthwhile for the shareholders (or the shareholder majority) if it instils trust in minority shareholders and other stakeholders that the corporation will respect their interests beyond complying with specific legal duties.[37]

There can therefore be good reasons for the shareholders to grant the directors some degree of responsibility and independence, without the right to interfere in the board's management. At first sight, there seems to be no objection to the shareholders surrendering their power over the corporation. In spite of this, many jurisdictions reserve a range of decisions to the shareholders' meeting in a mandatory way, including alterations to the articles of association, an increase or reduction of issued share capital, the adoption of the annual accounts as well as passing resolutions on distributions and share repurchases.[38] The rationale behind these restrictions very likely is minority protection: the law prevents the majority from transferring all decisions to the board, thereby removing them from any influence of the minority. Even if the minority can be outvoted in the shareholders' meeting, it still has to be invited and informed about the subject-matter for resolution. This can provide an opportunity to obtain protection from the courts against the measure pressed by the majority. In addition, the statute can stipulate special majority requirements for certain resolutions, for instance on structural changes.[39] The shareholders' meeting is thus employed as a vehicle of minority protection. Therefore, which competences should be reserved to the shareholders' meeting is ultimately a matter of minority protection,[40]

---

37 See A.III.2. above.

38 As in Art. 28(1) Draft SPE Regulation, supra (note 31). Similarly far-reaching provisions can be found in Art. 160 Ley de Sociedades de Capital and Art. 2479(2) Codice Civile. Sec. 46 GmbHG is optional within limits, see *Zöllner* in: Baumbach/Hueck, Komm. z. GmbHG, 19th ed., 2010, Sec. 46 margin no. 93 et seq.

39 As in Art. 28(2) Draft SPE Regulation, supra (note 31).

40 See Chapter 3.

which should be balanced against the higher transaction costs of shareholder resolutions.

II Controlling Directors' Behaviour

Directors are fiduciaries. Since closed corporations typically have few shareholders and shareholders frequently act as directors themselves, aligning the incentives of directors to shareholders' interests poses less difficulties as a practical matter than in the public corporation. Nonetheless, corporate law should furnish an incentive structure for passive shareholders to entrust the management of the corporation to professional directors.[41] The legal framework for controlling directors comprises specific-conduct duties but also indirect incentives for running the corporation's business in the interest of shareholders. In addition, the law should consider the interests of all stakeholders involved – shareholders and third parties, majority and minority. Yet following the argument made above, this balancing act should only result in specific-conduct duties imposed on the directors, if and to the extent that such duties can be stipulated and enforced.[42]

Specific-conduct duties can be derived from the directors' general duty of care or they can be imposed by the statute. They can originate from corporate law, but also the general law of tort, criminal law or public regulation (Section 1.). Beyond these specific boundaries, directors enjoy considerable leeway that is not directly constrained by the law. In this domain, directors' conduct can only be controlled indirectly. One such channel of influence is the right to appoint and remove directors (Section 2.), information rights of the shareholders (Section 3.), affirmative incentives through remuneration and other benefits (Section 4.) and rules for the avoidance of conflicts of interest, in particular the directors' duty of loyalty (Section 5.).

1 Specific-Conduct Duties

As fiduciaries, directors are inevitably bound by duties. While at the level of legal doctrine, many of these duties run to the corporation, it is nevertheless important to establish which stakeholder interests a given duty of the director serves

---

41 On the regulatory issues pertaining to this problem, see generally *Fleckner* supra (note 8), p. 79 et seq.
42 A.III. above.

so as to determine its precise meaning. The following analysis therefore looks separately at the protection of the shareholders as a class (Section a)), of the minority against the majority (Section b)) and of third parties (Section c)). In all three respects, an overarching issue is the extent to which entrepreneurial decisions should be subject to judicial review or, expressed otherwise, to what extent the directors should be granted a margin of judgement.

a) Protection of the Shareholders as a Class

Jurisdictions uniformly impose on the directors a general duty of care in relation to the closed corporation.[43] The care owed to the corporation above all benefits shareholders as a class because shareholders are the first to be affected by the corporation's profits and losses. In theory, the courts could derive a single permissible course of action from the general duty of care for every conceivable setting in which the board is called upon to decide. If this were the case, the law would, again only in theory, precisely predetermine the directors' course of action.

In practice, however, directors would very frequently be left in the dark as to what the general duty of care requires from them. Entrepreneurial activity inescapably involves decision-making under great uncertainty. The greatest advantage can often only be had by leaving the beaten track of how the business is or should be run, particularly when competing with other firms.[44] For example, at the time the decision is made, there is no way of knowing with any degree of certitude whether entering a new market will be worthwhile for the corporation. Subjecting business decisions to unlimited legal scrutiny would harbour the serious risk of an erroneous finding of a breach of the duty of care and director liability *ex post*. In addition, directors could hardly foresee *ex ante* whether their conduct would later possibly be considered in breach of duty. Consequently, directors would expose themselves to a considerable risk of liability even in case of careful behaviour, or in spite of their best endeavours. Such an unavoidable risk of liability is hard to reconcile with their fiduciary position: both the opportunities and risks of the business pertain to the corporation (and thereby primarily to the shareholders). If, in spite of their greatest endeavours regarding the duty of care, the directors exposed themselves to a non-trivial threat of liability for compensation, they would in effect bear part of the business risk. To avoid this, di-

43 See Sec. 174 Companies Act 2006; Art. L223–22(1) C.com.; Art. 2476(1) Codice Civile; Art. 225 Ley de Sociedades de Capital; Sec. 43(1), (2) GmbHG; Art. 2:9 Burgerlijk Wetboek.

44 The connection between the need for managerial discretion and competition is nicely made by *Hommelhoff* Konzernleitungspflicht, 1982, p. 168 et seq.: Liability should only be imposed for "evidently mistaken" decisions (p. 174) "in extremely rare situations" (p. 172).

rectors would shy away from worthwhile ventures and innovations. In addition, they would undertake measures to reduce their personal liability risk at the corporation's expense, even if this brings no material advantage (for instance: opinions by external advisors to secure their position). Furthermore, capable or wealthy persons would be less willing to act as directors or would demand higher remuneration.

The disadvantages of an intrusive duty of care would hardly be offset by benefits for the shareholders: to the extent to which they have the right to appoint directors and remove them from office, they can themselves punish poor entrepreneurial judgement or failures. In doing so, they can rely on their own subjective assessments and less tangible evidence which could not be used in litigation. With this sanction in hand and their right to instruct the board, they can closely monitor business development and individual management decisions. Performance-related remuneration can provide additional incentives. Shareholders therefore have effective instruments to discipline directors. It is thus not in their interests to call directors to account in court for (purportedly) wrong decisions.[45] Courts should be reluctant to review the decisions by corporate directors. Directors should be granted wide-ranging discretion under the "business judgement rule".[46]

In addition to the general duty of care, the statute could in principle contain specific-conduct duties. Again, however, it is difficult to stipulate such requirements on behalf of shareholders as a class in a manner that is sufficiently clear and predictable for directors, which is why they are rarely if ever encountered in the statute book. Bookkeeping duties may be an exception as they can at least in part be explained as an attempt to ensure careful management of the corporation also on behalf of the shareholders.

---

45 See *Myers* 5 J. Fin. Econ. 147, 157 (1977): "No sane lawyer attempts to write a contract requiring management to 'abstain from sub-optimal decisions'."

46 For the rationale of the "business judgement rule", see representatively *Fleischer* FS Wiedemann (2002), p. 827, 829 et seq.; *Enriques/Hansmann/Kraakman* in: Kraakman et al., The Anatomy of Corporate Law, 2nd ed., 2009, p. 79 et seq.; for an economic analysis, see *Engert/Goldlücke* Why agents need discretion: The business judgment rule as optimal standard of care, Working Paper, 2013. On the business judgement rule under French law, see *Redenius-Hoevermann* La responsabilité des dirigeants dans les sociétés anonymes en droit français et droit allemand, 2010, at 112 et seq. Similarly, liability for damages pursuant to Art. 2:9 Burgerlijk Wetboek presupposes a "severe accusation" (*ernstig verwijt*) against the director, *Van Schilfgaarde/Winter* Van de BV en de NV, 15th ed., 2009, Sec. 47, p. 168. On business judgement particularly in the closed corporation, see also Chapter 3 B.IV.2. and *Kuntz* GmbHR 2008, 121, 122 et seq.; *Fleischer* NZG 2011, 521, 522 et seq.

b) Protection of Minority Shareholders

Specific-conduct duties on behalf of minority shareholders (and of third parties, see below in B.II.1.c)) may have greater significance. The reason for this is that such duties are the only instrument by which the interests of minority shareholders can be brought to bear in the management of the corporation:[47] as the majority rules in the shareholders' meeting, it can influence the directors by issuing instructions or threatening to remove them from office. If necessary, majority shareholders can elect themselves or other persons of their choice to the board. The minority lacks rights of equal value.

To balance this, corporate law imposes specific-conduct duties on the directors. These duties primarily aim at ensuring proper procedures, reliable documentation and transparency. They include the duties to keep the shareholder list and the corporate books, to provide financial reports, to fulfil the inspection rights of individual shareholders and to convene the shareholders' meetings. The board is thus charged with responsibility for proper procedural standards within the corporation.

As managers of the corporation, the directors will easily find themselves caught in between the majority and the minority. If, for example, the dominant shareholder wishes to conclude a certain transaction with the corporation, this must take place through the board as the representative of the corporation. Other disputes in which the board may become involved concern the appropriation of profits or the issue of new shares (if the board can decide on a share issue).[48] To prevent the majority from abusing its influence on the board, the law can impose specific-conduct duties on the directors. Such duties can be stipulated by statute as in the case of a statutory pre-emption right for new shares. Beside such narrow rules, there should be broad standards from which specific-conduct duties on behalf of the minority can be derived. The directors' general duty of care in relation to the corporation again provides a suitable approach if the majority attempts to enrich itself – via the board – at the expense of the corporation. In addition, the corporation, the shareholders' meeting and the board – and hence also the directors – should be bound by a general principle of equal treatment of shareholders.[49]

Yet again, the general duty of care or the principle of equal treatment may be of little practical import if the directors are granted extensive discretion under the business judgement rule, as was advocated above with regard to sharehold-

---

47 See also Chapter 3 B.IV.2.

48 For an overview of important exploitation strategies of the majority, see Chapter 3 B.II.

49 Art. 813 Swiss Code of Obligations contains an express duty of equal treatment directed towards the directors. On the principle of equal treatment generally, see Chapter 3.

ers as a class.[50] The disadvantages of exposing even diligent directors to liability risk argue in favour of according the same unfettered margin of judgement. In the context of minority protection, however, there is the additional concern that the majority can exert its influence on the directors and should be balanced by a threat of sanctions. The optimal policy response ultimately rests on the function of the board in the particular setting of a conflict between the majority and the minority. As stated above, placing specific-conduct duties on the management can serve the purpose of relieving the shareholders of the same duties and the threat of sanctions.[51] If majority shareholders are to be released from their duties vis-à-vis the minority, directors would be the only safeguard on behalf of the minority. In fact, directors should be assumed to fully substitute for the (majority) shareholders when it comes to certain procedural duties, for instance the duty to keep records and the shareholder list. By contrast, as far as business decisions are concerned, a controlling shareholder should be subject to his/her own fiduciary duty even if the board represents the corporation in its dealings with the shareholder. For one thing, the shareholder actively participates in the transaction and indeed often controls it. A threat of liability therefore weighs less heavily on him/her than on a passive shareholder. For another thing, liability of a controlling shareholder for dealing with the corporation usually only means returning the unfair gain obtained at the expense of the corporation (and the minority). The mere risk that the fairness of a transaction is challenged after the fact does not justify substituting the directors for the controlling shareholder. To the contrary, the dispute should be dealt with by the shareholders themselves. This implies that there is no reason to curtail the margin of business judgement of the directors; of course, this does not apply to majority shareholders even if they are at the same time directors.[52] Hence, the directors' general duty of care in principle protects the minority against majority overreaching, but its practical impact is small because directors can usually invoke the business judgement rule. The same argument applies for the principle of equal treatment.

c) Protection of Third Parties

The directors substitute for shareholders mostly with regard to specific-conduct duties in favour of third parties: the board as corporate organ and "gatekeeper"

---

50 See also Chapter 3 B.IV.2.b).

51 A.III.1 above.

52 See Chapter 3 B.IV.2.b). Similarly, *Kuntz* GmbHR 2008, 121, 124 et seq. (unfettered business judgement of the external director, but stricter scrutiny in case of shareholder-directors); *Fleischer* NZG 2011, 521, 526 et seq. (likewise).

permits to spare shareholders the threat of liability. Instead of the shareholders as the economic owners, the directors are made responsible for the protection of third parties. However, shareholders can only be indemnified to the extent to which they respect the division of labour and the board's responsibility. Obligations can no longer be confined to directors when shareholders use their influence to induce the directors to breach their duty (see B.III.2 below).

There are two types of specific-conduct duties of the directors on behalf of third parties: firstly, the corporation's creditors and other stakeholders must have an interest in safeguarding the corporation's assets and, generally, in preserving its solvency (Section aa)). Secondly, the corporation's activities can affect contract partners and other third parties. In relation to them, the corporation should be held to fulfil its obligations and not to inflict harm on outsiders (Section bb)).

aa) Preserving the Assets and Solvency of the Corporation

Creditors (as well as employees and other contractual partners) have a vital interest in reducing the risk of insolvency of the corporation and, if insolvency nonetheless occurs, in limiting their losses. In this regard, limited liability creates a potential for abuse that corporate law should address. Safeguards include restrictions on asset diversion by limiting distributions to shareholders and a potential duty to initiate insolvency proceedings.[53] The content of such duties is dealt with extensively in Chapter 5.[54] For present purposes, it is important to note that these duties are imposed predominantly or even exclusively on the directors, even though the benefits of limited liability accrue to shareholders. As a particularly obvious example, consider the limitation on distributions of corporate assets to shareholders: while the directors incur full liability when they approve excessive distributions (in spite of their not having received anything), the liability of shareholders is restricted to mere repayment. Some jurisdictions even require that the shareholder knew or ought to have known that the distribution was impermissible.[55]

---

53 Such as provided for by Sec. 15a German Insolvency Code.

54 See in particular Chapter 5 D.III. (duty to file for insolvency proceedings), F. (asset shifts), G. (duties of information).

55 Likewise Art. 22 Draft SPE Regulation, supra (note 31); similarly under English law Sec. 847 (2) Companies Act 2006 and the liability for knowing receipt, see *Bachner* Creditor Protection in Private Companies, 2009, p. 117 et seq., 174 et seq.; stricter Art. L223–40 C.com. (no knowledge requirement); a nuanced solution is found in German law, see Sec. 31(1), (2) GmbHG; in addition, there is contingent liability pursuant to Sec. 31(3) GmbHG, which applies if repayment cannot be collected from another shareholder.

The most important issue in respect of the directors is whether – in addition to the duties provided for explicitly in the statute – the general duty of care also serves to protect creditors and other third parties.[56] Technically, the directors' general duty of care towards the corporation can be construed so as to encompass these stakeholders' interests in preserving the assets and solvency of the corporation.[57] Certain statutes, such as those in France and England, also contain broad provisions on director liability in favour of creditors.[58] However, there are divergent opinions about whether it is at all advisable to impose a general duty of care towards creditors on the board.[59] The question is of great relevance when a corporation suffers economic or financial distress.[60] In such a situation, it may well be in the shareholders' interests to pursue a risky business strategy even if this reduces the total value of the firm.[61] The risk incentive exists even before the equity capital has been depleted; it becomes considerably more acute if the corporation has become insolvent. An efficiency-minded corporate law must constrain the risk incentive in order to preserve the remaining value of the firm.[62] The directors' duty of care may be a means to this end. At the outset, therefore, the duty of care should be conceived as running not only to the shareholders but also to third parties; more particularly, it aims at preserving or increasing the total value of the firm.[63]

If director duties towards creditors nevertheless remain contentious, this may once again be due to the problem of business judgement. Granting the directors broad discretion is relatively easy to justify as long as it only affects

56 See also Chapter 5.

57 In English law, such a "duty to creditors" has been established in the important case *Liquidator of West Mercia Safetywear Ltd. v Dodd & Anor,* [1988] 4 B.C.C. 30, 33; see *Bachner* supra (note 55), p. 231 et seq.; for a comparative overview of German, US and English law, see *Klöhn* ZGR 2008, 110, 118 et seq.

58 See the French liability for *insuffisance d'actif* in Art. L651–1 et seq. C.com. and the English liability for wrongful trading in Sec. 214 Insolvency Act 1986.

59 The jurisprudence of the Delaware courts opposes such duties, see *North American Catholic Educational Programming Foundation v. Gheewalla,* 930 A.2d 92, 101 (Del. 2007); *Production Resources Group v. NCT Group,* 863 A.2d 772, 787 et seq. (Del. Ch. 2004); a duty only arises when the corporation is insolvent, ibd., p. 790 et seq. Any director duty to creditors is rejected by *Hu/Westbrook* 107 Colum. L. Rev. 1321 (2007).

60 See also Chapter 5 C.III.3.c).

61 On the shareholders' risk incentive, see seminally *Jensen/Meckling* 3 J. Fin. Econ. 306, 335 et seq. (1976); *Galai/Masulis* 3 J. Fin. Econ. 53, 70 et seq. (1976).

62 On the efficiency goal, see Chapter 2.

63 See also Chapter 5 III.3.b). On the increase of the expected total value of the firm – i.e. the sum of the value positions of all stakeholders – as regulatory goal, see *T. Smith* 98 Mich. L. Rev. 214, 243 et seq. (1999); *Engert* FS Heldrich, 2005, p. 87, 91 et seq.

shareholders because they can discipline directors in other ways, such as with the threat of removal from office. Creditors do not have such power and must assert themselves against the risk incentive of the more influential shareholders. In view of this, it might seem appealing to curtail the business judgement of directors and to use their duty of care as a bulwark against the shareholders' risk incentive. In view of the interests of creditors, one is tempted to recommend stricter scrutiny of the directors' decisions.[64] However, this is not a foregone conclusion. There is no inconsistency in viewing the duty of care as running to third parties but at the same time leaving the business judgement rule in full force. This would imply that the duty of care in relation to creditors would rule out only risk-taking that is evidently value-destroying.

At the heart of the debate, therefore, is the policy issue of whether directors should still be able to invoke the business judgement rule in corporate distress. A first point to note is that strict duty-of-care review without the benefit of the business judgement rule often would have limited effect on directors leading a corporation in crisis. Whether a threat of liability can guide director behaviour depends – roughly speaking – on a double precondition: firstly, the director must not suffer large losses if the corporation becomes insolvent because otherwise the director will seek to prevent the corporation's demise "at all costs". For this reason alone, shareholder-directors will seldom be impressed by the duty of care. Secondly, liability must place the director in a significantly worse position even if insolvency occurs because only then can it have a substantial effect on incentives. Even non-shareholder directors will therefore often not be susceptible to sanctions because their own fortunes are closely tied to the corporation and they may have little private wealth to lose.

Stringent liability from the duty of care only becomes important in the relatively rare case that a non-shareholder director has substantial assets outside the corporation. Yet even then liability need not bring about an overall improvement: without the business judgement rule, the director faces an increased likelihood that, in spite of his/her best efforts, liability cannot be avoided. He/she can avoid this risk by surrendering his/her office to persons less sensitive to sanctions (such as shareholders) or by initiating insolvency proceedings even when an out-of-court restructuring attempt would be preferable. Here as in the original

---

64 This contrasts with the widely held belief that directors have greater leeway if they were to serve "more than one master", *Clark* Corporate Law, 1986, p. 20, 679 et seq.; *Easterbrook/Fischel* The Economic Structure of Corporate Law, 1991, p. 38. For the opposite view regarding the duty of care and the business judgement rule, see for instance *Macey* 21 Stetson L. Rev. 23, 35 et seq. (1991); *Ribstein* 81 Notre Dame L. Rev. 1431, 1468 et seq. (2006).

setting, restricting the business judgement rule has damaging side effects.[65] Furthermore, large financial lenders win considerable influence in times of crisis and can restrain excessive risk-taking, which also benefits other stakeholders.[66] Precisely when it counts, creditors are therefore not helpless.[67] A final aspect concerns the difficulty of drawing a line between the stricter crisis duties and the domain of the unrestricted business judgement rule. Undesired ancillary effects would arise in the twilight zone between the two spheres. Ultimately, the better reasons support the conclusion that the business judgement rule should be left untouched, even in a crisis.

Summarising the results in respect of minority shareholders and third parties, an overall picture emerges: the directors' general duty of care serves the interests of shareholders as a class, minority shareholders, creditors and other third parties. This finding reflects the doctrinal structure of the duty of care, namely that it is owed not to the shareholders or to other stakeholders but to the corporation itself. The corporation represents the combined interests of all stakeholders, the total value of which is to be maximised.[68] While the duty of care serves the interests of all stakeholders, the business judgement rule remains in place in all settings. It follows that, in practical terms, the duty of care governs director behaviour only in rare and extreme cases.

bb) Compliance with the Corporation's Obligations and the Prevention of Injury

Apart from their interest in the continued solvency of the closed corporation, third parties are in many ways affected by the corporation's business activities. Just like other firms, the closed corporation must comply with numerous obligations under private and public law.

As regards directors, one first has to ascertain whether these provisions apply not only to the corporation itself, but also to the persons acting for it or

---

65 Of course, a stringent duty of care could be used to force the directors to initiate insolvency proceedings. But if this is the goal, the law should rather impose a duty to file for insolvency proceedings.

66 For a vivid description of how lenders make themselves heard in large corporations in the US, see *Baird/Rasmussen* 154 Pa. L. Rev. 1209, 1224 et seq. (2006). Empirical evidence on the (successful) influence of banks on medium-sized firms in the Netherlands in *Couwenberg/de Jong* 26 Int'l Rev. L. & Econ. 429, 442 et seq. (2007).

67 In smaller firms, however, shareholders typically have a greater informational advantage over creditors and thus better opportunities to steer the board. At the same time, directors in smaller firms will often be less sensitive to liability incentives.

68 On this goal, see note 63 above.

standing behind it.[69] For contractual obligations, this is usually not the case: as a general rule, the corporation alone is liable for the contracts concluded in its name. If the other party wishes to obtain the personal commitment of a shareholder or director, it must bargain for it in the contract. By contrast, duties from tort law often attach not only to the corporation but also to directors or shareholders.[70] Beside general tort law and criminal law, one should bear in mind as diverse fields as insolvency law, tax law, social security law and public regulation. It is not quite clear why other persons should be liable for breaches of duty alongside the corporation itself, which is responsible for the firm. The justification must be found in the shareholders' limited liability: for certain duties, liability only takes effect when the corporation has become insolvent. Shareholders have no interest whatsoever in ensuring compliance with such duties and will not induce directors to do so. Closed corporations could be employed as a scheme to shield oneself against liability in order to commit breaches of duty or at least to tolerate them. To prevent or at least mitigate such abuse, the law can extend liability to the persons behind the corporation.

In taking recourse to persons behind the corporation, one should, however, take into account the division of labour that corporate law aims to establish. Shareholders should be allowed to stick to the role of passive providers of capital. Beside not suffering from losses incurred by the corporation, they should also not be sanctioned for breaches of duty committed by the corporation. Providing this relief is perhaps the most important reason for establishing a board of directors as a separate organ of the closed corporation. As long as the shareholders do not interfere with the board,[71] only the directors should be liable for compliance with the duties of the corporation.

From the perspective of legal doctrine, it is often a matter of the pertinent legal field – for instance, tort law or criminal law – who can be held to account for complying with a given duty. But corporate law can develop its own devices to channel liability. An example is the French theory of *faute détachable*, which as a general rule denies directors' liability for breaches of duty of the corpora-

69 See also Chapter 5 B.

70 A borderline case between contract and tort is the question whether a director is liable himself/herself for negligently misleading the other party in contract negotiations with the corporation. German courts tend to dismiss such claims under the German doctrine of *culpa in contrahendo*, see BGHZ 126, 181, 183 et seq.; likewise from an English point of view (tort) *Williams & Anor v. Natural Life Health Foods*, [1998] 1 UKHL 17.

71 See B.III.2. below.

tion.[72] Conversely, corporate law expands directors' liability through a broad reading of the general duty of care: the duty of care is said to imply a "duty of compliance", under which the directors must comply with legal requirements when they act on behalf of the corporation.[73] The corporation's legal obligations are thus transformed into duties of the directors owed to the corporation. The duty of care is augmented by an additional dimension regarding the protection of third parties and the general public.

2 Appointment and Removal from Office

The analysis so far suggests that specific-conduct duties can control directors' behaviour only to a limited extent. Directors inevitably have broad discretion for which the law does not prescribe a particular course of action. The leeway enjoyed by directors primarily affects the shareholders (if they do not themselves serve as directors). Therefore, the law seeks to equip the shareholders with monitoring and control rights to align directors' interests with those of the shareholders. Beside a right of instruction (which can be contracted away)[74] there is, in particular, the right of the shareholders' meeting to appoint directors or remove them from office. For sake of simplicity, the default rule should be election with a simple majority. To save time and cost of shareholder meetings, directors should remain in office until they are replaced.

In principle, shareholders should be able to modify or restrict their right to appoint directors at will. For example, the articles of association may provide that only shareholders can be appointed as directors so as to guarantee a shared interest in the corporation's success. Alternatively, individual shareholders may

---

72 The director himself/herself is only liable if the breach is separable (*détachable*) from his/her function as a director, which the theory assumes for serious, deliberate breaches. See in detail *Vidal* supra (note 9), p. 225 et seq.; *Cozian/Viandier/Deboissy* Droit des sociétés, 24. Aufl., 2011, p. 161 et seq. German law has adopted the contrary principle that directors are generally liable for torts; it is less clear, however, under which conditions the duties of conduct arising under tort law apply to directors; for further detail, see BGHZ 109, 297, 302 et seq. ("Baustoff") and the more cautious approach in BGHZ 125, 366, 375 et seq.; for a distinction between "direct" and "indirect" breaches, see *Kleindiek* Deliktshaftung und juristische Person, 1997, p. 452 et seq. For unqualified liability of directors in tort under English law, see *Standard Chartered Bank v Pakistan National Shipping Corp*, [2002] UKHL 43, margin no. 20 et seq.; generally for the English discussion, see *Hannigan* Company Law, 2nd ed., 2009, margin nos. 3–72 et seq. with further references.

73 For the rationale of the duty of compliance, see *Thole* ZHR 173 (2009), 504, 509 et seq.; for the perspective of US law, see *Fleischer* ZIP 2005, 141, 146 et seq.; for a critical view from law and economics, see *Gelter/Grechenig* Wirtschaftspolitische Blätter (WPBl.) 2010, 35.

74 See B.I.2.a) above.

be granted a right to serve as directors themselves or to be entitled to name a director. Such a power can serve to secure the position of the minority or to reflect the special role of a shareholder, for instance that of the founder of the corporation. Finally, the appointment of directors can be delegated to another organ – such as a supervisory board – in order to involve external expertise or to preclude shareholder conflicts from impairing the selection process. The shareholders can even wish to offer other important stakeholders a say in the appointment of directors. Such representation of non-shareholder interests could take place in a special selection organ or through direct appointment rights for certain parties.

By contrast, the draft of an SPE Regulation reserves the shareholders' meeting the competence to appoint directors and remove them from office as well as to determine their terms of office.[75] It is hard to justify why the shareholders' autonomy should be pruned to this extent. The shareholders as owners (residual claimants) will typically have the strongest interest in the corporation's success, so that the control of the management would appear best placed in their hands. Yet if the shareholders choose to surrender their rights in the articles of association, they themselves bear the potential disadvantages. It is, therefore, not very convincing to adduce the corporation's optimal constitution as an objection to shareholder autonomy. Instead, one must assume that the shareholders will restrict their control rights only for good reason. An ultimate limit should be drawn where economic ownership of the corporate resources is irrevocably separated from control over them.[76] This restriction can be defended on the grounds that those exercising control may easily dissociate themselves over time from the shareholders who nonetheless remain entitled to the corporation's economic

75 Art. 27(1)(i) Draft SPE Regulation, supra (note 31). See also Art. L223–25(1) C.com. (mandatory right of the shareholders' meeting to remove directors, but directors are entitled to compensation if they are removed without cause); similarly Sec. 16(1), (3) öGmbHG; Art. 223 Ley de Sociedades de Capital (two-thirds majority must be able to remove directors from office). In Germany, the prevailing view is that the appointment of directors cannot be delegated to outsiders, see *Liebscher* Münchener Komm. z. GmbHG, 2012, Sec. 46 margin no. 180, 183. On mandatory rights of removal of the shareholders for public corporations in continental European jurisdictions, see *Cools* 8 Eur. Co. & Fin. L. Rev. 199, 206 et seq. (2011).

76 In the German debate, the issue is often discussed under the heading of the "sovereignty of an association" (*Verbandssouveränität*), see seminally *Wiedemann* FS Schilling, 1974, p. 105. A similar problem arises when a shareholder attempts to assign certain control separately from the share ("prohibition of separate assignment", *Abspaltungsverbot*), see *Schön* ZHR 159 (1994), 229, 251 et seq.; see particularly p. 257 for the perils of "logjam and reciprocal chicanery"; the problem is related to the "tragedy of the anticommons" as elaborated by law and economics scholars, see *Heller* 111 Harv. L. Rev. 621 (1998).

value and surplus. As a result, management of the corporation could become highly inefficient. Shareholders cannot sensibly make provision against this in the articles of association. However, it is sufficient for the shareholders to retain a final competence to recover their powers. This condition is satisfied if they can amend the articles of association to reclaim the right to appoint directors.[77]

The freedom of shareholders to frame the corporate constitution should be restricted in yet another respect, namely in view of an extraordinary right to remove a director from office for cause. Again, one might argue that the shareholders themselves suffer the consequences if they do not reserve a right of removal from office even in case of evident incompetence or gross, wilful breaches of duty by a director. It seems likely, however, that foregoing even such minimal protection results from a failure in the contracting process: firstly, shareholders may underestimate the dangers of surrendering the corporation to a director for better or worse.[78] Secondly, even if a removal right is needed, the shareholders may still rationally agree to exclude it when they negotiate with a particularly capable director and want to signal trust to foster a cooperative relationship.[79] Finally, mandating such a right can protect the minority against gross breaches of duty by a director appointed by the majority.[80] For this purpose, many jurisdictions enable individual shareholders to enforce removal from office in court.[81] If such a minority right is provided for, it should be mandatory.

3 Information of the Shareholders or a Supervisory Organ

To decide on a removal from office or to exercise other control rights, such as determining the directors' remuneration or suing them for damages, the shareholders need information about the state of the corporation and its business activities. For shareholders as a class, this does not pose a major difficulty in the closed corporation. The shareholders can use their right of instruction to obtain any information they need. They should be able to specify or restrict their monitoring rights in the articles of association. In a large corporation, it may be ad-

77 It is difficult to draw a precise boundary if the shareholders can change the articles of association, but this is made significantly more difficult, for instance, by a unanimity requirement.
78 On lack of rationality as a justification for mandatory rules, see Chapter 2 C.III.1.
79 On inefficient contractual provisions as "signals" in contract negotiations, see fundamentally *Aghion/Hermalin* 6 J.L. Econ. & Org. 381 (1990).
80 See Chapter 3.
81 As in Art. L223–25(2) C.com.; Art. 2476(4) Codice civile; Sec. 16(2) Austrian GmbHG; Art. 815 (2) Swiss Code of Obligations. In German law, Sec. 47(4) sent. 2 GmbHG excludes a shareholder-director from passing the resolution on his/her removal, BGH NJW 1969, 1483, 1483 et seq.

visable to establish a supervisory organ for the purpose of monitoring the board so as to protect confidential business information. Conversely, rights of information and inspection on behalf of individual shareholders or a minority can improve the monitoring of the board by saving shareholder coordination cost. If at all, mandatory rights to information are only needed in the context of minority protection.[82]

4 Remuneration and Other Benefits

In addition to carefully selecting directors, monitoring and replacing them if needed, the shareholders can use remuneration and other positive incentives to align the interests of directors with the business success of the closed corporation. The precise manner in which management performance is rewarded should be left to the articles of association and/or the employment contract.[83] There is far too much variance in how one defines business success and what contributes to it for a legislator to even try to provide default rules that closed corporations might find useful. There is little need for regulation because shareholders themselves typically decide on remuneration issues in the closed corporation.

5 Avoiding Conflicts of Interest

Conflicts of interest are the exact opposite of positive performance incentives: damage to the corporation would procure a private benefit for the directors. Conflicts of interest occur in so many different forms that the shareholders cannot regulate all of them in the articles of association. This gap is filled by the directors' duty of loyalty. It determines how to deal with conflicts of interest and must be sharply distinguished from duties prescribing a specific conduct, in particular the duty of care. The duty of loyalty generally consists of a duty to avoid conflicts of interest. It does not aim at prescribing a particular decision or course of action; in principle, it does not even restrict the director's business judgement. Instead, it only seeks to prevent the director from exercising his/her discretion under the influence of incentives that run counter to the interests entrusted to him/her. Corporate law provisions on conflicts of interest need not take the form of legal duties. An alternative approach is to restrict the director's powers to act when he/she likely is subject to a conflict of interest.

---

82 See Chapter 3.

83 But see Art. 218 Abs. 1 Ley de Sociedades de Capital (profit participation may at most amount to 10 % of the profit eligible for distribution and must be stipulated in detail in the articles of association).

a) Strategies in Dealing with Conflicts of Interest

We cannot discuss conclusively here how the law of the closed corporation should respond to conflicts of interest. All corporate laws contain provisions on well-known and frequent cases of conflicts of interest. In the following, we categorise examples of such rules.

aa) Simple Conflicts of Interest: Banning Private Benefits to the Detriment of the Corporation

The simplest form of a conflict of interest consists of seeking a private advantage at the expense of the corporation.[84] This essentially amounts to misappropriation: the director enriches himself by taking from the corporation without creating any potential benefit for the corporation. One can think of outright theft, the use of the corporation's property or the private consumption of services delivered by the corporation without consideration. The appropriate legal response is simple, given that the corporation stands to gain nothing from the transaction: stealing is never in the corporation's interests. Directors are therefore *per se* prohibited from seeking private advantages at the expense of the corporation. Difficulties can only arise in delimiting which assets belong to the corporation. The issue of when a business opportunity pertains to the corporation is a paradigmatic example.[85] Once it is clear that the business opportunity belongs to the corporation, it is beyond doubt that the directors cannot use it for themselves.

bb) Resolving Complex Conflicts of Interest

The solution is not so simple if the contemplated transaction can, but need not, result in a net gain for the corporation. An important example is an exchange of goods or services with the director, including his/her employment contract as director. Even the private benefits just discussed can involve an advantage for the corporation if, for instance, the corporation sells one of its business opportunities to the director for consideration or if this is the only way to prevent the di-

84 See Sec. 175(2) Companies Act 2006: exploitation of property, information or opportunity of the corporation as an instance of a conflict of interests. Similarly, Art. 228 Ley de Sociedades de Capital.

85 Criteria for attributing business opportunities are provided in *American Law Institute* Principles of Corporate Governance, 1994, Sec. 5.05(b); for English law, see *Gower/Davies* Principles of Modern Company Law, 9th ed., 2012, 16–148 et seq.; for a general overview, *Fleischer* WM 2003, 1045, 1054 et seq.

rector from terminating his/her employment (provided that the director's continued service is of value to the corporation).[86]

There are (at least) three possible responses to a more complex conflict of interest. The first strategy is to completely prohibit the directors from engaging in a transaction involving a conflict of interest. English corporate law originally adopted this approach, deriving from trust law an uncompromising prohibition of self-dealing transactions.[87] French law provides a contemporary example in its outright ban on loan contracts between the corporation and its directors.[88] Such a strict rule is based on the belief that the likely harm from the conflicted transaction typically outweighs any potential benefits for the corporation. This assumption seems too strong. No decision involving a conflict appears so dangerous that the shareholders cannot be allowed to approve it, provided they are fully informed. An absolute prohibition of certain types of transactions is unwarranted.

The second regulatory option consists of controlling the conflict of interest without precluding the transaction from the outset. To this end, the law can divest the director of his/her decision-making power and introduce additional actors, such as other, disinterested directors or the shareholders. Under Netherlands law before the reform of 2012, the corporation was generally represented by the supervisory board in cases of conflicts of interest affecting the director.[89] Similarly, the shareholders' meeting in the French SARL must approve contracts outside the ordinary course of business or subject to unusual conditions between the corporation and a director.[90] English law requires a shareholders' resolution for loans to directors and for contracts concerning substantial assets.[91] As a general matter, in the closed corporation the shareholders suggest themselves as the party best suited to deal with directors' conflicts of interest. Still, it should be

---

86 On this, see *American Law Institute* supra (note 85), Sec. 5.05(a) (abandoning a business opportunity requires a decision by the disinterested directors or the shareholders); Sec. 175(5), (6) Companies Act 2006 (authorisation by a majority of disinterested directors); Art. 228 Ley de Sociedades de Capital (director must not influence the corporation's decision).

87 *Aberdeen Railway v. Blaikie,* (1854) 1 Macq. 461, 471 et seq.; on overcoming the prohibition (in Great Britain by contracting out, in the US by the courts) *Kershaw* The Path of Fiduciary Law, 2011, p. 25 et seq., available under http://ssrn.com/abstract=1874763.

88 Art. L223–21 C.com. Likewise Sec. 43a GmbHG (but only insofar as a loss of the loan would cut into the issued share capital).

89 See the former Art. 2:256 Burgerlijk Wetboek. On the practical problems of this broad rule, see *De Kluiver* 3 Eur. Co. & Fin. L. Rev. 45, 67 et seq. (2006). The prohibition of self-dealing in Sec. 181 German Civil Code follows a similar approach but is much more formal.

90 Art. L223–19, L223–20 C.com.

91 See Sec. 197 Companies Act 2006 (loans) and Sec. 190–196 Companies Act 2006 (substantial property transactions).

possible to transfer this competence to a potential supervisory organ or to other, disinterested directors in the articles of association.

A third regulatory response to conflicts of interest is even more conservative. Under it, the only requirement is that the directors must disclose a conflict of interest to impartial persons or the shareholders' meeting. English law demands that a director must disclose his/her own interests in proposed transactions to the other directors if they could lead to a conflict of interest.[92] Even without an approval requirement, such a duty mitigates incentive misalignment by exposing the directors to critical scrutiny, litigation and other possible sanctions, such as removal from office. Disclosure is particularly suitable in enabling the shareholders or co-directors unaffected by the conflict to examine whether they want to make the decision themselves.

cc) Preventing the Emergence of Conflicts of Interest

All policy options so far address an existing conflict of interest and attempt to neutralise it. Another strategy attempts to prevent conflicts of interest from arising in the first place. The underlying idea is that the director should not be allowed to put himself/herself in a position in which his/her own interests diverge from those of the corporation. A straightforward example is the prohibition on accepting benefits or bribes from third parties.[93] Precluding the director from competing with the corporation falls in the same category. Competing with the corporation inevitably creates a constant conflict of interest because it reduces the director's incentive to give the corporation an edge over its competitors. At the same time, a permanent temptation arises to exploit the corporation's business opportunities as a competitor, rather than for the corporation to which they belong. Some corporate laws accordingly contain a general prohibition on competition.[94] However, some flexibility may be needed if the corporation depends on a particular director who does not wish to give up a competing activity. The shareholders' meeting should therefore be able to exempt the director

92 See Sec. 177, 178 Companies Act 2006.

93 Sec. 176 Companies Act 2006 prohibits benefits from third parties even if other directors or the shareholders authorise them; on German law, see BGH NJW 2001, 2476, 2477 (corporation entitled to benefits pursuant to Sec. 667 note 2 German Civil Code if effect on the director may harm the corporation).

94 See, for instance, Art. 230 Abs. 1 Ley de Sociedades de Capital; Art. 812(3) Swiss Code of Obligations; Sec. 24(1) öGmbHG; in Germany, an unwritten prohibition is assumed for the GmbH, *Zöllner/Noack* in: Baumbach/Hueck, Komm. z. GmbHG, 19th ed., 2010, Sec. 35 margin no. 41; English law is less clear on the matter, *Gower/Davies* supra (note 85), margin no. 16–166 et seq.

from the prohibition on competition.[95] This can be generalised: for its own benefit, the corporation should be able to accept certain conflicts of interest that the law would otherwise rule out.

b) Should the Statute Contain a General Provision on Conflicts of Interest?

As to legislative technique, it seems advisable to make specific provision in a corporate law statute for the most important types of conflicts of interests. It seems less clear whether there should be a general standard for managing other instances of conflicts of interest. According to Section 175 Companies Act 2006, directors must avoid any situation in which they have, or can have, a direct or an indirect interest which are, or may be, contrary to the interests of the corporation.[96] As the law cannot offer specific rules for the variety of conceivable conflicts of interest, a general duty of loyalty is unavoidable. It is not clear, however, what an express statutory regulation could stipulate beyond a very general duty to avoid conflicts of interest. If the statute specified a particular means of resolving conflicts of interest – usually the involvement of the shareholders' meeting[97] – there would still be uncertainty as to when a relevant conflict of interest exists.[98] In any event, a general provision could show the directors an incontestable way to avoid a conflict of interest and the liability risk associated with it. At least as a safe harbour, a general statutory provision could be useful.

c) Contracting Away the Duty of Loyalty

The duty of loyalty primarily serves the interests of shareholders as a class. This suggests that the shareholders should be able to contract away the duty of loyalty in the articles of association.[99] However, it would often seem doubtful

---

95 As expressly provided in Art. 230(1) Ley de Sociedades de Capital; Sec. 24(1), (2) öGmbHG.

96 Similarly Art. 229(1) Ley de Sociedades de Capital and (after the 2012 reform) Art. 2:239(6) Burgerlijk Wetboek.

97 Sec. 175(4)(b), (5), (6) Companies Act 2006 requires consent from the directors not involved in the conflict. Similarly Art. 229(1) Ley de Sociedades de Capital (approval by the board or the shareholders' meeting without the director's participation); Art. 2:239(6) Burgerlijk Wetboek (decision to be taken by the remaining directors, the supervisory board or the shareholders' meeting).

98 According to Sec. 175(4)(a) Companies Act 2006, consent does not have to be obtained from the other directors if "the situation cannot reasonably be regarded as likely to give rise to a conflict of interest".

99 As Delaware law generously provides for the limited liability company, see Sec. 1101(c) Del. LLC Act (but no contracting out of the duty of good faith and fair dealing). The current Chief

whether the shareholders really anticipated the implications of comprehensively abolishing the duty: without a duty of loyalty, directors would obtain *carte blanche* to pursue their private advantage at the expense of the corporation. This is hardly what shareholders would want especially in view of the fact that many possible conflicts of interest cannot be foreseen in detail.[100] An attempt to regulate conflicts of interest conclusively would invite a quest for loopholes and a methodical approach at exploiting the corporation.[101] As in the case of the right to remove directors from office for cause, extensive contracting-out therefore is usually attributable to a disruption of the contracting process.[102]

These considerations advocate limitations on the ability to contract away the general duty of loyalty.[103] It can nevertheless make sense for the shareholders to address conflicts of interest in the articles of association. They may wish to relieve the director of precautions that they consider unnecessary and awkward, such as the duty to submit any conflicted transaction to the shareholders' meeting. The shareholders should thus have control over the way in which conflicts of interest are treated. In particular, they should be able to exempt certain decisions from the duty of loyalty and to stipulate in general terms how conflicts of interest should be dealt with;[104] this could go so far as to stipulate that conflicted transactions are only examined in a subsequent dispute to see whether they ultimately disadvantaged the corporation. In sum, the shareholder would remain capable of contracting away the general duty of loyalty in each and every aspect, but they would have to replace the duty's open-ended standard by specific provisions.[105]

Justice of the Delaware Supreme Court goes even beyond this by advocating that duties of loyalty apply only if affirmatively agreed upon by the shareholders, *Steele* 46 Am. Bus. L.J. 221 (2009). For the US debate about contracting out of duties of loyalty, see *Ribstein* 2005 U. Ill. L. Rev. 209, 211.

100 See Chapter 3 B.III.3.; *Hellgardt* FS Hopt, 2010, p. 765, 771 et seq.

101 "[D]evious people can smell a loophole a mile away", *Bishop/Kleinberger* Limited Liability Companies, Chapter 14.05[4][a][ii], cited from the commentary on Sec. 110(d) ULLCA 2006.

102 B.II.2 above, in particular the text on note 78 et seq.

103 See Sec. 110(d)(1)(B) ULLCA 2006 (no "obviously unreasonable" contracting out). Sec. 232 (1), (4) Companies Act 2006 is nebulous, see *Gower/Davies* supra (note 85), margin no. 16–201 et seq. On German law, see for instance *Winter* Mitgliedschaftliche Treuebindungen im GmbH-Recht, 1988, p. 216 (only particular aspects of the shareholders' duty of loyalty can be contracted away); similarly *Wiedemann* Gesellschaftsrecht, Volume II, 2004, p. 198; for a differentiated analysis, see *Hellgardt* FS Hopt, p. 765, 774 et seq.

104 See Sec. 103(b)(3)(i) Uniform Partnership Act 1997 ("the partnership agreement may identify specific types or categories of activities that do not violate the duty of loyalty, if not manifestly unreasonable").

105 See Chapter 3 B.III.3.; *Ribstein* 2005 U. Ill. L. Rev. 209, 219 et seq.

III Sanctions

If directors are required to follow a specific course of action, breaches must be linked to perceptible sanctions; the same is true for duties to avoid conflicts of interest or to comply with the competence system.

1 Type of Sanction

Various sanctions can be imposed to ensure directors' compliance. The most important private law sanction is liability for damages. At least at the outset, it promises a strong deterrent effect because the director must answer for losses with his/her own assets, although he/she acts as a fiduciary and any possible benefits from his/her activity thereby accrue to others.[106] In addition to liability for damages, common law jurisdictions often provide for the surrender of profits in case of a breach of the duty of loyalty.[107] This is an important complement because the corporation sometimes cannot prove the damage resulting from a conflict of interest, but the director should in all cases be held to avoid the conflict.[108] A comparable incentive effect is often accomplished if a breach of duty or the transgression of a power makes a legal transaction invalid, so that advantages received must be returned (for example, due to a lack of power of representation).

Neither damages nor the return of benefits or the disgorgement of profits is sufficient to ensure that directors always behave in accordance with their duties. Not all claims are enforced: invalid contracts are not reversed in all cases, compensation claims only pursued if the breach of duty is discovered. Above all, private law liability is hollow to the extent to which the debtors' assets are insufficient (the "judgment-proof problem"[109]). In order to achieve an adequate deterrence of directors with small private wealth, serious breaches of duty should also be sanctioned under criminal or administrative law. In this context, many legal systems resort to the possibility of disqualifying a person from serv-

106 On the undesired consequences of this asymmetry as the main reason for the broad business judgement rule, see B.II.1.a) above.

107 On this general principle relating to fiduciary duties, see Sec. 100 Restatement (Third) of Trusts (Tentative Draft Nr. 6, 2011); Sec. 8.01 Restatement (Third) of Agency (2006), Comment d.(1). See (also on German law) *Rusch* Gewinnhaftung bei Verletzung von Treuepflichten, 2003.

108 *Cooter/Freedman* 66 N.Y.U. L. Rev. 1045, 1051 et seq. (1991) (compensation not sufficient as an efficient deterrent); for a more nuanced analysis, see *Easterbrook/Fischel* 36 J.L. & Econ. 425, 441 et seq. (1993); *Smith* 55 Vand. L. Rev. 1399, 1493 et seq. (2002); see also *Wiedemann* supra (note 103), p. 195 et seq.

109 *Shavell* 13 J. Legal Stud. 357, 360 et seq. (1984); *Shavell* 6 Int'l. Rev. L. & Econ. 45 (1986).

ing as a director in the future.[110] However, not infrequently disqualified directors later again manage a corporation as the de facto directors: this only comes to light after the next insolvency. The deterrent effect of this sanction therefore also remains limited.

2 Extending Director Sanctions to Shareholders

The sanctions considered so far are directed at the directors. Particularly in relation to third parties, directors are held to account in lieu of the shareholders;[111] the division of labour between capital providers and professional managers extends to liability for breach of the law. In one respect, calling the directors to account enhances the enforcement of legal duties because (non-shareholder) directors do not participate in the corporate profits and thus have no countervailing benefit to the risk of personal liability. Yet the shift can also lead to abuse: the shareholders can deliberately appoint directors with limited private wealth who, as a consequence, respond little to the threat of sanctions. In addition, shareholders can exert pressure in critical cases to induce the directors to breach their duties. The law typically imposes some form of vicarious liability on the principal to address these risks from the use of agents.[112] These general rules do not, however, apply for the shareholders of a closed corporation in relation to the directors. Instead, only the corporation itself can be seen as the "principal".[113] As has been discussed earlier, an important tenet of closed corporation law is to enable the shareholders to delegate the conduct of the business as well as the concomitant duties and liabilities to professional managers.

---

110 A well-known example is the British Company Directors Disqualification Act 1986. See also Art. L653–1 et seq. C.com., Art. 213(1) Ley de Sociedades de Capital in conjunction with Art. 163 et seq., 172(2) no. 2 Ley Concursal, and the disqualification provision (expanded in 2008) in Sec. 6(2) sent. 2 GmbHG.

111 By contrast, the duties of loyalty of the majority to the minority should not in principle be capable of privative transfer to the directors, see above in more detail B.II.1.b).

112 From a law and economics perspective, see seminally *Sykes* 93 Yale L.J. 1231 (1984). Strict vicarious liability even in the absence of negligence on the part of the principal is the rule, for instance, in France (Art. 1384 Code Civile), Italy (Art. 2049 Codice Civile) and England (see in more detail *Hannigan* supra (note 72), margin no. 3–66 et seq.); this also includes corporations with regard to their organs. By contrast, German law differentiates between organ liability (Sec. 31 German Civil Code) and liability for agents or employees (Sec. 831 German Civil Code), likewise Swiss law (Art. 55(2) Civil Code in contrast to Art. 55(1) OR).

113 Sensu strictu, the corporation is not a "principal" to the directors, see supra notes 9 et seq. and accompanying text.

For this reason, corporate law needs to strike a balance between on the one hand appropriately protecting the shareholders from liability and on the other hand restricting the potential for abuse. A plausible approach is to sanction shareholders as quasi directors if they effectively usurp the role of a director.[114] In this vein, many jurisdictions recognise the notion of a de facto director, but they differ considerably in how to define it.[115] French law considers a person a *gérant de fait* if he/she engages in the management of the corporation, either directly or through others, with the support of, or in place of, the actual directors.[116] By contrast, German case law gives far less room to the doctrine of the de facto director.[117] The courts require that a de facto director "engages in acts which are *observable* outside the corporation and which are usually attributable to the management of the corporation".[118] Shareholders can also be subject to accessory liability for aiding and abetting a tort committed by directors (Sec. 830(2) German Civil Code). English corporate law in turn uses two different concepts of quasi directors. A person is liable as a de facto director if he/she behaves as a director (and is portrayed as such by the corporation) without being it.[119] By contrast, the shadow director is characterised by the amount of his/her influence, because the true directors are "accustomed to act" "in accordance with [... the shadow director's] directions or instructions".[120]

There are two conflicting goals in defining the circumstances under which shareholders should be treated as de facto directors. In principle, the shareholders can only be exempt from liability if they do not interfere when directors attempt to comply with their duties. On the other hand, apart from specific-con-

114 See also Chapter 5 E.I.

115 For an overview, see *Fleischer* AG 2004, 517, 519 et seq.

116 See Art. L241–9 C.com. (extension of the criminal provisions to "*toute personne qui, directement ou par personne interposée, aura, en fait, exercé la gestion d'une société à responsabilité limitée sous le couvert ou au lieu et place de son gérant legal*"); see also the definition in *Dedessus-le-Moustier* Rev. Soc. 1997, 499, 506: "*est un dirigeant de fait celui qui, en toute souveraineté et indépendance, exerce une activité positive de gestion et de direction*".

117 For an up-to-date discussion, see *Fleischer* GmbHR 2011, 337, 340 et seq.; *Strohn* DB 2011, 158, 160 et seq.

118 BGHZ 104, 44, 48 ("*eigenes, auch nach außen hervortretendes, üblicherweise der Geschäftsführung zuzuordnendes Handeln*"); see also BGHZ 150, 61, 69 et seq.

119 See *Hydrodam (Corby) Ltd, Re,* [1994] B.C.C. 161, 163 ("A *de facto* director is a person who assumes to act as a director. He is held out as a director by the company, and claims and purports to be a director, although never actually or validly appointed as such.")

120 Sec. 251(1) Companies Act 2006; but see the broad exception for corporate groups in paragraph (3); see also Sec. 251 Insolvency Act 1986. The shadow director need not exercise his/her influence in secret, see *Secretary of State for Trade and Industry v. Deverell* [2001] Ch. 340, 355.

duct duties in the interest of third parties, shareholders are entitled to direct the management of the corporation. They are thus allowed to exercise a strong influence on the directors on a regular and firmly established basis, even if doing so endangers the fulfilment of the directors' duties. By requiring an outward appearance of shareholder influence, German law effectively gives the shareholders a free hand on using their power on the directors internally. This is too generous: to justify comprehensive shareholder influence in the closed corporation, we argued above that the shareholders could always appoint themselves as directors if this were the only way to implement their desired course of action.[121] Yet if they did, they would expose themselves to director liability. It follows that there is no need to exempt shareholders from all liability if, instead of acting as directors themselves, they internally influence the appointed directors. However, shareholders should not expose themselves to liability when they monitor and control the directors without hampering compliance with the directors' duties.[122] They should also be allowed to express their own view of the legal scope and content of the directors' duties. The shareholders cross the line only when they, as a general practice or in a particular case, defeat the ability or the willingness of the directors to conform to their duties under their own responsibility. As a consequence, shareholders should be liable as quasi directors if they enforce a breach of duty *in concreto,* such as by means of an (illegal) instruction or the threat of removal from office.[123] Above and beyond individual decisions, the law should use a structural element in line with the concept of shadow director under English law: if there is a regularity of sustained and intensive intervention in the management of the corporation, this should give rise to a refutable presumption that the directors were no longer fully independent in their decisions to comply with their duties and that, accordingly, a breach of duty was triggered by the shareholders.

3 Enforcement

Criminal and administrative law sanctions are imposed by the courts or other public authorities. Claims for damages can in principle be brought by the corporation or by the individuals affected by the breach (which could be individual shareholders or third parties). At the first stage of analysis, this depends on whether the corporation or the individuals are entitled to compensation.[124] Allo-

121 See A.III.2. above.
122 See also Chapter 5 E.I.
123 See also Chapter 5 E.I.
124 On shareholders' right to sue, see Chapter 3 B.V.1.b).

cating the claim to the corporation has the advantage of avoiding a wasteful race for the limited private assets of the directors. On the other hand, there can be too little enforcement if individuals cannot bring suit or – if they are granted standing to sue on behalf of the corporation[125] – have only little to gain from doing so.[126] In any case, the corporation can only be entitled to compensation if a breach of duty reduces its assets. If directors commit a tortious act against a third party or inflict harm on individual (minority) shareholders, there can only be a direct claim that the injured party can enforce himself/herself against the directors.

4 Modifying Director Sanctions in the Articles of Association

Should shareholders be allowed to alter director liability? In particular, should it be possible that the articles of association alleviate director liability? As a matter of course, such a modification can only relate to the private law liability of the directors for compensation or disgorgement of profits. Answers differ across jurisdictions.[127] In terms of policy, the issue resembles that of whether the corresponding duties should be mandatory.[128]

Limiting the director liability would be of little concern insofar as it only affects the shareholders as a class. However, if we follow the considerations discussed above, directors' duties in relation to the corporation also exist on behalf of minority shareholders, creditors or other third parties.[129] In particular, the directors' duty of care precludes favourable treatment of majority shareholders at the expense of the corporation; it also aims at reducing the risk of insolvency, thereby protecting the interests of creditors. At first blush, it appears that neither

125 On the shareholders' standing to sue, see Chapter 3 B.V.1.b); of the creditors, see Chapter 5 C.III.3.a). For creditor standing only under the condition that the corporation's assets are insufficient, see Sec. 93(5) AktG (for the public corporation) and Art. 240 Ley de Sociedades de Capital.
126 See *Schmolke* ZGR 2011, 398, 406 et seq. on the weak incentives of shareholders to assert claims on behalf of public corporations. Because closed corporations tend to have fewer shareholders, this is a lower hurdle. Similar incentive problems arise for creditors.
127 In the US, the shareholders can limit or waive director liability for breaches of the duty of care but not for breaches of the duty of loyalty, see Sec. 102(b)(7) Del. Gen. Corp. L.; Sec. 110(g) ULLCA 2006; Sec. 1101(e) Del. LLC Act goes even further by insisting only on liability for "bad faith violation of the implied contractual covenant of good faith and fair dealing". By contrast, English and French law preclude any restriction of liability in the articles of association, Sec. 232 (1)–(3) Companies Act 2006; Art. L223–22(4) C.com. Under German law, the issue is unsettled, see *Fleischer* BB 2011, 2435.
128 On the mandatory nature of the duty of loyalty, see B.II.5.c) above.
129 From the point of view of creditor protection, see also Chapter 5 C.III.3.a).

the incorporators nor later a qualified majority should be able to diminish the protection afforded to minority shareholders and third parties. On the other hand, there may be legitimate reasons for wishing to modify director liability in the articles of association. The law should not light-heartedly abandon freedom of contract, which operates as a check on statutory and judicial overreaching.[130] One should also take into consideration that the overarching goal of the duty of care is to preserve and increase the total value of the firm, which is typically in the common interest of all stakeholders. Shareholders as residual owners are primarily affected by a violation of the duty of care. By alleviating director liability, they primarily – albeit not exclusively – affect their own interests. At least as an approximation, shareholders can be considered as representing the interests of all stakeholders collectively. This justifies permitting the shareholders to regulate director liability with effect for all participants in the corporate enterprise.

> It would be insufficient if the shareholders were to limit damage claims against the directors only to the extent to which the creditors do not rely on them for full compensation. As the directors can never preclude insolvency with certainty, a limitation of liability would be worthless for them in relation to creditors if it did not cover this contingency.[131]

The argument developed so far relates to the directors' general duty of care. It does not extend to duties that aim specifically at the protection of third parties. In this context, the shareholders themselves are no longer affected. Compliance with such duties may at times even run contrary to their interests as, for instance, in the case of limitation of distributions; in this regard, they cannot be counted upon to represent the interests of all stakeholders in the firm. Although based on the general duty of care, the same applies to the "duty of compliance", i.e. the precept of complying with the corporation's legal duties when acting for the corporation.[132] As a matter of course, the articles of association can only modify or exclude director liability owed to the corporation but not claims of individual shareholders or third parties.

---

130 On the primacy of default rules, see Chapter 2 C.III.1.

131 Sec. 9b, 43(3) sent. 2 GmbHG contains a restriction to this effect but only for particular duties that specifically aim at protecting creditor interests.

132 On the duty of compliance, see note 73 above and the accompanying text. By contrast, corporate laws in the US prevent the exclusion of liability only for knowing violations of the law, Sec. 102(b)(7)(ii) Del. Gen. Corp. L.; even more generously, Sec. 110(g)(5) ULLCA 2006 (only intentional violations of criminal law).

Finally, it would make little sense if there were restrictions on modifying the duty of loyalty,[133] but liability were to be eliminated with the same effect. In line with the solution advocated above, the shareholders should only be able to alter sanctions for specific instances of conflicts of interest. A closely related question is whether the shareholders should be able to waive liability for intentional breaches of duty. If a director wilfully inflicts damage on the corporation, his/her incentives will typically be severely distorted, whether out of a peculiar disregard for the corporate interest or because of a conflict of interest that cannot be demonstrated in court. As with the general duty of loyalty, liability for intentional breaches should not be capable of exclusion.[134]

C Results

1. The board of the closed corporation serves three functions. Firstly, it permits shareholders to delegate management to particularly capable persons. Secondly, as a corollary of the first function, the board serves as the primary acting organ of the corporation. Thirdly, the law can harness the board to safeguard the interests of minority shareholders and third parties in relation to the (majority) shareholders.
2. Corporate law conceives the board not as a a mere agent but as an organ of the corporation. The main reason is the board's third function, that is its role as a mediator between the interests of the shareholders and the other stakeholders. Instituting the board as a corporate organ can be of indirect benefit to the shareholders: as part of an organ, directors themselves are subject to duties in relation to minority shareholders and third parties. This can justify releasing the (majority) shareholders from the risk of liability for breaches of duty. In addition, the board as a separate organ can promote the trust of minority shareholders and third parties in the closed corporation if the directors act as guardians of their interests.
3. The directors should be held to safeguard the interests of minority shareholders and third parties to the extent to which a specific course of action can be prescribed ("specific-conduct duties"). Beyond such clearly specified duties, closed corporation law should not conceive the board as a neutral intermediary. Shareholders themselves, however, should be free to vest the board with

133 See B.II.5.c) above.

134 This is provided for in Sec. 276(3) German Civil Code; Sec. 102(b)(7)(ii) Del. Gen. Corp. L.; Sec. 110(g)(4) ULLCA 2006. As mentioned in note 127, even Delaware LLC law preserves liability for bad faith violations of good faith and fair dealing, see Sec. 1101(e) Del. LLC Act.

greater independence, for example by abandoning their right to instruct the directors or by securing the directors against removal from office.

4. As the corporation's primary acting organ, the board should be the mandatory representative of the corporation in relation to third parties. The board should be responsible for all matters insofar as neither the law nor the articles of association reserve them to the shareholders. At the same time, the shareholders' meeting should have a right to issue instructions to the board. Subject to certain minority rights and the board's mandatory duties, the articles of association should be free to alter the competence allocation.
5. The directors are subject to a general duty of care to the corporation. At the same time, however, they are entitled to broad discretion under the business judgement rule so that the duty of care only rarely imposes or prohibits a specific course of action for the management of the corporation. The business judgement rule also applies if decisions specifically affect the interests of minority shareholders or third parties, such as, for example, when the corporation is in crisis or when a decision touches on the equal treatment of shareholders. A more stringent obligation only arises from more specific duties, often imposed by the statute, such as the duty of keeping records, restrictions on distributions to shareholders, a duty to initiate insolvency proceedings, etc.
6. Apart from specific-conduct duties, it is mostly through indirect incentives that the law and the shareholders seek to ensure that directors manage the corporation successfully. The most important means of control is the right to appoint directors and to remove them from office. Even with regard to this right, shareholders should be largely free to reallocate competences in the articles of association.
7. Corporate law addresses conflicts of interest under the directors' duty of loyalty. The law should make specific provisions for certain frequent conflicts of interest. In addition, the statute should contain a safe harbour on how a conflict of interest can be avoided, namely through approval by the shareholders' meeting. Shareholders cannot contract away the general duty of loyalty. By contrast, shareholders should be able to regulate particular instances of conflicts of interest.
8. A breach of duty leads to liability for compensation under private law. This sanction should be complemented by criminal and administrative law provisions, including disqualification. Director liability should extend to shareholders (and other persons) if the latter prevent the actual directors from complying with their duties; there is a refutable presumption to this effect if shareholders constantly and significantly interfere with the management of the corporation. Directors' private law liability to the corporation should

in principle be subject to modification and alleviation in the articles of association. An exception applies for duties that specifically protect minority shareholders or third parties.

Chapter 5 Creditor Protection in the Closed Corporation*

Table of Contents

* The text is based on a draft by *Schön*.

A Limited Liability and Contractual Freedom

I Limited Liability – Doctrinal and Policy Considerations

Shareholders' limited liability for the corporation's debts forms one of the pivotal characteristics of the (closed) corporation. It is to be found in public and private limited companies throughout Europe as well as in the United States and Asia.

Policy analysis of creditor protection in the corporation should not assume that the limitation of liability constitutes *a priori* a mandatory element of the legal person in general or the corporation in particular.[1] Members' limited liability cannot be considered a rule of natural law for the legal person or for the corporation as such, and piercing the veil to call to account shareholders or executive members should not be considered an exception requiring justification. Admittedly, the categorisation of certain (entrepreneurial) legal forms as legal persons suggests at first sight that all debt relationships arising from their activities are primarily attributable to them, not to their members or the natural persons acting for them, but this first look says nothing about the rationale and the scope of additional liability of shareholders and acting persons. Instead, a glance at legal history and comparative law reveals this assumption to be a fallacy.

From the viewpoint of German legal tradition, the differentiation between the corporation being a legal person on the one hand and the partnership as a form of joint ownership lacking legal capacity on the other hand appears doubtful. Independent legal personality has always been a trait of commercial partnerships (Section 124 German Commercial Code (HGB)) and nevertheless involves full personal liability of the members; conversely, tried and tested legal practice with non-profit associations without legal capacity shows that a corporate body's lack of formal legal capacity does not necessarily result in members' personal liability. Against this background, the overarching concept of a "legal entity" in civil law theory has emerged, which encompasses all commercial and non-commercial partnerships as forms of joint ownership as well as associations or corporations and in each case declares the association of persons to be

1 In detail, *Grigoleit* Gesellschafterhaftung für interne Einflussnahme im Recht der GmbH, 2006, p. 8 et seq; the formation of separate assets is, however, a precondition for limited liability (*Dubarry/Flume* ZEuP 2012, 128 on the sole trader with limited liability).

the focal point of legal relations.[2] Therefore no direct conclusions for the members' (or the acting persons') liability position can be drawn from the dichotomy between the legal person and the joint ownership of partners. This agnostic position is endorsed by the fact that in the late 19th century, the path-breaking legislation on the German GmbH explicitly left the issue of categorising the corporation with limited liability as a "legal person" up to academic discussion[3]. This shows that liability limitation as such is not necessarily associated with the category of the legal person.

From a comparative law point of view, scepticism about "natural" or "logical" standards on liability limitations with regard to the commercial partnership is increased by a glance at Romanist legal systems, which have always classified the commercial partnership as a "*personne morale*" without this categorisation changing anything about the personal liability of the owners; from the viewpoint of the British legal system, original forms of corporation include not only the company limited by shares with limited liability but also the unlimited company with unlimited liability of the shareholders, without any differentiation with regard to the legal capacity of the company in relation to third parties;[4] in more recent British and US-American corporate law legislation, the limited liability partnership (LLP) has been introduced, which is considered a partnership with its flexibly structured internal relations and precedence of non-delegated management, and which nevertheless (contrary to the German limited partnership *Kommanditgesellschaft* or professional partnership *Partnerschaftsgesellschaft*[5]) does not expose (some of) its shareholders to unlimited personal liability.[6] Moreover, the LLP in turn appears phenotypically close to the limited liability corporation (LLC) categorised as a legal person under US law;[7] in the light of this diversity of forms, any conceptual or otherwise categorical standards seem devoid of any value.

If we consider European corporate law, we can cite two further examples for the uselessness of dogmatic categories: the indifference of the EEIG Regulation

2 *K. Schmidt* AcP 209 (2009), 181.

3 Evidence in *Fleischer* Münchener Komm. z. GmbHG, 2010, Introduction margin no. 6 et seq.

4 *Gower/Davies* Principles of Modern Company Law, 9th ed., 2012, I – 21.

5 The law on German professional partnerships has been modernised recently. As a reaction to the increasing number of UK-based LLPs in Germany, lawyers, patent lawyers, tax accountants and auditors will be allowed to opt for limitation of professional liability under German law.

6 *Gower/Davies* supra (note 4), I – 4.

7 See Section 104 (a) *Revised Uniform Limited Liability Company Act 2006*; on contractual control of the *managers* and *members* in the Delaware LLC: *Di Matteo* 46 Am. Bus. L.J. 279 (2009).

in relation to the categorisation of the EEIG as a legal person or partnership (it lightly leaves this categorisation issue up to the Member States in Art. 15 EEIG Regulation) or the legal policy programme of the Directive on single-member private limited-liability companies, which mandatorily dictates to the Member States the duty to introduce a legal form with limited liability for sole traders but considers it unimportant whether this takes the form of an independent legal person or whether the "entrepreneur with limited liability" is entitled to separate business assets and private assets from each other.[8]

Against this background, the economic function of the legal form on the one hand and the safeguarding of the interests involved on the other hand must be decisive for the design of creditor protection in the law of closed corporations. When addressing the underlying regulatory issues, there should always be asked, whether and to what extent the basis and structure of the protection of persons affected can be left up to private autonomous negotiation and structuring.

II Function of Limited Liability in the Closed Corporation

The function of liability limitation in the closed corporation differs in grades, but not in principle, from the function of liability limitation in the public corporation. In both cases, it is all about providing an incentive for financiers to invest a limited amount of their own assets in a (risky) project without being liable with their entire remaining assets in case of failure for the liabilities incurred.[9] In this way, the closed corporation extends with a clear purpose the variety of possible forms of investment; otherwise, certain investments which are desirable for the economy would possibly not be made.

The fundamental difference to the public corporation lies in the typological assumption that the investors which invest in shares of public corporations in the open capital market (portfolio shareholders and institutional investors) do not at the same time act as members of the management and also do not hold a share of the voting capital to an extent which secures each of them significant

8 *Schön* RabelsZ 64 (2000), 1.

9 *Haas* Gutachten E zum 66. DJT 2006, p.E 13; *Fleischer* supra (note 3), Introduction GmbHG margin no. 281 et seq; see also EuGH NZG 2011, 183, 185 et seq margin no. 47 et seq – C-81/09 (*Idryma Typou*) on unlimited liability as an obstacle to the economic development in the European Single Market, *Schön* Festschrift Peter Hommelhoff, 2012, p.1037 et seq., and *Pfennig* Gläubigerschutz bei der Europäischen Privatgesellschaft, 2011, p. 42 et seq. For a differentiated discussion of the rationale for limited liability in public and private companies in English literature, see *Gower/Davies* supra (note 4), 8–1 et seq.

influence on the operative management of the company due to their members' rights of cooperation and information. By contrast, it can regularly be assumed in a closed corporation that all or individual shareholders either personally undertake the task of management or can at least exercise substantial influence on the operative business within the framework of a shareholders' meeting or of other decision-making bodies (supervisory boards, advisory boards, etc.).

This influence of the shareholders of a closed corporation on the basis of the status of an organ or membership in the corporation does not, however, call into question their fundamental need for a legal form with limited liability. Otherwise, neither the invention nor the triumphant success of the limited liability corporation in the world could be explained.[10] There are no empirical grounds for seeing a necessity of generally debating the liability limitation of "owner-managed" enterprises as a problem. For this reason, over-simplifying considerations on the synchronisation of control and liability,[11] which would tend to restrict the option of liability limitation for controlling shareholders, are unconvincing. The real-life instances of the closed corporation, namely the family business, the joint venture, the group subsidiary or the start-up-company, thrive on the combination of both limited liability and far-reaching control exercised by the shareholders. This model has not proved to be fundamentally damaging to public welfare.[12] The clear mandate in European corporate law in favour of the single-member limited liability company forcefully underlines the significance of the closed corporation for corporate law policy.

For this reason, the fundamental issue of creditor protection in the closed corporation cannot be whether there should be liability limitation in closed corporations at all, but rather one must ask how such liability limitation should be structured, in particular with the aim of controlling opportunistic behaviour by the members and directors of the corporation in relation to its creditors.

10 In further detail, *Fleischer* supra (note 3), Introduction GmbHG margin no. 210 et seq; *Grigoleit* supra (note 1), p. 31 et seq.

11 Against those considerations, see also *Spindler* JZ 2006, 839, 840; *Grigoleit* supra (note 1), p. 18 et seq; on the discussion in the 1930s, see *Fleischer* supra (note 3), Introduction GmbHG margin no. 88.

12 *McCahery/Vermeulen* Corporate Governance of Non-Listed Companies, 2008, p. 6 et seq, 24 et seq.

III Limited Liability – a Privilege?

Thus we cannot assume that in the legal person, personal liability of the participants is an exception requiring justification. Conversely it is just as illogical to construe the limitation of liability of a corporate form as a "privilege"[13] which has to be "earned" or "paid for". Since the legal framework for the setting up of legal persons has left behind the system of discretionary concessions and moved into a system of compulsory statutory requirements in all relevant corporate law systems, the exceptional character of the formation of a legal person (by *royal charter* or a comparable act of approval) no longer exists, and the formation of a legal person has since been accepted as a natural expression of private autonomy. From the German perspective, freedom of association is a constitutional right according to Art. 9 (1) Basic Law. It also means that this formation cannot be made dependent on a *quid pro quo* which has to be provided by the founders. In European law, the Directive on single-member private limited-liability companies dating from 1989 also confirmed this stance for the wholly-owned limited liability corporation. The same idea is, for example, finally formulated in "Directive concerning indirect taxes on the raising of capital" of the European Union, which permits only the payment of the costs-related fees for registration in the Commercial Register as a fiscal barrier to registration. The idea of a further-reaching "entrance fee" for the founders of corporations, or another type of payment, is irreconcilable with this regulation.

For this reason, the assumption that the limitation of liability must be "recompensed" through the raising of minimum capital[14] or earned by the willingness to disclose corporate data is not acceptable if the idea is linked to consideration for an expensive privilege. Any minimum capital requirement or any mandatory rules on corporate disclosure have to be objectively justified in order to protect specific interests of the corporate creditors or other persons;[15] liability limitation as such in any case does not *per se* require the founders of the corporation paying a price.

It also follows from this that any recourse by the creditors against the shareholders by "piercing the corporate veil" cannot be justified by the idea that the "privilege of limited liability" is a *quid pro quo* with respect to good conduct of the shareholders. Every instance of veil piercing[16] presupposes a specific damage done to creditors, which results from specific unacceptable behaviour of direc-

13 Most recently *Schall* Kapitalgesellschaftsrechtlicher Gläubigerschutz, 2009, p. 294 et seq.
14 *Lutter* in: Lutter, Legal Capital in Europe, 2006, p. 1, 4.
15 See *infra* H.II.
16 For an overview, see *Merkt/Spindler* in: Lutter, supra (note 14), p. 166.

tors and shareholders, and its legal consequences must be tailored to the recovery of these losses. In view of this, veil piercing will not be analysed in this chapter as an independent legal institution; rather, the relevant groups of cases will be discussed in the respective material context.

IV Limited Liability and Freedom of Contract

A closer look at legal forms providing limited liability shows that these institutions are ambivalent from the viewpoint of the founders' private autonomy. The starting point seems to be that no civilised legal system provides founders with the right to set up corporate bodies in a completely unrestricted manner. Rather, a *numerus clausus* of corporate forms is available in every jurisdiction, involving – depending on policy and legal tradition – differently characterised choices between several corporate forms provided for, but without the possibility of deviating from them.[17] In view of this, statutory provisions on legal forms containing limited liability can on the one hand be classified as *enabling* or *facilitating law*, i.e. as rules which enable access to certain advantageous legal structures in the first place. In this sense, the pre-ordained statutory corporate forms can be understood as an offer by the respective legal system to extend the legal freedom of action of natural persons and give them the option of a (collective or – in case of the single-member company – individual) liability limitation.

On the other hand, the existence of a *numerus clausus* granting the choice between several legal types, but without the possibility of fundamentally deviating from them, can be understood as an expression of a deep-seated prohibitive provision which prevents the founders from freely structuring legal forms with limited liability. From this point of view, the *numerus clausus* indirectly secures a core area of mandatory law within the framework of the respective corporate forms offered under the relevant statutes and opposes the free formation of bodies corporate. Its effects are similar to the law on the general terms of business which – by declaring specific contractual clauses invalid – lowers transaction costs but also limits freedom of individual contracting.

From the perspective of German law, the ambiguity of the "enabling" and the "prohibitive" elements of a corporate law system was discussed with regard to

---

17 For a discussion of so-called *Typenzwang* in German corporate law, see *K. Schmidt* Gesellschaftsrecht, 4th ed., 2002, p. 96 et seq.

the contractual creation of a civil law partnership with limited liability.[18] The question was whether the partners of a joint partnership pursuant to Section 705 German Civil Code can establish a limited liability legal form alongside the established statutory corporate forms simply by declaration to the general public, by limitation of the representative authority of the shareholder-directors and by inclusion of limited liability stipulations in contracts with third parties. The *Bundesgerichtshof* rightly considered this impermissible.[19] Freely structured liability limitation in the civil law partnership would call into question all mandatory rules which supranational or national legislation has introduced for the protection of third parties, e.g. rules on disclosure, representative authority, raising and maintenance of capital, duties of care and loyalty, duties to file a petition for insolvency and so on. Liability limitation would be insulated from the system of corresponding statutory provisions. If and to the extent to which statutory corporate law establishes mandatory law within the framework of the legal forms on offer, the *numerus clausus* – which ensures broad-based security of the respective mandatory framework conditions for creditor protection in a particular legal form – is also justified.

This also sheds light on a further specific component of private autonomy, namely free choice of the applicable law. Precisely from the point of view of creditor protection, the issue has repeatedly flared up in ECJ case-law about the extent to which the Member States of the European Union can extend their specific legislative stipulations about the technique and scope of creditor protection to foreign legal forms in which enterprises are active within their sovereign territory.[20] Admission of enterprises employing foreign legal forms according to the "incorporation theory" means a substantial increase in the number of legal forms available to economic agents, so that the policies of foreign legislatures also gain relevance for the level and technicalities of creditor protection at home. This once again highlights the close connection between private autonomy and the statutory level of protection.

Finally, it must also be borne in mind from the viewpoint of private autonomy that there is no conceptual antagonism between the existence of statutory requirements for a legal form and the individual stipulations of a contractual relationship. They rather complement each other fruitfully. Depending on the individual real-life case, contractual arrangements may extend liability beyond the corporation's assets (for example with shareholders' guarantees) or limit it

18 *K. Schmidt* supra (note 17), p. 1794 et seq.
19 BGHZ 142, 315.
20 *Eidenmüller* FS Heldrich, 2005, p. 581, 585 et seq.

to individual parts of the corporation's assets (for example by specific contract with an individual creditor). This perspective makes it clear that every choice of a legal form also involves an element of "collective agreement": the founders decide in favour of a legal form as a "standard contract" with third parties, which can be supplemented by more detailed individual agreements at the parties' request within the framework of mandatory law. For this reason, the following analysis is based on the assumption that the rules provided by statutory corporate law offer a partly optional, partly binding "standard contract" between founders/shareholders on the one hand and creditors on the other hand.[20a]

The existence of such a partly optional, partly binding "standard contract" also ensures that – when conflicts come up – the courts do not hastily feel obliged to substitute the necessary protection of individual groups by vague judge-made concepts ("piercing the veil", "abuse of law").[21] The more specific the institutional rules which are offered to creditors by statutory law, the less recourse to judicial lawmaking is likely to be necessary.

B Limited Liability and Variety of Creditors

It is generally acknowledged that the statutory rules on limited liability have different functions depending on a creditor's characteristics and the legal background for her claims. A helpful distinction has been put forward by *Bebchuk/Fried* who regard *adjusting* and *non-adjusting creditors* as two different types of creditors – assessing the creditors' need for protection against the background of their own capacity to contractually secure the satisfaction of their claims.[22] The role model for an *adjusting creditor* is the debtor's bank, which can to a great extent secure its claims or compel adequate risk premiums, using its superior knowledge and *de fa*cto power. By contrast, *non-adjusting creditors*, in particular tort creditors, become creditors involuntarily and without preceding nego-

20a It has recently been exposed that one of the main deficiencies of pure covenant-based creditor protection lies in the fact that corporate bond covenants are not enforceable against third parties (directors, shareholders). Insofar, statutory law is more effective unless we introduce binding third-party effects of contracts (*Adler/Kahan*, 161 U. Pa. L. Rev. (2013), p. 1773 et seq.).

21 *Böckmann* Gläubigerschutz bei GmbH und *close corporation*, 2005, p. 317 et seq.

22 For futher detail, see *Armour/Hertig/Kanda* in: Kraakman/Armour/Davies/Enriques/Hansmann/Hertig/ Hopt/Kanda/Rock, The Anatomy of Corporate Law: A Comparative and Functional Approach, 2nd ed., 2009, p. 115, 120 et seq; for a critical view of this distinction, see *Grigoleit* supra (note 1), p. 42 et seq.

tiation, along with other statutory creditors or economically weaker contractual partners (namely employees or small suppliers and craftsmen).

From these *non-adjusting creditors* one should not expect that they decline to enter into a contract with a limited liability corporation even if they are not strong enough to negotiate balanced or at least individually suitable contractual clauses.[23] Against this background, there are good reasons for securing the position of these contractual creditors by protective provisions outside corporate law which are specific to this sub-group; a case in point are employees who enjoy priority in insolvency and insurance policies for pensions and other instruments. In many cases, minimum protection will also result from the right to retaining liens or contractor's liens.

In addition, there are some other statutory debt relationships which can be either tort-like or contract-like, depending on their structure, e.g. claims based on unjust enrichment, strict liability claims or public law duties such as tax duties. The holders of these claims are regularly in a *non-adjusting* position. However, precisely the example of tax claims shows that the dual definition of *adjusting/non-adjusting creditors* is ambivalent.[24] On the one hand, the treasury appears to be the superior creditor because – in the context of legislation – it can freely define taxable events and can establish fiscal privileges in bankruptcy and other securing measures. On the other hand, when it comes to the application of the law by the tax authorities, the rule of law does not grant the administrative bodies any discretion as to whether they wish to enforce a tax claim. Parliaments as tax legislators are therefore *adjusting creditors*, whereas the tax authorities engaged in enforcement are not. Thus, there is much to be said in favour of subjecting these types of cases to special regulation. This applies similarly for other mandatory contributions under public law, such as, for example, social insurance contributions, which on the one hand give rise to a claim to benefits under appropriate circumstances (and are therefore similar to contractual claims), but whose existence and enforcement cannot be merely optional.

23 For greater detail, see *Haas* supra (note 9), p. E 95 et seq; *Mülbert* in: Eidenmüller/Schön, The Law and Economics of Creditor Protection – A Transatlantic Perspective, 2008, p. 361, 370 et seq.

24 For greater detail, see *Schön* FS Westermann, 2008, p. 1469; most recently *Altmeppen* FS Goette, 2011, p. 1; *Weiland* DZWiR 2011, 224.

C Contractual Creditors

I Regulatory Aims

If a person acquires a claim to payment or other performance against a corporation on a contractual basis, this claim is usually (apart from the rare case of a gift) based on performance by the creditor. When it comes to securing this claim, a distinction must be made between a simultaneous exchange of performances and cases of one-sided advance performance. An example is the grant of a loan in return for the promise of repayment of the capital amount and payment of interest or other fees for the provision of capital for a limited period. Further cases relate to purchase, work performance or services and the transfer of possession of items for use, to the extent to which performance and counterperformance are not exchanged simultaneously but the creditor instead provides advance performance. It is typical for this constellation that the creditor transfers value to the corporation's assets for a particular period of time and in turn relies on repayment (loan) or counterperformance (interest and other performance or delivery fees) being forthcoming from these corporate assets. If the creditor has not obtained individual collateral by negotiation (such as a lien on real estate belonging to the corporation or a shareholders' guarantee), the economic value of this claim mainly depends on the corporation's solvency. The creditor therefore has an interest in its solvency (at the latest by the time the claim falls due). From the legislative point of view, this raises the question whether this interest is a sufficient reason for the creation of statutory provisions (mandatory or optional).

This requires an economic assessment of entrepreneurial activity which assumes that the voluntary combination of production factors provided by the corporation's founders (know-how, high-skilled labour, equity capital, etc.) and production factors provided by the creditors (debt capital, advance provision of goods, work or services) can lead to the efficient allocation of resources and thus to an increase in overall welfare. It is therefore the task of the legal system to provide a framework which enables this convergence and in particular efficiently allocates the costs for the corporation's founders on the one hand and the costs for the creditors on the other hand.[25]

If we start this assessment with regard to the position of the creditor, we find that she will make the provision of debt capital or other advance performance dependent on the extent to which solvency is secured for the future; otherwise,

25 *Myers* 5 J. Fin. Econ. 147 (1977); *Nash/Netter/Poulsen* 9 J. Corp. Fin. 201 (2003).

the risk of insolvency must be taken into consideration by risk premiums on the agreed interest.[26] However, not every risk can be compensated by such premiums. It will frequently prove more efficient to exclude particular risks (such as opportunistic behaviour of shareholders) by statutory or contractual prohibitions than to price them with high risk premiums.[27] On the other side, the entrepreneur must consider which restrictions on her freedom to act she is willing to accept in order to obtain the desired debt capital at all or to be able to press for low debt charges. Finally, it must be borne in mind that both corporation founder and debt capital provider depend for their economic success on the management operating the enterprise with skill and energy; however, their attitudes towards risk by degrees differ from one another because the debt capital provider fundamentally bears only the risk of the corporation's insolvency, whereas the founder (and equity provider) internalises the further-reaching opportunities and risks of the business model with her share in the liquidation assets and the profit shares attributed to her.

Close scrutiny shows that this difference as to risk in particular has an effect in case of success: the equity capital provider alone benefits from the residual profit, whereas the debt capital provider typically receives fixed interest only. In case of entrepreneurial failure, both the equity capital provider and the debt capital provider typically suffer losses once the (primarily liable) equity capital has been used up.

II Central Issues

In view of this, the equity capital provider (corporation founder) and the debt capital provider will usually be affected by the same questions:[28]

- Who exercises control over the corporate assets? In particular:
  - Who sets the business strategy of the corporation?

---

26 *Brealey/Myers/Allen* Principles of Corporate Finance, 9th ed., 2008, Chapter 24, p. 646 et seq; *Haaker* ZGR 2010, 1055, 1061–1065; for a discussion of the different financial risks (liquidity, risks of value loss), see *Handschin* 22 Eur. Bus. L. Rev. 189 (2011); on the calibration of the risk surcharge depending on the owner structure, see *Sánchez-Ballesta/García-Meca* 20 Eur. Acct. Rev. 389 (2011).

27 *Tirole* The Theory of Corporate Finance, 2006, S .80 et seq; *Mülbert* in: Eidenmüller/Schön, supra (note 23), p. 374 et seq.

28 For fundamental questions of creditor protection in corporations, see the overview in *Armour/Hertig/Kanda* in: Kraakman et al., supra (note 22), p. 115 et seq.

  - What are the consequences of wrong entrepreneurial decisions (by directors or shareholders) for the debt capital provider's position?
  - Does the content of the directors' duties change in a crisis?
  - Which legal constraints exist for a major entrepreneurial change of strategy?
  - At which point in time is it advisable to shift control over the corporation's assets to the creditors?
  - What are the consequences of a late change of control (in particular the case of delayed filing of a petition for insolvency proceedings)? Who is responsible (directors, shareholders)?
- To what extent are payments from the corporation's assets to shareholders (or persons close to them) permissible; in particular:
  - When can dividends be disbursed?
  - What limits apply to hidden asset transfers to shareholders?
  - Which further self-interested interventions by directors or shareholders in the operation and assets of a corporation must be penalised?
- Which rights of information should be accorded to the creditors?
- Which functions are fulfilled by the rules on raising and maintaining capital? This question is consciously posed at the end of the preceding list. After all, one of the primary aims of the following analysis is to clarify the relationship between the general rules of creditor protection in case of limited liability corporations and the particularities of a "legal capital" regime. It will be seen that the policy issue of "capital" does not have the central control function usually attributed to it.

III Control of the Corporate Assets

In a first step, it must be clarified how control over the corporate assets, and in particular the business policy, is to be determined in relation to the shareholders, creditors and directors. In this context, it must be noted that the issue is characterised by a total of four fundamental framework conditions:
- Purpose of the enterprise (for-profit or not-for-profit)
- Object of the enterprise (field of activity, risk profile)
- Scope of the corporation's assets available for investments and current operations (provision of debt and equity capital)
- Standards of good business management

1 Corporate Purpose and Activity

German law on corporations starts from the assumption that the purpose of the enterprise and its scope of activities are defined by the corporation's founders in the articles of association. By contrast, it is possible to completely waive specifying the aim of the corporate purpose in a company's articles of association in the United Kingdom (Section 31(1) Companies Act 2006) and in the United States (Section 102(a)(3) Del. Gen. Corp. L.). This raises two questions: firstly, whether the founders (on creditor protection grounds) must be placed under an obligation to stipulate the purpose and scope of an enterprise's activities at all (with substantive precision), and secondly whether and to what extent debt capital providers must be granted a voice in such stipulation.

The answer to both questions presupposes that, from the point of view of the debt capital provider, the aim and the object of the enterprise have significant importance for the decision to provide capital, as well as the type and amount of the capital fee. This assumption seems to be true:

- Due to the management's aim of profit maximisation, a for-profit corporation will always tend to focus its sights on securing the corporation's solvency; by contrast, a corporation serving charitable or public purposes or a mixed-economy corporation by definition precisely pursues the aim of the consumption or exhaustion of the corporation's assets. From the lender's point of view, such a corporation with the sole aim of covering costs (or less) also has a different risk profile from a corporation which offers its goods and/or services at market prices with profit margins and is therefore in a better position to generate reserves which protect creditors.[29]
- The same applies to the scope of activities of the enterprise. Depending on the choice of business model, the corporation will have a different risk profile irrespective of the positive anticipated value of the investment (with higher or lower volatility), which has a specific (in part asymmetric) effect on the risk profile of the debt capital provider. For this reason, the corporate purpose and the scope of activities of the enterprise are important factual bases for an investment decision by the debt capital provider.[30]

---

29 *Schön* ZGR 1996, 429, 452 et seq; on the relationship between profit aim and liability limitation, see the detailed discussion in *Grigoleit* supra (note 1), p. 55 et seq.

30 *Wicke* Münchener Komm. z. GmbHG, 2010, Section 3 margin no. 10; explicitly from the point of view of new equity capital providers: *Fleischer/Schmolke* ZHR 73 (2009), 649, 674; on new regulation by the German Act on the Modernisation of GmbH Law and the Combat of Abuse (Gesetz zur Modernisierung des GmbH-Rechts und zur Bekämpfung von Missbräuchen), see *Schröder/Cannive* NZG 2008, 1; see *Schön* Der Nießbrauch an Sachen, 1992, p. 51 et seq. for the similar necessity to set a "specific purpose" of property subject to a usufruct.

It is advisable to primarily grant to the corporation's founders the defining competence for the aim of the enterprise and object of the enterprise and not (also) to the debt capital providers. In the case of the corporation and its debt capital providers, it must be taken into account that not just one bilateral relationship comes into existence (between the corporation and one single debt-provider), but that the equity capital provider(s) usually face(s) a potentially unlimited number of debt capital providers which will establish contact with the company at different times present and future. Their capital contributions will be mingled inextricably within the corporation as business assets and operating capital.

It seems to be virtually impossible in practical terms to split up the respective capital amounts according to different purposes, scopes and risk profiles. High transaction costs prevent ever new negotiations with each debt capital provider about the aim of the enterprise and purpose of the enterprise with the aim of achieving a collective uniform result. It is therefore advisable for the corporation's founders to define the aim and the object in a first step and let the debt capital providers (including future new debt capital providers) decide on the basis of their freedom to contract whether they wish to contribute to financing this enterprise. Although the debt capital provider cannot legally enforce the establishment of a new aim or object of the enterprise, she can refuse to provide debt capital and (depending on the importance of her financing contribution for the corporation) is therefore indirectly in a position to achieve a modification of the aim and object.

An interesting question concerns the option for debt-providers to inject their funds only into a specific area of activities undertaken by the corporation. In this respect one has to distinguish between general business risk and insolvency risk. The capital provider is free to restrict her capital input to particular activities of the enterprise by individual contractual agreement, e.g. only to enter into a "silent partnership" with regard to a partial business of the enterprise[31], and therefore not to expose herself to the business risks of the entire enterprise. However, participation in the insolvency risk of the overall enterprise cannot be avoided on a contractual basis due to the fact that when insolvency proceedings start, all assets of the corporation are liable for all its liabilities. Only the LLC statutes of several U.S. federal states provide for internal separation into further series (e.g. Section 18–215 Delaware Limited Liability Company Act), but the liability law and insolvency law consequences of such treatment have ultimately not

---

31 *K. Schmidt* Münchener Komm. z. HGB, 2nd ed., 2007, Section 230 margin no. 39.

been clarified (for this reason, the *Revised Uniform Limited Liability Company Act 2006* does not contain these rules).[32]

Given the high importance of the corporate goal and the scope of activity of a corporation for its creditors, it seems advisable not only to establish the purpose and the scope and risk profile of the enterprise internally, but also to make it public in the Commercial Register, thereby providing *ex ante* certainty to an infinite number of future contractual partners. Such publication not only lowers transactions costs. It is also advisable because individual contractual bargaining with different corporate creditors might have different outcomes as to the risk profile of the company, which will give rise to conflicts between creditors and the corporation (or its directors and shareholders) as well as conflicts between different groups of creditors which can lead to a paralysis of the corporation's activities. These coordination losses should be avoided in advance so that the creditors are reciprocally aware of the fact that they accept certain parallel risks on the basis of the corporation's articles of association.[33]

In the light of this, it can be assumed that the purpose of the enterprise and the envisaged scope of activities of the enterprise announced in the Commercial Register at the time of negotiation of debt becomes the "basis of the transaction" for debt capital provision. Given well known problems of collective action, it would be excessive to require the full consent of all creditors in case the shareholders want to modify these elements of the corporate charter at a later stage. However, the creditors should have the right to terminate the loan for cause – as under the French law on debentures – in case of a corresponding alteration of the articles of association by the shareholders.

Nevertheless, there is ultimately no reason to oblige the founders to such specification of the aim and object of the enterprise in the articles of association – thus lowering transaction costs – against their will. The creditors remain free to decide against doing business with an enterprise if it refuses to disclose its object and therefore the risks associated with its activities. Insofar, it is advisable to follow the law in the U.S. and the United Kingdom, where there is no statutory duty to restrict the object of the enterprise in the articles of association.

---

32 For a critical view of the series concept, see *Kleinberger/Bishop* 62 Bus. Law. 515, 541 et seq. (2007); for a contrary view, see *Ribstein* 3 Va. L. & Bus. Rev. 35, 36 et seq. (2008).

33 See also *Hirte* FS Hüffer, 2010, p. 329.

2 Scope of the Corporate Assets

The creditors' risk position is established in a second step by the scope and composition of the corporate assets, namely the relationship between equity and debt capital at the time of financing. Subsequent alterations to the financing structure therefore also result in modifications to the value of the creditors' claims. This leads to the question of whether and to what extent the creditors can be granted an influence on changes to the financing structure of the enterprise.

In principle, corporate law does not recognise reservations of consent by creditors in case of alterations on the equity capital side. This appears completely natural in case of a recapitalisation, because an issue of new stock increases the assets of the corporation and therefore enhances the value of the creditors' claims to repayment. By contrast, claims to secure creditors' rights in case of formal reductions of capital, mergers or split-ups of corporations are provided for by statute in many cases. When compared to a wide-reaching reservation of consent by the creditors, such individual securing appears the better solution. A statutory reservation of consent to all or individual creditors would be extremely burdensome for negotiations between shareholders, directors and third parties in restructuring and would not result in material added value for the creditors of a sound enterprise. The statutory claim of a creditor to ask for collateral in case of a lowering of statutory capital appears to be a milder and therefore more suitable solution because it is oriented towards the specific threats to creditors' rights in the individual case. This does not prevent powerful creditors from demanding further-reaching reservations of consent or rights of termination in their individual debt covenants with the corporation.[34]

Statutory corporate law currently seems to set no restrictions – even in a comparative view – on the issue of whether the corporation can later collect further debt capital, thereby "diluting" recourse by the earlier creditors to its assets (debt dilution).[35] However, this is in any case not a problem specific to corporate law, but a legal issue of lending in general, as it concerns neither the limited liability of the corporation nor particular principal-agent conflicts in relation to the shareholders: a difference between debt dilution in the case of natural persons and legal persons does not exist. Both earlier and later debt capital providers acquire their claims against the corporation's assets on the basis of individual debt contracts. Any far-reaching statutory prohibition of debt dilution would thus be equivalent to a prohibition to the further assumption of debt in addition to existing obligations (with the

34 *Bratton* in: Eidenmüller/Schön, supra (note 23), p. 37, 47 et seq.

35 *Armour/Hertig/Kanda* in: Kraakman et al., supra (note 22), p. 127.

reservation of the right to consent for creditors). Imposing this prohibition on contracting would create serious adverse effects on the contractual freedom of debtors, given the fact that in most cases there is no material damage on the creditors' side. It therefore appears sensible and sufficient to let creditors who are significantly affected in an individual case to enter into specific contractual arrangements if they see the necessity to do so.[35a]

3 Business Management

The establishment of the purpose of the enterprise, the scope of the enterprise and the financing of the corporation creates a common basis for the corporation's day-to-day business activity both for equity and debt capital providers. In a next step, it must be clarified who shall be entitled to control the current management of the corporation – the directors, the shareholders or the debt capital providers.

At this point one must introduce a fundamental distinction for this analysis: the following discussion exclusively concerns ordinary management measures with regard to the assets and operation of the corporation, which are in principle aimed at realising the purpose of the enterprise. These measures are primarily the task of the management, which must choose and implement them under the general duty of care with the application of business judgement. The underlying rules on current management do not concern transactions between the corporation and the shareholders or between the corporation and the directors in which assets are shifted out of the corporation's sphere to the detriment of the creditors. Such measures – dividends, tunnelling and other forms of self-dealing of the directors and shareholders with regard to the business opportunities and assets of the corporation – will be examined in another section below.[36]

a) Management in Sound Enterprises

Theory and practice of the closed corporation assume that the shareholders in principle have control over the current management. They have the choice to either undertake the management themselves or to delegate this task to professional non-shareholder directors chosen by them according to their working capacity and entrepreneurial skills. This at the same time involves the assumption that the directors (whether shareholder-directors or non-shareholder directors) pri-

---

35a For third-party effects of such covenants see *Adler/Kahan*, supra (note 20a), p. 1798 et seq.
36 See F. below

marily focus on the shareholders' interests in the fulfilment of their management tasks. From the creditors' point of view, this is acceptable. The shareholders' financial interests are directed at dividends and liquidation proceeds whose disbursement depends on reasonable consideration for the interests of the debt capital providers. As long as an enterprise does not get into economic difficulties, there is a natural correlation between the interests of the shareholders and the creditors: both groups are interested in increasing the corporation's assets – the debt capital providers to secure their repayment claims and the equity capital providers to increase their residual profit.

The directors' general duty of care therefore benefits both the debt capital providers and the equity capital providers as regards the material result.[37] Nevertheless, there is the fundamental question of who derives compensation claims from a breach of these duties – the corporation as such, the shareholder or even the creditor?[38]

The starting-point for considering this question is the assumption that the directors – from a doctrinal point of view – owe their services to the legal person "corporation" and must therefore pay compensation into the corporation's assets if they breach their duty of care (taking into consideration the business judgement rule), thus causing a reduction of the corporation's assets or preventing their increase.[39] From the perspective of creditors and shareholders, the first question to be raised is whether they should additionally be granted a personal compensation claim in case of misconduct by the directors. This is not the case: the shareholders' own pecuniary loss (reduction of the share in the profits and liquidation share) and the creditor's loss (reduction of the repayment amount) primarily reflects the pecuniary loss of the corporation as such.[40] If the directors who have caused the damage place the corporation in the position in which it would have been in case of proper management, this automatically leads to correct compensation of the reflective loss of the creditor and the shareholder. This concept is fully enforced in French law with the *responsabilité pour insuffisance d'actifs* (following on from the previous *action en comblément de passif*).[41]

The only issue still in question is whether the shareholder and the creditor shall be entitled to individual standing to sue for compensation payments owed

---

37 *Davies* in: Eidenmüller/Schön, supra (note 23), p. 303, 332; *Adler/Kahan* supra (note 20a), p. 1777–1778.

38 In detail *Drygala* in: Lutter, supra (note 14), p. 232, 238 et seq; *Klöhn* ZGR 2008, 110.

39 *Wiedemann* ZGR 2011, 183 (197 et seq); for a detailed discussion of the significance of the business judgement rule, see Chapter 4 B.III.

40 For a recent discussion of reflective losses, see *De Wulf* in: FS Hopt, 2010, p. 1537.

41 *Cozian/Viandier/Deboissy* Droit des Sociétés, 22nd ed. 2009, margin no. 298 et seq.

to the corporation. For shareholders, this can make sense by means of the *actio pro socio* if the majority of shareholders (such as a (majority) shareholder participating in the management) refuses to enforce a compensation claim. However, it is not necessary for the creditor to have own standing to sue, at least not usually in the case of a "healthy" enterprise. The difference between the two groups is that the shareholder as a "residual claimant" feels every damage caused by careless management to the corporation's assets indirectly in the value of his shares, whereas the creditor is only economically affected by misconduct if and to the extent to which her claim to the repayment of the debt capital (or the interest payment) is at risk. This picture changes if the creditors obtain no satisfaction for their claims (due to business management misconduct by the directors) *via* the corporation: in this case, independent authorisation of the creditors to sue in favour of the corporation appears sensible, in particular when formal insolvency proceedings are not carried out for lack of funds. This idea, which is capable of generalisation, is set forth for stock corporations in Section 93(5) German Stock Corporation Act (*Aktiengesetz*).[42]

The question of the construction of an independent duty of care in relation to the creditors comes sharply into focus in particular if the shareholders are willing to indemnify the directors against liability for faulty business management decisions either from the outset or subsequently, while the creditors do not agree with this measure. The legal situation in Delaware is a good example: there the shareholders can also waive adherence to the duty of care to the creditors' detriment so that negligent management remains without sanction (although breach of the duty of loyalty does not).[43] According to recent caselaw,[44] this exclusion of liability cannot be called into question by a creditor's independent right to sue; for this reason, the notion of a self-standing fiduciary duty of the directors in relation to the creditors cannot be accepted.

To date, German corporate law has no clear line on this issue.[45] It is clear that the liability of the executive board of a stock corporation for "gross" breaches of duty cannot be excluded with prejudice to the creditors (Section 93(5) sentence 1 *Aktiengesetz*). This also cannot be circumvented by a resolution of the shareholders' meeting or a subsequent waiver or settlement (Section 93(3), (5) *Aktiengesetz*). The relevant law on privately-held limited liability companies

---

42 *Haas* supra (note 9), p. E 38 et seq.

43 Section 102(b)(7) Del. Gen. Corp. L.; on leeway for disposition under UK law, see *Steffek* Gläubigerschutz in der Kapitalgesellschaft, 2011, p. 309 et seq.

44 See *Adler/Kahan* supra (note 20a), p. 1782 et seq.; on the even further-reaching indemnifications in the LLC, see: *Miller* 46 Am. Bus. L.J. 243 (2009).

45 *Klöhn* ZGR 2008, 110, 131 et seq.

does not offer such a strict rule for the *closed corporation*; instead, the law on limited liability companies indemnifies the directors against liability for measures executed upon the instructions of the shareholders.[46] The dominant view is also that the duty of care can be reduced in the articles of association;[47] such regulations on release from liability have an indemnifying effect unless the directors shift assets to the shareholders to the detriment of the share capital (Section 43(3) sentence 2 *GmbH-Gesetz*). It is in any case disputed that the creditors have their own right to sue.[48] The risk to creditors by faulty business management decisions of the directors is therefore not sanctioned in the private limited company for the benefit of the creditors.

If we consider this situation *de lege ferenda*, we need to distinguish. First of all, it must be clear that the extent of directors' liability with effect for and against the creditors cannot be fixed by a unilateral resolution of the shareholders. From the viewpoint of the debt capital provider, shareholders and directors constitute one single management precisely in the closed corporation.[49] A disadvantageous instruction by the shareholders to the directors to implement a particular measure may endanger the creditors' claims, just like the subsequent indemnification against liability for breach of the duty of care. On the other hand, the creditors must accept the corporation and the enterprise operated by it as they find it at the time of the conclusion of the loan contract. This applies not only to the purpose and the object of the enterprise, but also to the standards governing the ongoing business management. If and to the extent to which the shareholders of a closed corporation extend the directors' range of business judgement by contractual agreement from the outset, the creditors of debt capital must accept this if they were aware of this circumstance at the time of the provision of the debt capital. For this reason, the regulation in the State of Delaware permitting full exclusion of liability for the duty of care in the articles of association is a sensible example if this regulation in the articles of association is disclosed to the general public in the Commercial Register. The creditors then know what they are getting into. If, by contrast, the shareholders only decide to indemnify the directors against liability for breach of the duty of care after the time of provision of debt capital or if they themselves issue disadvantageous in-

46 For a detailed discussion, see *Paefgen* in: Ulmer/Habersack/Winter, Komm. z. GmbHG, 2006, Section 43 margin no. 113 et seq.

47 *Paefgen* supra (note 46), Section 43 GmbHG margin no. 122 et seq; in further detail, *Fleischer* BB 2011, 2435.

48 *Paefgen* supra (note 46), Section 43 GmbHG margin no. 174.

49 *Armour/Hertig/Kanda* in: Kraakman et al., supra (note 22), p. 117 et seq, 135; *Fleischer* supra (note 3), Introduction to the GmbHG margin no. 277.

structions, the situation is different. While it would be excessive to require the consent of every single debt capital creditor, depending on the individual case this should be a justification for the creditors to terminate the loan agreement for good cause and to require the immediate repayment of the capital provided. Moreover, it has, of course, to be accepted that the creditors can include a further-reaching positive commitment of the standards of management in their debt covenants.

b) Management in Crisis

Current issues of creditor protection in corporate law include the issue of whether and from which point in time onwards a deterioration in the economic circumstances of the enterprise results in a change of content in the management's duties, in particular when stronger emphasis on the creditors' interest must be demanded.[50] Such a shift in coordinates is often justified by the argument that a further-reaching loss of equity leads to a divergence between creditors' and shareholders' interests. Both creditors and shareholders in principle remain interested in maximising the value of the enterprise. However, whereas creditors may tend to focus on careful management and the swift winding-up of the enterprise in order to secure the highest possible repayment on their claims, shareholders primarily benefit from the positive result of risky transactions which lead them back into the profit zone, whereas a negative business result no longer affects them in economic terms. In the U.S.[51] and in the United Kingdom[52] this has resulted in the question whether directors *in the vicinity of insolvency* are primarily obliged to act as trustees for the debt capital providers.

In answering this question, the need for conceptual clarity leads to a distinction. The particular risk to the creditors' interests which can arise in the vicinity of insolvency by the shift of assets from the corporation's assets to the shareholders or directors or affiliated persons forms a separate issue and must be left to

---

50 *Armour/Hertig/Kanda* in: Kraakman et al., supra (note 22), p. 119 et seq, 134 et seq; *Davies* in: Eidenmüller/Schön, supra (note 23), p. 303, 329 et seq; *Mülbert* in: Eidenmüller/Schön, supra (note 23), p. 361, 407 et seq; *Spindler* in: Eidenmüller/Schön, supra (note 23), p. 341; *Baums* ZHR 174 (2011), Issue 2+3; see also Chapter 4 B.II.1.c)aa).

51 See the recent leading case of the Supreme Court of Delaware in *North American Catholic Educational Programming Foundation, Inc., v. Rob Gheewalla, Gerry Cardinale and Jack Daly* 930 A.2d 92; from the literature, see *Bainbridge* 1 J. Bus. & Tech. L. 281 (2007); *Hu/Westbrook* 107 Colum. L. Rev. 1321 (2007); *Ribstein/Alces* 1 J. Bus. & Tech. L. 529 (2007); *Böckmann* supra (note 21), p. 202 et seq.

52 *Keay* 4 J. Corp. L. Stud. 307 (2004); *Davies* in: Eidenmüller/Schön, supra (note 23), p. 303; *Steffek* supra (note 43), p. 263 et seq.

one side. Our current discussion exclusively concerns the issue of whether the directors' business judgement in the pursuit of the aim of the enterprise is narrowed down in the vicinity of possible insolvency. This primarily concerns the conclusion of risky transactions which tend to be damaging to the creditors but advantageous for the shareholders, because the latter constituency is hardly affected by the downside risk in the period after the (far-reaching) loss of equity capital in any case.

In considering this question, we first note that the creditors of a corporation have entered into a contractual agreement according to which business losses can have an adverse effect on them. There is no strict repayment guarantee, just as there is no personal liability on the directors or shareholders for the amounts owed by the corporation. For this reason, in a crisis the creditors cannot complain that the purpose of the enterprise was pursued using their money within the framework of the corporate statute in a way which has eventually led to the loss of their repayment claims.[53]

However, there are two corresponding restrictions. Firstly, the purpose of the enterprise usually pre-programmes the orientation towards profit maximisation. For this reason, directors may only take measures, in particular enter into obligations and make investments, which have a positive net present value for the corporation. In addition, directors must remain within the framework of the object of the enterprise. This usually means that the risk profile of the business activity is constrained in a sufficiently transparent way. Finally, general rules of good governance require the diversification of risks within an enterprise, including the establishment of a functioning risk management.[54] In many cases, this framework will by itself prevent directors of healthy enterprises from entering into "cumulative risk" and will be all the more effective in a crisis situation.

Having said this, the directors are, however, not in principle prohibited from implementing measures which include the risk of adverse effects on creditors. An example is the concentration of the enterprise's financial resources on the development and marketing of a particular core product with which the directors – in their business judgement – hope to achieve its permanent launch in a particular market. The failure of this project can lead to total loss, without such a strategy being capable of prohibition from the outset.[55] The assumption of a gen-

53 *Haas* supra (note 9), p. E 13 et seq; *Mülbert* in: Eidenmüller/Schön, supra (note 23), p. 378 et seq; *K. Schmidt* in: Lutter, supra (note 14), p. 144, 145.

54 See the (careful) tendency in *Fleischer/Schmolke* ZHR 73 (2009), 649, 674 et seq; on the 'correlation risk' in which the risks from liabilities and investments correlate, see *Squire* 123 Harv. L. Rev. 1151 (2010).

55 Persuasive: *Hu/Westbrook* 107 Colum. L. Rev. 1321, 1378 et seq (2007).

eral prohibition on endangering the "existence" of the corporation by management measures therefore cannot be upheld. Creditors must accept this; we can only assume that directors must obtain the internal consent of the shareholders for such fundamental business decisions.[56]

"Gambling for resurrection" is the counter-example of a prohibited measure: the management undertakes unusually risky activities in order to save a failing enterprise in a crisis.[57] Close inspection usually reveals that such investments are not covered by the object of the enterprise and are hardly acceptable in business terms in view of the requirement of risk diversification. The directors are therefore not permitted to engage in them under the general rules. If a creditor desires an even further-reaching restriction of the directors' business judgement, she must negotiate specific stipulations for this in the debt covenant; it is difficult to stipulate general criteria for all enterprises and sectors for this under "objective law". Conversely, the directors can negotiate a "break-out" measure with shareholders and creditors about whether such an excessive risk can be taken.

At first sight, there is no reason to modify this duty in the vicinity of insolvency. As long as the directors pursue the aim of the enterprise, do not depart from the framework of the object of the enterprise and comply with the general business rules of risk diversification, risks arising in this context are in principle covered by the agreements with creditors.

However, in this situation it is necessary to define the direction of entrepreneurial activity towards the aim of "profit maximisation" more specifically. The starting-point is the assumption that both creditors and shareholders have an interest in generating profits, because every increase in the corporation's assets provides the creditor with more security for the repayment claim and the shareholder with an increase of her residual share.[58] In times of crisis, the directors may therefore only start projects with positive net present values. However, the asymmetry of risk allocation in a corporation in crisis can lead to a situation in which, given several possible projects with positive anticipated values, the respective anticipated values for the shareholders and creditors do not correlate, because the upside risk and the downside risk of the possible measures are unequally distributed. Should the director in this situation choose between the options depending on which project most benefits the shareholders, which project maximises benefits for the creditors or which project focuses on the overall yield

---

56 *Drygala* FS Hopt, vol. 1, 2010, p. 541, 545 et seq.
57 *Haas* supra (note 9), p. E 83 et seq.
58 *Engert* FS Heldrich, 2005, p. 87, 91 et seq.

of the investment? This problem arises in the closed corporation in particular due to the considerable influence of the shareholders on its management.[59]

The shareholder value approach appears to come close to the first option; however, this neglects the fact that the provision of debt capital by the corporation's creditors takes place under the (implicit) precondition that the enterprise is managed according to principles of good business management. One-sided emphasis on the creditors' interests does not, however, appear advisable, because they have not switched to the position of the enterprise's owners from a legal point of view; even if the shareholders have (temporarily) lost their financial contribution, they still hold their original position as holders of the shares and therefore have a *call option* on the future value of the enterprise above the liabilities capable of repayment.[60]

The management's business decision must thus be directed at the option which has the highest anticipated value from an "objective" point of view, regardless of how its opportunities and risks are allocated between shareholders and creditors.[61] As long as directors act within the framework of the risk profile defined in the articles of association, they are not obliged to choose a less risky project with a lower anticipated value for the benefit of the creditors. However, they are not permitted to take risks above and beyond the implicit agreement.

A genuine problem only arises in the rare case in which several alternative investments carry identical anticipated net present values but have different allocation effects between creditors and shareholders.[62] Here, the law must positively formulate a preference for one of the two capital providing groups (which can subsequently become the basis for risk assessment and interest calculation for the grant of the loan). If we consider the information asymmetry between shareholders and directors on the one hand and creditors on the other hand as regards the valuation and risk analysis for this investment, there are good reasons for giving preference to the creditors' interests in case of doubt. Directors' duties in a crisis therefore do not take a different direction from the framework of duties with which they must comply in a "healthy" enterprise.

A completely different question is whether unfavourable development of the business forces the directors to initiate a change in entrepreneurial strategy in the interests of all participants or to attempt the re-capitalisation of the corporation. This will be discussed in the following chapter.

---

59 *Davies* in: Eidenmüller/Schön, supra (note 23), p. 310 et seq; *Spindler* in: Eidenmüller/Schön, supra (note 23), p. 344 et seq.

60 *Hu/Westbrook* 107 Colum. L. Rev. 1321, 1382 et seq (2007).

61 *Baird/Henderson* 60 Stan. L. Rev. 1309, 1323 et seq. (2008).

62 *Klöhn* ZGR 2008, 110, 131 et seq.

D Transfer of Control to Creditors

The issue of the extent to which the directors of a closed corporation must give due consideration to the creditors' interests must be separated from the further question of whether, from a certain time onwards, control over the corporation's assets should be taken out of the hands of the shareholders and their directors and transferred to the creditors or persons acting as trustees for them. This affects the initiation of insolvency proceedings, the facts and circumstances triggering them and the personal entitlement and/or duty to file for insolvency proceedings.

I Facts and Circumstances Initiating Proceedings

Upon the initiation of the insolvency procedure or any other proceedings aiming at the realisation of the corporation's assets, core control over the enterprise is transferred to the creditors or a person acting as trustee for them (trustee in bankruptcy, administrator, receiver etc.).[63] It must therefore be clarified which facts and circumstances can legitimate this deprivation of rights of the holders to date (shareholders, directors) and who is entitled to initiate such proceedings.[64]

In virtually all legal systems, the decisive facts and circumstances for the initiation of such realisation proceedings refer to the corporation's cash-flow-based insolvency. In many jurisdictions, this is joined by "over-indebtedness".[65] This rule is based on the hypothetical assumption that repayment of the creditors' claims out of the assets is fully secure until the onset of cash-flow-based insolvency or over-indebtedness. Control by creditors should therefore start at the time from which they can only expect reduced satisfaction of their claims. From this "moment of truth" onwards, competition stiffens on the one hand between the individual creditors (so that an overarching procedure for even-handed enforcement appears advisable in order to maintain the *par conditio creditorum*) and on the other hand between creditors and shareholders, so that a shift of control rights to the first group appears necessary.[66]

We must realise that the rules according to which the transfer of control is based on cash flow-based insolvency or over-indebtedness are not predetermined by the nature of the matter, but merely reflect positive legal conventions.

63 For a detailed discussion, see *Haas* supra (note 9), p. E 19 et seq.
64 *Eidenmüller* in: Eidenmüller/Schön, supra (note 23), p. 241.
65 For a comparative law discussion, see *Haas* supra (note 9), p. E 21 et seq; *Steffek* supra (note 43), p. 67 et seq; in further detail *K. Schmidt* in: Lutter, supra (note 14), p. 150 et seq.
66 *Haas* supra (note 9), p. E 19 et seq.

They form a central element of the statutory "standard contract" between creditors and shareholders, which grants creditors the right to obtain control over the enterprise from a certain loss of value onwards.[67] This is an answer provided by current law – being one of several possible answers – to the question of the point in time which would typically been agreed for the transfer of control from shareholders to creditors in a debt covenant between the shareholders and creditors designed from the standpoint of efficiency. The statutory stipulation of this "moment of truth" in turn decisively determines the creditor's willingness to make debt capital available in the first place, as well as the amount of the risk premium which the loan creditor requires from the debtor in addition to the risk-free capital market interest rate.

Against this background, one should not complain about the fact that the current trigger for insolvency fails to guarantee the full satisfaction of the creditors in every single case or even in the majority of cases. The aim of the choice of trigger is not the full satisfaction of the creditors under all circumstances, but the choice of a point in time that provides incentives promoting efficiency for the preceding conduct of the participating actors, including creditors, shareholders and directors.

In order to provide legal certainty for the parties, the trigger for a change in control under a benchmark of cash-flow-based insolvency or over-indebtedness has to be laid down in the law in an unambiguous manner, so that the facts and circumstances of over-indebtedness are objectively dependent on the statutory calculation method (e.g. break-up values, going concern values, historical values). Nevertheless, the test of over-indebtedness or cash-flow-based insolvency is frequently supplemented by an element of forecast which reflects the economic outlook of the enterprise and therefore plays a central role in the transfer of control.[68]

Three fundamental requirements must be borne in mind if one decides whether the main test should refer to over-indebtedness (balance sheet test) or to solvency (solvency test):

- The first criterion relates to the "objectivity" of the trigger, which must be ascertained with the aid of outwardly visible characteristics if possible – due to its significance for directors, creditors and shareholders. From this point of view, the test of cash flow-based solvency proves superior to over-indebtedness.[69] Moreover, the initiation of proceedings as early as the company en-

67 *Tirole* supra (note 27), p. 84 et seq; *Klaus Schmidt* in: Eidenmüller/Schön, supra (note 23), p. 87, 91 et seq; *Christensen/Nikolaev* 50 J. Acct. Res. 75 (2012) ("Performance Covenants").
68 *K. Schmidt* in: Lutter, supra (note 14), p. 144.
69 *Eidenmüller* in: Eidenmüller/Schön, supra (note 23), p. 241.

ters a "crisis" in the vicinity of actual insolvency would prove even less manageable than a link to over-indebtedness.[70]

- However, opposing requirements are imposed if one wishes to increase creditor satisfaction or enable the company to enter restructuring. Any attempt to increase creditor satisfaction has to accept that this is least fulfilled if the trigger is linked to cash flow-based insolvency. To the contrary, the initiation of a realisation of assets or a restructuring procedure might be more promising upon the onset of over-indebtedness. The idea of creditor protection may even make it appear sensible to move the facts and circumstances triggering the procedure even further forward, in order to guarantee greater or even full satisfaction of the creditors' claims. From the point of view of the equity capital provider, this could, however, lead to the destruction of their profit prospects at a time at which there is still hope of leading the enterprise into a successful future in the interests of all participants.[71] The change of control must therefore not take place too soon.
- Thirdly, it is sensible to introduce an element of forecast alongside the calculated facts and circumstances of cash flow-based insolvency or over-indebtedness when considering the initiation of insolvency proceedings, in order to avoid arbitrary effects under the relevant accounting rules and at the same time to supplement the lack of foreseeability of later developments at the time of the conclusion of a debt covenant by a current look at the entrepreneurial situation.

This prognostic element[72] can take effect in two directions:

- According to the German tradition, a positive going-concern forecast which is applied within the framework of the test of over-indebtedness may give rise to the application of going-concern valuation of the corporate assets and therefore exclude insolvency.[73] In spite of accounts-based insolvency, the positive outlook prevents the initiation of insolvency proceedings. In other words, the creditors cannot force the directors to file for insolvency proceedings in spite of balance-sheet insolvency, but instead have to give them the opportunity to undertake further rescue attempts.
- By contrast, according to the British rules on wrongful trading a negative forecast can give rise to shareholders' duties to act even in the vicinity of ac-

---

70 *Eidenmüller* in: Eidenmüller/Schön, supra (note 23), p. 244 et seq; *Haas* supra (note 9), p. E 31.

71 *Davies* in: Eidenmüller/Schön, supra (note 23), p. 322.

72 For a differentiated comparative law view, see *Steffek* supra (note 43), p. 468 et seq.

73 *Hüttemann* FS Karsten Schmidt, 2009, p. 761; *K. Schmidt* in: Lutter, supra (note 14), p. 156 et seq.

tual insolvency. In other words, the directors cannot be satisfied with continuing the business as before given the existing solvency, but must take measures to bring the corporation back to a favourable forecast through alterations to the business model and/or re-capitalisation.[74] However, it is not absolutely clear from the literature whether, under British law, the corporation's solvency is ascertained only by the standard of cash-flow-based insolvency or also by the standard of over-indebtedness for the purposes of wrongful trading.[75]

This shows that the point in time triggering insolvency is not to be determined by legislation primarily according to the prospect of full creditor satisfaction, but according to the efficient allocation of behavioural incentives for the participating groups. It must still be combined with a forecast of the enterprise's capacity for survival and statements about behavioural duties of the management in crisis – particularly in view of specific business decisions.

Balanced regulation could contain the following elements:

- Prior to the point in time of accounts-based over-indebtedness of the corporation on the basis of break-up values, the right to continue the corporation does not depend on a special positive forecast or a change of behaviour by the directors. Even in case of immediate winding-up, there is no risk for the creditors.
- If insolvency has arisen on the basis of break-up values, over-indebtedness may not yet occur on the basis of going-concern values in case of a positive forecast for continued existence. The directors must then examine the measures to be taken in order to avoid insolvency permanently. The initiation of proceedings is not necessary at this point in time, but continuing observation of the development of the going-concern value and an adjustment of the business model is necessary to avoid insolvency.
- If the forecast is unfavourable and over-indebtedness cannot be avoided either by the use of break-up values or the use of going-concern values, the management has to seek a further extension of the time limit to save the enterprise or wind up the corporation. Here, informing the shareholders and the most important creditors about the financial situation – to avoid insolvency proceedings – and negotiating with them about re-capitalisation or

---

74 *Davies* in: Eidenmüller/Schön, supra (note 23), p. 313 et seq.

75 *Bachner* 5 Eur. Bus. Org. L. Rev. 293 (2004); *Davies* in: Eidenmüller/Schön, supra (note 23), p. 319 et seq; *Habersack/Verse* ZHR 168 (2004), 174, 213 et seq; *K. Schmidt* in: Lutter, supra (note 14), p. 156 et seq; on French law *Haas* supra (note 9), p. E 27 et seq.

other rescue measures is a necessary requirement.[76] In this situation, the creditors must already be given the opportunity to file for insolvency proceedings in order to have meaningful leverage in the negotiations. However, special rights of termination in the context of the underlying debt covenant which would lead to the immediate cash flow-based insolvency of the corporation can *de facto* replace any statutory right of creditors to apply for insolvency proceedings.
- Insolvency proceedings must be initiated at the latest upon the cash-flow-based insolvency of the enterprise.

II Right to File a Petition for Insolvency Proceedings

In the light of this, the right to file a petition for insolvency proceedings requires specific differentiation:
- A creditor's right to file a petition for the commencement of insolvency proceedings is a considerable encroachment on shareholders' and directors' control. Filing for insolvency proceedings is therefore only legitimate at the time of insolvency. On the other hand, this encroachment must be possible in order to avoid continuing damage to creditors in case of unfavourable economic development of the business resulting from misjudgement by the directors and the consequent delay in realisation of the corporate assets.[77] Making the commencement of proceedings dependent on a negative continuation forecast for the enterprise protects shareholders and directors in their genuine endeavours to lead the corporation out of crisis.
- The directors' right to file a petition for the commencement of insolvency proceedings is important for another reason. From their point of view, the opening of the formal insolvency proceedings serves to ensure an ordered winding-up of the company[78] – or an ordered restructuring, depending on the individual circumstances – as well as to inform the general public even-handedly about the corporation's financial position. This at the same time releases the directors from a precarious collision of duties. Once insolvency proceedings have started, the corporation is protected from uncontrolled intervention by the creditors and, if necessary, is granted the opportunity to free itself from burdensome liabilities. For this reason, there is intense de-

76 Most recently *Kleindiek* FS Uwe H. Schneider, 2011, p. 617, 618 et seq.
77 *Armour/Hertig/Kanda* in: Kraakman et al., supra (note 22), p. 122, 143 et seq.
78 On British law *Steffek* supra (note 43), p. 139 et seq.

bate about whether the directors can be granted the right to file a petition even at an early stage – in the vicinity of insolvency – in order to enable the early entry into ordered reorganisation or restructuring.[79]

- Particularly in closed corporations, this brings up the issue of the position of the shareholders (individually or jointly). It initially introduces the problem of whether the directors require the shareholders' consent to exercise the right to file. It will not be possible to award them this entitlement in the situation of over-indebtedness or cash-flow-based insolvency, because the commencement of insolvency proceedings here primarily serves to secure creditors' claims. However, shareholders must be able to ward off the premature filing of a petition for insolvency proceedings if they are concerned that the directors unfoundedly take the risk of a devaluation of the corporation's assets in order to make sure they are "on the safe side" or carry out reorganisation or restructuring to the shareholders' detriment without compulsory consultation with the shareholders.[80] Given the fact that the deliberate liquidation of an entity can only be carried out on the basis of a (qualified) shareholders' approval, the same should be said about filing for insolvency in the vicinity of insolvency.
- Finally, there is the question whether the shareholders of a closed corporation should also be in a position to independently file a petition for the conduct of insolvency proceedings. There are good reasons for this: the conduct of insolvency proceedings serves to satisfy the creditors on the one hand and also serves the ordered winding-up, restructuring or reorganisation of the enterprise on the other hand (depending on the relationship between the liquidation value and the going concern value). Both are in the direct or indirect interests of the shareholders, who may have to counteract self-interested conduct by the directors. For this reason, the shareholder majority or a qualified majority should be in a position either to file such a petition or to instruct the directors accordingly.

---

79 *Armour/Hertig/Kanda* in: Kraakman et al., supra (note 22), p. 143; on the dysfunctionality of Section 18 German Insolvency Code, see *K. Schmidt* in: Lutter, supra (note 14), p. 148.

80 *Baird/Henderson* 60 Stan. L. Rev. 1309, 1320 et seq. (2008); this corresponds to the dominant view in German law on the relationship between the right to file and the duty of submission (*K. Schmidt* in: Schmidt/Uhlenbruck, Die GmbH in Krise, Sanierung und Insolvenz, 4th ed., 2009, Section 5.43 et seq.).

III Duty to File a Petition for Insolvency Proceedings

As in most continental European legal systems,[81] German law is familiar with a general duty to file a petition for insolvency proceedings imposed on the management bodies of a legal person, namely the executive board of a stock corporation and the directors of a GmbH. The breach of this duty is sanctioned under civil and criminal law.[82] However, such a duty to file a petition for insolvency proceedings is not self-evident, as a glance at the U.S. shows. There, the directors of a corporation are entitled but not obliged by statute to file an insolvency petition and – depending on the situation – to seek protection under Chapter 11 or aim for regular winding-up pursuant to Chapter 7 of the Bankruptcy Code. This is not least supported by the argument that the directors should not be led into a conflict between creditors' interests and shareholders' interests. British law has developed a middle-of-the-road solution: the provision on wrongful trading (Section 214 Insolvency Act) does not provide for a duty to file a petition for insolvency proceedings, but imposes civil law liability on the directors if they do not file the petition in spite of the crisis of the enterprise and also do not ensure by their way of managing the firm that the damage to the creditors resulting from the delay in the commencement of insolvency proceedings is minimised. Ultimately, this enforces indirect pressure on filing a petition even if there are no criminal law consequences.[83]

In a careful assessment of the interests involved, a statutory duty on the directors to file a petition is primarily supported by the constraints of information asymmetry and collective action. Creditors do not know the corporation's financial position as well as directors (and, in the closed corporation, as well as shareholders) and it is difficult for them to coordinate their interests in advance of formal insolvency proceedings. Particularly in the case of small creditors, the time, effort, expense and risk of filing a controversial petition for insolvency proceedings can thwart any initiative. Therefore, there are good reasons for primarily imposing a duty on directors to file a petition for insolvency proceedings upon the onset of over-indebtedness and cash flow-based insolvency. In this way, directors are also indirectly obliged to disclose the financial situation to the most important creditors at an early stage and negotiate on relief measures (voluntary subordination of debt, debt-equity swaps, partial waivers). In case of late filing, the

---

81 *Kalss/Adensamer/Oelkers* in: Lutter, supra (note 14), p. 112.

82 In more detail *Wagner* FS Karsten Schmidt, p. 1665; on the aim of prevention *Casper* in: Bachmann/Casper/Schäfer/Veil, Steuerungsfunktionen des Haftungsrechts im Gesellschafts- und Kapitalmarktrecht, 2007, p. 33.

83 *Davies* in: Eidenmüller/Schön, supra (note 23), p. 316; *Keay* 25 J. Legal Stud. 431 (2005); *Steffek* supra (note 43), p. 342 et seq.

directors should therefore have an obligation to make up for any damage which has arisen as a result of the delay. The British solution (through wrongful trading) and the German solution (through Section 823(2) German Civil Code in conjunction with Section 15 a Insolvency Code) hardly differ from one another as regards this result.[84]

In this constellation, it is decisive who is responsible for making the forecast about the continued existence or failure of the enterprise.[85] Whereas in German law the court is primarily responsible for such a forecast within the framework of an insolvency investigation (possibly with the help of expert opinions), British law primarily leaves this forecast up to the directors, who must nevertheless act with the necessary care. We cannot avoid finding a generic inefficiency here: directors are better informed than the court about the development of the enterprise and its economic environment, but at the same time face the risk of false perceptions (over-optimism) and misguided incentives (avoidance of liability; job security) to the detriment of the creditors. By contrast, the court is impartial in its assessment; however, it not only lacks any detailed knowledge, but also has to avoid the temptation of hindsight bias in its assessment.[86] An optimal solution is therefore structurally impossible. Instead, we have to live with a compromise solution which primarily leaves the forecast about the economic future of the business up to the management, but requires substantiation of this assessment in subsequent court proceedings and documentation of the decisive considerations.[87]

This also includes an obligation on directors to do everything necessary in the vicinity of final insolvency in order to lead the enterprise back to success.[88] This involves visible measures such as a review and possibly a revision of the business concept, negotiations with equity and debt capital providers on the re-capitalisation of the corporation, etc. The advantage of not having to file a petition for insolvency proceedings in spite of calculated over-indebtedness in case of a favourable going concern forecast must be balanced by a corresponding duty to take the measures necessary to realise this forecast.

84 *Davies* in: Eidenmüller/Schön, supra (note 23), p. 321 et seq; *Haas* supra (note 9), p. E 29; *Mülbert* in: Eidenmüller/Schön, supra (note 23), p. 386 et seq; *K. Schmidt* in: Lutter, supra (note 14), p. 159 et seq.

85 *Spindler* JZ 2006, 839, 846 et seq.

86 *K. Schmidt* in: Lutter, supra (note 14), p. 150.

87 On the burden of proof, see *Strohn* NZG 2011, 1161, 1162.

88 For a different view, see *Haas* supra (note 9), p. E 33 et seq.

IV Administration by Directors and Shareholders?

A separate question is whether there can be reasons to oblige the managers to direct the enterprise in the creditors' interests upon the initiation of insolvency proceedings, but not to take the operation of the enterprise away from the existing directors. A comparative law view shows that many legal systems are familiar with self-management, as shown by the example of Chapter 11 of the U.S. Bankruptcy Code; German law also increasingly supports a combination of insolvency proceedings and directors remaining in office.[89]

Regarding this issue, one distinction seems to be useful. Self-management must not be established primarily in the directors' interests of continuing their professional position; in addition, the fundamental transfer of control over the enterprise to the creditors must not be called into question. Self-management is then ultimately a type of fiduciary administration of the current (or of new) management, which acts as "trustee" for all the creditors jointly like an insolvency administrator. It therefore requires the consent of the majority of the creditors and at the same time changes the status of duties of the directors towards primary safeguarding the interests of all the creditors as a group.

E Liability of the Shareholders

A strong influence of the shareholders on the management is typical for the closed corporation. This means that the question of personal liability of the shareholders (towards the corporation) for their involvement in the day-to-day management of the company is of greater relevance here than in the case of public corporations.[89a] In a limited liability corporation, it must be accepted that general entrepreneurial influence of the shareholders as such and the stipulation of certain business concepts for the management is not sufficient to trigger personal liability by the shareholders.[90] Instead, two aspects are important in this context: liability for wrong business decisions by the shareholders and their liability for the delayed filing of a petition for insolvency proceedings.

89 For a recent detailed discussion, see *Eidenmüller* ZHR 175 (2011), 11; *Jaffe* ZHR 175 (2011), 38.
89a *Rock*, 161 U. Pa. L. Rev. (2013) p. 1907 et seq., at p. 1926 et seq.
90 *Mülbert* in: Eidenmüller/Schön, supra (note 23), p. 368.

I Liability for Intervention in the Management

The issue of liability by the shareholders for intervention in the management comes up not only in Germany but also in other countries under the label of a *de facto* organ[91] (*de-facto director/dirigeant de fait*) or from the perspective of the indirect exercise of influence (*shadow director*).[92] The question is whether shareholders who exercise influence on the corporation's activities can be subject to such an obligation instead of or alongside the directors.

The starting-point is the consideration that, according to the statutory division of tasks in the corporation, shareholders "as such" are not subject to any duty apart from the fulfilment of their obligations under the articles of association (namely the provision of a capital contribution).[93] They are not "organs" in the sense of assuming responsibility for the day-to-day fulfilment of duties in the corporation. A shareholder who puts up his capital contribution and then withdraws completely from the corporation's activities does not in principle act in breach of duty. This in particular enables a shareholder in a closed corporation – like a shareholder in a public corporation – to reduce his activity to the position of mere capital provider. It seems advisable to give capital providers the opportunity to acquire such a share without "work duties". This should in principle also apply to the owner of a wholly-owned firm: If the statutory duties of directors are reasonably well-established and sanctioned, there is no reason to burden the shareholders with special supervisory obligations. This avoids inefficient bundling of capital and labour.

On the other hand, it will often precisely be the case with a closed corporation that one or more shareholders do in fact exercise influence on the actual management. If and to the extent to which they issue disadvantageous business instructions, the question is whether and to what extent there is a duty to pay compensation to the corporation. This does not involve examining the – likewise frequent – conflicts between majority and minority shareholders; instead, we investigate whether, for example, the sole shareholder of a closed corporation should be liable to the corporation for disadvantageous instructions.

The analysis must build on the point of view of *ex ante* negotiations between creditors, directors and shareholders. Creditors assume (in the usual statutory case) that directors comply with the standards of proper management (within the framework of the business judgement rule) and that the corporation's assets

---

91 For a recent detailed discussion, see *Strohn* DB 2011, 158; see also Chapter 4 B.III.2.

92 In detail and from the viewpoint of comparative law *Merkt/Spindler* in: Lutter, supra (note 14), p. 180 et seq, 205 et seq; *Steffek* supra (note 43), p. 499 et seq.

93 *Haas* supra (note 9), p. E 100 et seq.

are not reduced by improper measures. If shareholders had the possibility of issuing instructions to directors without being liable to the corporation for disadvantageous instructions, directors would feel the full force of the conflict of interest between creditors and shareholders: shareholders would face the temptation to speculate to the disadvantage of the creditors but without the risk of personal liability, and the functionality of the governance system would depend exclusively on the directors' personal backbone (in particular their personal independence from the shareholders). The same applies if a shareholder undertakes management measures directly with regard to the corporation (and employees, customers, suppliers, etc. of the corporation follow his instructions). The outward appearance is not decisive here.[94]

It therefore appears sensible to make the shareholders personally liable to the corporation for instructions which are negligent from a business point of view and which are disadvantageous for the company to the same extent as measures taken by the actual directors. This not only corresponds to the view repeatedly put forward in the German academic discussion with different reasons;[95] Italian law has also recently included this liability rule in Art. 2476(7) *Codice Civile* for "decisions" and "authorisations" by the shareholders.[96] Those seeking to avoid this liability must avoid such involvement. However, liability for breach of the duty of care can once again be excluded, either as a whole or in part, in the published articles of association (but only if directors' liability is also limited in the same fashion). Creditors are then aware of the modes of governance they can expect. Moreover, the usual threshold of the business judgment rule does apply.

II Shareholder Liability for Delayed Filing of a Petition for Insolvency Proceedings

The picture is more complicated regarding the liability of shareholders for delayed filing of a petition for insolvency proceedings or failure to file such a petition at all. This involves an "omission" which can in principle be punished only if there is a clearly allocated legal duty. Again we must assume that a shareholder is not automatically obliged on the basis of his position as shareholder to

94 See also *Davies* in: Eidenmüller/Schön, supra (note 23), p. 314; *Spindler* in: Eidenmüller/Schön, supra (note 23), p. 348; likewise in JZ 2006, 839, 847 et seq.
95 On the one hand *Wilhelm* Rechtsform und Haftung bei der juristischen Person, 1981; on the other hand *Grigoleit* supra (note 1), p. 289 et seq.
96 *Sangiovanni* RIW 2011, 744.

inform himself about the corporation's financial situation and possibly work towards a petition for insolvency proceedings. This would be incompatible with the picture of the shareholder as purely a capital provider. The situation is no different in case of significant shareholdings. In this context, the law should assume a clear division of labour between management and shareholders.

The mere knowledge of the corporation's financial situation also cannot be sufficient for such liability. Shareholders have the right but not the duty to inform themselves about the financial situation of the enterprise. If they do so, it will not be possible to derive a duty to file a petition from "interference" unless we wish to deter the shareholders from informing themselves about management conduct and the enterprise's economic situation.

The assessment is more difficult if the shareholders participate more or less in the management. Occasional instructions by the shareholders assembly will probably be insufficient to trigger liability for delaying to file a petition for insolvency proceedings, in contrast to full interference in the corporation's daily work. However, any obligation would have to be combined with a shareholder's personal right to file.[97] A different but clear case concerns the situation in which a shareholder actively prevents a petition for insolvency proceedings being filed – here the shareholder is surely liable for his intervention.[98]

F Open and Hidden Distributions to Shareholders

I General Limit to Disbursements

The interests of the creditors and the corporation clash directly in case of payments out of the corporation's assets to the shareholders. Such payments – whether an open dividend or a hidden asset shift – reduce the liable funds of the corporation and increase the consumption funds of the shareholders. This effect is reinforced even further if the law – for instance as with dividends drawn in good faith – excludes the demand for repayment by the company against the shareholders to the detriment of the creditors.

The framework for the permissibility of disbursements to shareholders is therefore a fundamental basis of the "standard contract" between creditors and shareholders as provided by statutory corporate law.[99] Depending on the

97 See above and *Haas* supra (note 9), p. E 47 et seq.
98 *Haas* supra (note 9), p. E 44.
99 *Kalay* 10 J. Fin. Econ. 211 (1982).

scope of the right of shareholders to remove assets from the corporate entity, it will be easier or more difficult to obtain equity capital, but on the other hand the creditors will typically require higher interest rates as payment for the risks to their claims caused by shareholder withdrawals.[100] However, the risk of opportunistic conduct is particularly high in this area, so it may be worthwhile to include mandatory provisions in corporate law which generally prevent withdrawals of the corporation's assets completely if they work to the creditors' detriment.[101] Alternatively, there is also the option of extending the law on "fraudulent transfers" to disbursements to shareholders.[102] This technical question – whether insolvency law or corporate law is the right *sedes materiae* for this subject-matter – is also relevant in cases of conflicts of laws but will not be discussed here.[103]

Legal systems from Roman law right until the 19th century have established particularly high barriers for asset transfers by endorsing the disbursement of profit shares only upon liquidation of the corporation and after the prior satisfaction of all creditors' claims; however, this prohibition of interim payments led to an inefficiently high level of creditor protection in permanent corporations, which did not pay due respect to the interests of the shareholders in regular midstream payouts which not only provided means of consumption to the shareholders but also the option to reinvest the monies outside the realm of the corporation.[104] Against this background, the truth lies somewhere in the middle: it must be possible to make regular dividend payments and to shift other assets in the corporation's current course of business to a limited extent. "Standard contracts" must be codified which – in order to balance the involved interests –

---

100 *Rickford* et al., 15 Eur. Bus. L. Rev. 919, 967 (2004).

101 *Armour* in: Eidenmüller/Schön, supra (note 23), p. 10 et seq, 14 et seq; *Spindler* JZ 2006, 839, 843 et seq; in many legal systems, the question of these limits to disbursement is linked to the issue of the maintenance of a corporation's share capital; however, it is raised regardless of the existence of a statutory capital protection scheme (*Lutter* supra (note 14), p. 5; *Schön* DK 2004, 162, 164 et seq).

102 In further detail *Eidenmüller/Engert* FS Karsten Schmidt, 2009, p. 305; *Grigoleit* supra (note 1), p. 153 et seq; *Paulus* in: Lutter, supra (note 14), p. 325; *Thole* Gläubigerschutz durch Insolvenzrecht, 2010, p. 89 et seq; *Wagner* in: Eidenmüller/Schön, supra (note 23), p. 217; on U.S. law, see *Baird* in: Eidenmüller/Schön, supra (note 23), p. 199.

103 This distinction acquires a certain material significance if we understand corporate law distribution limits as prohibitions which take effect *ex ante*, but only let insolvency law rules intervene *ex post*. In my view, however, (from a legal policy point of view) an insolvency law rule can also be accorded a certain 'advance effect', which, for example, makes directors liable ex post for challengeable disbursements.

104 *Schön* in: Hommelhoff/Rowedder/Ulmer, Max Hachenburg – Fünfte Gedächtnisvorlesung 2002, 2003, p. 17 et seq.

define the disbursement limits in such a way that an efficient issuance both of equity and debt capital can be expected.[105]

Generally speaking, existing legal systems distinguish between two different boundaries for corporate distributions: the limit of the subscribed capital on the one hand and the limit of over-indebtedness or solvency on the other hand. The concept that all payments and other disbursements which eat into the subscribed capital under a balance sheet test are prohibited fundamentally rests on the traditional system of raising and maintaining legal capital as formulated in the European Capital Directive and in many continental European legal systems. The merits of legal capital are discussed under a separate point below.[106] By contrast, the boundary of over-indebtedness or solvency exists in all known legal systems.[107] It is part of the core of corporate law or insolvency law that corporations with limited liability must not make any payments to their shareholders if this renders the fulfilment of the enterprise's obligations uncertain (see, for example, Section 6.40 *Revised Model Business Corporation Act*). Of course, this could be left up to the individual creditors to negotiate – but in view of the considerable transaction costs, the lack of market power of individual creditors and the known problems of collective action, it appears more advisable to provide for a fixed minimum limitation for disbursements with effect for and against all participants and to leave to the participants the opportunity to formulate higher disbursement limits contractually.[108]

If we recognise that this boundary performs the function of a "standard contract" which substitutes a typical debt covenant, it becomes clear that the advantages and disadvantages of the discussed concepts result in different risk allocations between the shareholders and the creditors (or individual groups of creditors) respectively. Individually secured major creditors (banks) will have no interest in standardised disbursement limitations because they can enforce their own priority rights and can also formulate their own disbursement regulations in covenants. As regards the other creditors, a distinction can be made between the interests of short-term and long-term creditors:[109] Whereas the holders

105 *Armour/Hertig/Kanda* in: Kraakman et al., supra (note 22), p. 132 et seq.; *Adler/Kahan* supra (note 20a), p. 1788 et seq.

106 See below par. H.

107 *Haas* supra (note 9), p. E 121 et seq; *Mülbert* in: Eidenmüller/Schön, supra (note 23), p. 392 et seq; *Rickford* in: Eidenmüller/Schön, supra (note 23), p. 135, 144 et seq; on the discussion within the framework of the SPE, see *Hennrichs* NZG 2009, 921, 926, *De Erice/Gaude* NZG 2009, 857, 860 et seq.

108 *Spindler* JZ 2006, 839, 841.

109 *Schön* in: Eidenmüller/Schön, supra (note 23), p. 181, 189 et seq.

of short-term claims will focus their attention on the current liquidity of the enterprise (checked by a "solvency test"), the holders of long-term unsecured claims (pension commitments, provisions for waste clean-up) will be interested in a "balance sheet test" which takes a view on the capacity of the corporation's assets to cover its debt including all existing liabilities and provisions. If we apply a "balance sheet test", we can use particularly conservative balance sheet rules stressing the downside risk in an asymmetrical fashion stronger than the opportunities, or we can go for information-oriented rules such as IFRS, which focus more on the current situation and market value orientation instead of the definition of long-term profits amenable to distribution.

A "balance sheet test" oriented towards the principle of conservatism is principally supported by considerations which focus on the risk of opportunistic behaviour by directors and shareholders. We should bear in mind that the application of these specified tests is initially in the hands of the management and is frequently ratified by the group of shareholders. External gatekeepers like auditors or courts only come into play at the next level. For this reason, tests should be applied which are open to as little manipulation as possible by the interested directors and shareholders.

In this context, the balance sheet test has a clear advantage over the solvency test, which to a large extent depends on the management's personal assessment of the enterprise's future development, whereas the balance sheet test is primarily oriented to historic data.[110] In selecting the balance sheet rules, it must be possible to refuse the shareholders' request to report and distribute profits in case of an uncertain course of business without their having to repay these payments in case of the realisation of the downside risk. A balance sheet in accordance with IFRS therefore cannot be a solution, even in combination with a solvency test.[111] Conservative accounting which recognises the realisation of losses earlier than the realisation of gains, by contrast, offers a borderline which is less susceptible to manipulation by shareholders and directors than a borderline according to IFRS or a solvency test. In the context of restrictions on dividend payouts, "conservative" accounting to date has proved its value

110 *Hennrichs* NZG 2009, 921, 926; *Spindler* JuristenZeitung (JZ) 2006, 839, 843 et seq; *Haaker* Deutsches Steuerrecht (DStR) 2010, 663, 667; likewise in ZGR 2010, 1055, 1061–1065; *Pfennig* supra (note 9), p. 113 et seq.

111 Although a contrary view is found in *Lutter* supra (note 14), p. 9 et seq and for the SPE: *Hommelhoff/Teichmann* GmbHR 2010, 337, 340; by contrast *Hennrichs* ZGR 2008, 361; *Schön* in: Eidenmüller/Schön, supra (note 23), p. 196 et seq.

and is also practiced in "voluntary" debt covenants to this day.[112] It should not be supplemented by an obligatory cumulative solvency test.[113]

II Dividends: Protection of Good Faith

As regards dividends out of the corporation's assets, the fundamental question arises about whether and to what extent good faith of the participants in the correctness of the payment can counterbalance the need to protect creditors. An example is a payment made on the basis of objectively incorrect annual accounts (e.g. failure to recognise the need for a reserve for considerable environmental protection obligations without subjective fault). At first sight, the dividend recipients may not appear in need of protection, because they did not acquire a certain claim to certain disbursements upon making their capital contributions in the first place. On the other hand, the willingness of investors to provide equity can be seriously reduced if they have to anticipate that open dividends received in good faith can subsequently be reclaimed from them. For this reason, a limited protection of good faith has to be granted by the law which gives rise to an exclusion of repayment demands at least in case of a balance sheet prepared by the management in good faith and dividends received in good faith by the shareholders.[114]

III Hidden Asset Shifts

Several problems arise in the case of hidden asset shifts.[115] The first question is whether this sort of self-dealing should generally be prohibited as it reduces the corporate funds available for creditors. This approach is in line with German stock corporation law which places all assets of the corporation under protection, even in case of corporations not listed on the stock exchange.[116] This rule has some merits from the viewpoint of shareholder protection (namely of the minority shareholders who have to be protected against "tunnelling" by majority shareholders), but it is irrelevant from the creditors' point of view. On the other hand, the difference between the open dividend and the hidden asset shift is not obvious with regard to creditor protection. Both payments are intended to

---

112 *Nikolaev*, 48 J. Acct. Res. 51 (2010); *Li* 48 J. Acct. Res. 1103 (2010).
113 *Pfennig* supra (note 9), p. 130 et seq.
114 *Schön* FS 50 Jahre Bundesgerichtshof, 2000, vol. 2, p. 153 et seq.
115 *Armour/Hertig/Kanda* in: Kraakman et al., supra (note 22), p. 132 et seq.
116 Critically *Schön* FS Röhricht, 2005, p. 559.

withdraw value from the corporation without adequate counterperformance. For this reason, hidden asset shifts must be subjected – from the creditors' viewpoint – to the balance-sheet test applicable to regular dividends. If statutory law provides for a balance sheet-oriented test for distributions, this must be applied not only to open dividends but also to hidden asset shifts.[117] A solvency certificate issued in advance would not be suitable in such cases, but the directors must be placed under an obligation (and have the right) to subsequently prove that a hidden asset shift was permissible once it is discovered. Whether a certain flexibility with regard to self-dealing should be granted in a corporate group situation if disadvantageous legal transactions appear justified in the context of a wider entrepreneurial strategy is another question.[118]

IV Other Forms of Self-Dealing

In addition to open dividends and hidden asset shifts between the corporation and the shareholders, there is a "grey area" of measures which are likely to increase the personal income of directors and shareholders to the detriment of the corporation's profits and assets. An example is the capture of business opportunities of the corporation by directors and shareholders or other entrepreneurial decisions, e.g. the closure of a business division, the removal of fixed assets essential to the business or the redrafting of a set of contracts, all of which cannot be seen as an asset shift in the narrower sense, but which display a correlation between assets of the corporation and assets of the shareholders/directors.[119]

From the creditor protection perspective, the special feature of these cases is that the corporation's assets are not factually transferred to the shareholders, but instead the corporation is deprived of the prospect of certain earning opportunities in the future. For this reason, a "balance sheet test" designed for distributions cannot sensibly be applied to these measures. This once again raises the question how the statutory "standard contract" between the shareholders, directors and creditors is to be "read".

The starting point for the contractual agreements between the creditors and the corporation is – as has been repeatedly emphasised – not only the protection of the existing assets but the corporation's entire business model as expressed in the articles of association of the enterprise. The creditors assume that the corpo-

---

117 *Armour* in: Eidenmüller/Schön, supra (note 23), p. 6 et seq; on the SPE, see *Wicke* GmbHR 2011, 566, 572 et seq.

118 *Fleischer* in: Lutter, supra (note 14), p. 94 (with a comparison of laws).

119 *Paefgen* supra (note 46), Section 43 GmbHG margin no. 45.

ration actively operates within this framework and uses the business opportunities available there. The shift of business opportunities outside the enterprise, the removal of significant bases of operation or even the extraction of entire fields of business take effect against future profits and are not covered by the common goal of creditors and equity holders. Directors or shareholders can only appropriate these advantages if they are outside the sphere of the object of the enterprise or if they amend the corporation's articles of association accordingly. In this respect, unanimous approval by all of the shareholders to a change in business policy can be sufficient to clear the behaviour of the directors. However, as creditors have extended loans to the company *rebus sic stantibus*, any subsequent change of the corporation's basic texture or a corresponding shareholders' resolution should trigger an immediate right of termination for the debt contracts by the corporation's creditors.

Any kind of self-dealing – which also includes some of the constellations discussed in Germany under the heading of *Existenzgefährdung*[120] – must be sharply distinguished from simply negligent and faulty business conduct. This applies in particular to the capacity to contract away duties. Whereas the duty of care – as described above – can be contracted away, including with effect against the creditors, this does not seem possible for the duties of loyalty in order to exclude opportunistic behaviour or moral hazard. Self-interested encroachments of the directors or the shareholders on the corporation's business operations must therefore in any case be sanctioned with liability of the parties in favour of the creditors *via* the corporation. A precondition must be that the creditors are at risk at all as a result of this self-dealing. It is therefore advisable to apply this liability only in case of insolvency (and to leave the enforcement of the claims up to either the insolvency administrator or the creditors).

By contrast, German law provides for directors' liability in the case of "payments triggering insolvency" (sec. 64(3) *GmbH-Gesetz*); this has given rise to major controversies, in particular with regard to the issue of "causality" between payments and insolvency.[121] This should not serve as a role model for future legislation. Therefore only three distinctive sets of facts and circumstances should lead to liability of directors and shareholders:

- Dividend payments which do not pass the "balance sheet test";
- Hidden asset shifts under the same preconditions;

120 *Habersack* ZGR 2008, 533; *Schall* supra (note 13), p. 213 et seq; *Schön* ZHR 168 (2004), 268; *Osterloh-Konrad* ZHR 172 (2008), 274; *Tröger/Dangelmayer* ZGR 2011, 558, 568 et seq.

121 In further detail *Altmeppen* FS Hüffer, p. 1; *Kleindiek* FS Karsten Schmidt, 2009, p. 893, 900 et seq.; *Schall* supra (note 13), p. 184 et seq.; *Strohn* ZHR 173 (2009), 589; likewise in NZG 2011, 1161, 1168 et seq., *Wiedemann* ZGR 2011, 183, 204 et seq.

- Other self-dealings by shareholders and creditors in the vicinity of insolvency.

G Duties of Information towards Creditors

The creditors' desire for timely and substantial information about the respective economic situation of the enterprise is one of the central concerns of the discussion about adequate creditor protection. This on the one hand concerns regular mandatory disclosure by the corporation and on the other hand ad-hoc information in crisis. There are differing views on both subjects:

I Mandatory Disclosure of the Corporation

1 The Disclosure Framework

In the European debate, the duty to publicise corporate accounts and other data is traditionally justified by the aim of creditor protection.[122] In many cases, there exists the underlying assumption that liability limitation in the corporation must be "earned" by the willingness regularly to disclose the corporation's figures. This stipulation, which has – for decades – been set forth in the First and Fourth Directives, is considered more or less self-evident. However, an alternative route has been taken in the United States, where the laws of the individual states for closed corporations stipulate hardly any disclosure rules for the corporation's accounts; under federal law, only capital market-oriented enterprises are subject to numerous disclosure obligations.[123]

Upon closer inspection, we find that any generalized duty of non-listed corporations to disclose their key numbers to the general public ultimately has disadvantageous effects: it primarily benefits the competitors of an enterprise formed as a corporation, for which there is extensive evidence.[124] By contrast, for the individual creditor it would be perfectly sufficient if the law were to grant him a personal claim to get hold of the audited annual accounts of a corporate entity. Anyone who is not yet a creditor but negotiates a loan contract can

122 *Merkt* in: Eidenmüller/Schön, supra (note 23), p. 93; *Haas* supra (note 9), p. E 105 et seq; *Mülbert* in: Eidenmüller/Schön, supra (note 23), p. 383 et seq.
123 *Armour/Hertig/Kanda* in: Kraakman et al., supra (note 22), p. 124 et seq.
124 *Schön* 6 J. Corp. L. Stud. (2006) p.259 et seq.

in any case make his/her willingness to grant the loan dependent on such submission, even without any statutory basis in the law.[125]

2 Liability for Non-Disclosure

The production and adoption of the annual financial accounts is usually the duty of the directors and shareholders. This raises the question of their liability for loss to creditors who have granted a loan in reliance on the correctness of the statements in the annual accounts of the corporation or have otherwise come into contact with it on a business level. This question, which is primarily discussed in German law as whether the directors' duties under accounting law benefit third parties,[126] must be answered positively *de lege ferenda.* It does not make sense to hold the directors only liable towards the company if they draw up wrong financial statements. The creditors would derive no advantage from such an internal liability since the corporation's assets are already available to them as liable assets.[126a] Moreover, in case of wrong financial statements, the damage done to the corporation is probably not congruent with damage done to the creditors. In order to be able to provide sensible incentives for proper corporate disclosure, any wilful or negligent drawing up of a false balance sheet should result in personal liability of the directors. In order not to overwhelm the directors with deterrent liability, due account should be taken of their business judgment when it comes to the factual identification and assessment of risks.

Shareholders should always be subject to a similar liability towards creditors if and to the extent to which they have exercised active influence on the drawing up of the balance sheet. If they have merely approved the calculations produced by the directors and attested by the auditors, they are in principle not liable because they cannot be expected to bear a duty of examination. It can only be assumed otherwise in case of wilful acts or clear evidence of fault.

Finally, an extreme case of this information liability is a specific liability for "mixing assets", often referred to as "liability for piercing the corporate veil", which primarily exposes the creditor to the risk that a transparent allocation of assets to the shareholders' assets and the corporation's assets with the aid

---

125 *Allen/Kraakman/Subramanian* Commentaries and Cases on the Law of Business Organizations, 3rd ed., 2009, Section 6.1, p. 133.

126 See for instance *Schnorr* ZHR 170 (2006), 9; for a dissenting view: *Grigoleit* supra (note 1), p. 136 et seq; *Merkt* in: Eidenmüller/Schön, supra (note 23), p. 118.

126a For a fundamental analysis of this issue see: *Adler/Kahan*, supra (note 20a), p. 1778 et seq.

of accounting is no longer possible.[127] This refers to situations where outsiders cannot find out which assets belong to the corporation and which assets belong to the shareholder. However, personal liability of the shareholder or the director is justified not by the mixing of asset spheres as such, but by the resulting information problem.

II Disclosure of "Crisis"

Under German statutory law, the critical state of an enterprise either becomes clear from the information disclosed through the filing of accounts with the public register or by the publicity effect of the commencement of insolvency proceedings. *Ad-hoc* disclosure is more or less limited to public corporations towards private investors under capital market law but is not provided for at the non-listed corporation level, not even as a supplement to the far-reaching rules on corporate disclosure under European corporate law.

However, such a duty of information is recognised in the Netherlands and in the Scandinavian countries[128] and directors' liability was practised over many years in Germany on the basis of judge-made rules on *culpa in contrahendo*. Current German law achieves a similar effect as directors are liable towards creditors under tort law if a corporation does not apply for formal insolvency proceedings in a situation of insolvency or over-indebtedness (as the commencement of insolvency proceedings would clearly be known to the creditors).[129]

We should consider whether such creditor-oriented *ad-hoc* publicity makes sense. Insofar, the directors of a company would have to be placed under an obligation to notify the start of an economic crisis (in the run-up of outright insolvency) to the general public or at least to all known creditors. This appears inadvisable. Instead, this would expose an enterprise in a difficult situation to the general suspicion of imminent insolvency and thereby counteract the directors' *bona fide* endeavours to put the enterprise back on track. For this reason, a general duty of disclosure regarding a critical situation of the company cannot be advocated.[130]

This leads to the specific question of whether directors have an obligation to inform creditors about an existing economic crisis of the enterprise in the course

127 *Merkt/Spindler* in: Lutter, supra (note 14), p. 172 et seq.
128 Evidence in *Kalss/Adensamer/Oelkers* in: Lutter, supra (note 14), p. 129, 130 and 135.
129 On this relationship, see *Casper* in: Ulmer/Habersack/Winter, Komm. z. GmbHG, 2008, Section 64 margin no. 154 et seq.
130 See also *Mülbert* in: Eidenmüller/Schön, supra (note 23), p. 387.

of specific negotiations with the creditors. In all legal systems, it is self-evident that the directors may not engage in misrepresentation: all positive information about the situation of the enterprise must be truthful at the risk of personal liability. Omitting to provide such information in the vicinity of insolvency is the real issue. We must ask if there should be a legal duty to inform counterparties in negotiations in advance about a critical current situation.

If we take a closer look at this, we find that the issue of a duty of information is closely connected to the time at which the duty to file a petition for insolvency proceedings applies. It has already been pointed out that – *de lege lata* and *de lege ferenda* – the point in time for a petition for insolvency proceedings is not so early that all outstanding claims can definitely be fulfilled in the insolvency proceedings. Instead, the directors are permitted – both by the application of particular accounting rules to the status of over-indebtedness and by taking into consideration a forecast element – to delay filing a petition for insolvency proceedings in such a way that creditors' claims are effectively put at risk. However, this directors' right to take measures, in particular to acquire new orders and new capital in order to save the enterprise in spite of calculated insolvency, leads to a situation of asymmetry: directors know the enterprise's situation and (potential) creditors do not, meaning that directors speculate at the expense of these creditors. This weighs in favour of a legal rule according to which the directors must positively point out the corporation's credit-worthiness risk to their business partners in a crisis.[131] Of course, it can be argued that this duty of information lessens the chances for recovery of the corporation, but we then have to accept that such general exclusion of this duty of disclosure in the vicinity of insolvency will also tend to scare off potential creditors of healthy corporations and can therefore lead to adverse selection on credit markets.

This results in the directors of an enterprise having to draw the attention of potential business partners to the potential insolvency of the corporation in a serious economic crisis. Personal liability of these directors is the only appropriate sanction which comes to mind, because liability of the corporation would not extend beyond the amount owed and the liable assets anyway. Shareholders should be personally liable either if they have personally conducted negotiations with potential creditors or have instructed the directors not to disclose the true circumstances.

131 For a dissenting view: *Mülbert* in: Eidenmüller/Schön, supra (note 23), p. 386 et seq, who believes that duties of information only arise at the time of insolvency.

H Capital

I Introduction

In some jurisdictions, the policy discussion on the future of creditor protection in corporate law focuses on the framework of legal capital and the statutory rules on the raising and maintenance of the corporation's capital – being the shareholders' contribution to financing the enterprise.[132] The reason why this subject is only discussed at the end of this chapter is because all preceding issues – behavioural duties of directors and shareholders, the right and the duty to initiate insolvency proceedings and the disbursement limits on the basis of a balance sheet test or solvency test – are not automatically affected by the concept of capital. A capital protection system should only be understood as a supplement to the preceding elements of creditor protection – but not as the conceptual starting-point for any creditor protection system established according to the general rules set forth above.

The debate on legal capital can be subdivided into three fundamental issues:[133] the regulatory value of a statutory "minimum capital", the rules on the raising and maintenance of the capital voluntarily fixed in the articles of association and finally the general function of a disbursement limit. All three aspects are not logically linked to one another: a differentiated capital protection system does not require minimum capital if and to the extent to which the majority of enterprises voluntarily agree on a substantial capital amount. Likewise, the control of distributions also does not require a capital system, as evidenced by the comments above. Instead, it is sufficient to introduce control for dividends and asset shifts oriented to a solvency test or a balance sheet test.

II Minimum Capital

It is hard to add anything new to the national[134] and international[135] discussion on the advantages of statutory minimum capital. Whereas the desire for a sub-

---

132 *Lutter* supra (note 14), p. 1.

133 *Schön* DK 2004, 162.

134 *Lutter* supra (note 14), p. 3, 6 et seq; *Eidenmüller/Grunewald/Noack* in: Lutter, supra (note 14), p. 17; *Fleischer* in: Eidenmüller/Schön, supra (note 23), p. 27; *Mülbert* in: Eidenmüller/Schön, supra (note 23), p. 389 et seq; *Schall* supra (note 13), p. 101 et seq.

135 *Armour* in: Eidenmüller/Schön, supra (note 23), p. 3, 15 et seq.; *Gower/Davies* supra (note 4) 11–8 et seq.

stantive "entrance fee" for corporate founders to ensure their reputability still exists in the academic debate[136] and the idea of a "quality signal"[137] in the sense of commitment by the shareholders to their own business model is advocated, another direction has long since been perceptible in reality and in the competition between European corporate law systems. Not only has it at all times been impossible to install a harmonised minimum capital rule for closed corporations in Europe corresponding to the Second Directive where a minimum capital is set for stock corporation law; moreover, under the laws of many European States, the legislative option of small corporations without minimum capital has steadily increased over the past ten years.[138] If we consider how little protection any minimum capital amount can offer and how largely irrelevant it looks when insolvency comes up, there are good reasons for not stipulating a mandatory minimum capital by statute.[139] Moreover, it does not make sense to require for every company some "adequate equity funding" since it is highly difficult to develop standards which might trigger any shareholder liability with regard to "substantive undercapitalisation" of a corporate entity.[140]

Whether and to what extent the amount of the capital stipulated in the articles of association should be disclosed,[141] in particular – as in Germany – by singling out low-budget corporations, is another question. The idea that the corporate name should signal the financial stability of the company to other market participants is in line with the concept of contractual freedom and symmetrical information.

III Statutory Capital

1 Statutory Capital as a "Collective Liability" Commitment

In recent years, it has been proposed to keep the classical capital protection system in place even without the stipulation of statutory minimum capital and simply to apply it to the respective capital in the corporate statute chosen by the

136 For the SPE, see for instance *Haaker* ZGR 2010, 1056, 1065, 1092; *Hommelhoff* ZHR 173 (2009), 255, 262 et seq; *Hommelhoff/Teichmann* GmbHR 2010, 337, 338 et seq; *Pfennig* supra (note 9), p. 101 et seq; *Wicke* GmbHR 2011, 566, 572; on the new ideas for a Member States option, see *Freudenberg* NZG 2010, 527, 527 et seq; *Wedemann* EuZW 2010, 534, 537.

137 *Eidenmüller/Engert* GmbHR 2005, 433.

138 Overview in *Witt* ZGR 2009, 872 (also with comments on Switzerland as an exception).

139 *Armour/Hertig/Kanda* in: Kraakman et al., supra (note 22), p. 130 et seq; also for the SPE: *Davies* FS Hopt, 2010, p. 479, 487 et seq.

140 For the contrary view, see *Bitter* in: Bachmann/Casper/Schäfer/Veil, supra (note 82), p. 57.

141 *Hommelhoff/Teichmann* GmbHR 2010, 337, 339.

founders or shareholders.[142] This proposal has both a factual and a legal background. On the factual side, we see that most corporations take up equity capital to an extent which far exceeds the statutory minimum capital in any event. The capital provided for in the articles of association can therefore also have the function of protecting creditors. From the legal side, this capital can be seen as having the character of a "collective liability commitment" – not in the sense of a direct contract between the shareholders and the creditors, but in the sense of self-commitment which allows the withdrawal of this capital only under the particular provisons of formal reduction of capital (with corresponding publicity and security mechanisms), thus working for the benefit of corporate creditors.

The designation of a certain amount of "capital provided for by the articles of association" therefore permits the founders or shareholders of a corporation to place funds at the disposal of the corporation which are specially committed in favour of the creditors in addition to the individual provision of shareholder guarantees, letters of comfort and so on. Viewed in this way, the capital protection system is not an atavistic and paternalistic element of ancient legal systems, but simply an extension of contractual options for the shareholders. It is up to them whether and to what extent they use this instrument in order to send a signal of credit-worthiness to all potential and current creditors. If and to the extent to which they provide such capital, mechanisms to control the raising and maintenance of this capital must clearly be established.[143] It can also be left up to the shareholders (but should be disclosed) whether they pay up this capital directly or merely guarantee for a particular amount.[144]

This concept has frequently been criticised in the literature or declared useless because the creditors are still able to use private law contract covenants to individually regulate the provision of equity capital, compliance with debt and equity capital ratios or limit disbursements.[145] But against this, it remains to be said that these individual contractual regulations are not benefitting all potential creditors and such creditors do not obtain a reliable legal position as free riders on the back of negotiations of major creditors; in particular, there is

142 *Schön* ZHR 166 (2002), 1, 4 et seq; likewise in DK 2004, 162; likewise in 5 Eur. Bus. Org. L. Rev., 429, 438 et seq (2004).

143 For further detail on the reform of raising capital in European law, see *Pentz/Priester/Schwanna* in: Lutter, supra (note 14), p. 42; *Jung* EuZW 2012, 129; likewise in EWS 2012, 25; *Pfennig* supra (note 9), p. 59 et seq; for a recent discussion of simplification, see *Hentzen/Schwandtner* ZGR 2009, 1007.

144 *Bayer* GmbHR 2010, 1289 et seq.

145 *Armour* in: Eidenmüller/Schön, supra (note 23), 19 et seq.

a failure to recognise that precisely such covenants can be understood as a meaningful supplement rather than a contrast to collective contractual minimum protection by a capital figure chosen voluntarily. Subscribed capital continues to be understood as a collective liability commitment in relation to the general public and can be correspondingly earmarked.

2 Differentiation between "Liable Capital" and "Free Capital"

The most important objection to this conception addressed in the literature to date originates from *Eilis Ferran.*[146] She points out that the choice of the equity capital figure by the founders or shareholders is in practice based more on business requirements and less on the liability function of the equity capital. Anyone who starts a medium-sized or large enterprise or works as the director of such a corporation faces the choice between taking up equity or debt capital and makes this decision on the basis of the financial aspects of the respective financial instrument (profit relatedness, participation in liquidation proceeds) or according to other legal aspects (voting rights), but not according to the scope of creditor protection triggered by it.

This argument is partly convincing; for this reason, it must partly be taken into consideration. On the one hand, definitions of equity capital under all legal systems involve the rule that all equity capital liabilities rank lower than all debt capital liabilities in insolvency. In this context, the function of equity capital protecting creditors is self-evident, otherwise the entire distinction between equity and debt capital would be put at risk. However, the equity capital character of the financing funds does not necessarily lead to a full application of the rules on capital formation and capital maintenance. It is perfectly conceivable that a financier is willing to make available some equity capital ranking lower than debt capital, but does not desire formal commitment of these funds for creditor protection.

In view of this, it appears advisable to further differentiate the "contractual" character of the equity capital commitment. To achieve this, it is merely necessary to categorise the "equity capital" represented by the shares into "liable" and "free" equity capital. Whereas the "liable" equity capital is registered as such in the Commercial Register, must be raised under strict rules, is subject to stringent disbursement limits and can only be reduced in a formal procedure, "free" equity capital is not so strictly committed. It can also be withdrawn with-

146 *Ferran* 3 Eur. Co. & Fin. L. Rev. 178, 196 (2006); in agreement *Armour/Hertig/Kanda* in: Kraakman et al., supra (note 22), p. 131 note 91.

out formalities by the shareholders. However, it does not have the same rank as debt capital in the corporation's insolvency but shares the rank of liable equity capital.

This model would indirectly follow a distinction which we find in the law on limited partnerships. i. e. the distinction between the liable amount promised towards the creditors and the amount promised as a contribution to the partnership's working capital. The entire capital amount promised and paid up by a partner represents the contribution he made in order to get the partnership going. If and to the extent to which the partners designate this amount as "liable equity capital", it is subject to the traditional rules on the raising and maintenance of the corporation's capital. The other part of the capital is "free capital" and can be withdrawn without any formality.

The law of the State of Delaware is familiar with a comparable distinction as Delaware corporations are granted the right to divide the funds paid in for the shares into corporate capital and a free surplus (see Sections 154, 170 Delaware General Corporation Law).

Under such a liberal system, reality will then show whether and to what extent the shareholders and directors make use of the option to equip their corporations with a more strictly committed "liable capital" and to which extent they only use "free capital".[147] Only if it transpires that this option is not used to a significant extent, can the complete abandonment of the concept of liable capital be considered. Empirical studies in the USA showing lower loan costs for states with a capital protection system point to a direction favourable for the capital system.[148]

However, an important aspect relating to the indemnification of the described "free" capital from the function of creditor protection is the insolvency law assessment of disbursements out of such non-committed equity capital to the shareholders in the vicinity of insolvency. It is clear that on the one hand the strict rules on capital maintenance and formal capital reduction do not apply.[149] It is also clear that the general barriers of the "balance sheet test" or the "solvency test" must be applied to every type of equity capital disbursement. In addition, there is the important question of whether there must be a time limit

147 On the practice in Delaware, see KPMG, Feasibility Study on an Alternative to the Capital Maintenance Regime established by the Second Company Law Directive 77/91/EEC of 13 December 1976, and an examination of the impact on profit distribution of the new EU-accounting regime, Main Report, 2008, p. 161 et seq.; *Rock* supra (note 89a), p. 1947 et seq.

148 *Mansi/Maxwell/Wald* 52 J.L. & Econ. 701 (2009); *Wald/Lang* 83 J. Fin. Econ. 287 (2007); critical *Rock* supra (note 89a), p. 1983 et seq..

149 See also in the UK: Section 642(1) Companies Act 2006; *Witt* ZGR 2009, 872, 893 et seq.

for the repayment of "uncommitted" equity capital positions which – as in current German insolvency law for shareholders' loans – subjects all disbursements to shareholders within the year prior to the commencement of insolvency proceedings to "fraudulent transfer" rules.

An analogy with shareholder loans points in favour of the application of insolvency law rights to demand repayment for "free" equity capital. In addition, there is also the information asymmetry between the shareholders and the creditors, which already permits a separate action for rescission for silent partnerships (Section 136 German Insolvency Code); it must also once again be taken into consideration that a rule on the duty to file a petition for insolvency proceedings permitting the directors to undertake rescue attempts at the expense of the creditors' quota in a crisis harbours the danger of the withdrawal of substantive "free capital" in the vicinity of actual insolvency. Sole reliance on the "balance sheet test" for payments in such a situation is risky. There are therefore good grounds for the insolvency administrator to require the repayment of all capital withdrawals from the period of one year before the formal commencement of insolvency proceedings.

IV Shareholder Loans

The "free capital" is thus very similar to the actual shareholder loans, but ranks even lower in insolvency. From a comparative view, treatment of such shareholder loans is currently very diverse. Both Germany and the U.S. as well as many other countries, are familiar with special rules which provide for the subordination or re-characterisation of such shareholders' loans, but this group of countries does not include England or France.[150]

The justifying basis for these special rules is seen in the incentive structure for the shareholders.[151] Do we want to concede to them that if their debt capital is used in a crisis, they can benefit from (virtually) the upside potential of the risk, but only participate to a limited extent with regard to the downside potential of the risk? A shareholder-lender who only receives a fixed repayment amount plus interest on her loan can still take all the profits in case of success as the residual profit goes to him anyway by way of the equity shares.

150 *Böckmann* supra (note 21), p. 210 et seq; *Witt* ZGR 2009, 872, 886 et seq, 922 et seq; *Huber/Habersack* in: Lutter, supra (note 14), p. 308 et seq; *Skeel/Krause-Vilmar* in: Eidenmüller/Schön, supra (note 23), p. 261; *Cahn* in: Eidenmüller/Schön, supra (note 23), p. 289; for the SPE see *Hommelhoff* ZHR 179 (2009), 255, 270 et seq.

151 *Engert* ZGR 2004, 813.

For this reason, it is not only – as initially proposed by *Mülbert*[152] – the repayment of shareholders' loans in the vicinity of insolvency which must be dealt with by statute; instead – following the new German rules – shareholder loans should rank below the genuine debt capital and only take precedence in satisfaction above the actual equity capital.[153] The alternative – treating shareholders' loans and third-party loans with equal rank and steering the difficult incentive structure through behavioural duties of the directors – appears, by contrast, difficult to put into operation.

I Results

According to the arguments developed above, creditor protection in the law on closed corporations is based on the following pillars:

1. Shareholders and creditors conclude their contracts on the basis of a particular "business model" of the corporation that contains the purpose and the scope of the enterprise, the duties of care and loyalty and – depending on the corporate statute – indemnifications against liability for the directors and shareholders. Alterations to the articles of association in these points entitle the creditors to terminate the loan relationship for cause.
2. Directors operate the enterprise of the corporation with the aim of maximising the enterprise's value. This aim also does not change in the vicinity of insolvency. Directors are also entitled and obliged to enter into risky transactions within the framework of the object of the enterprise and in compliance with the general rules on risk diversification. Breaches of duty lead to liability to the corporation which can also be asserted by the administrator or the creditors in insolvency. In exceptional cases, such claims can also be brought against shareholders who intervene in management.
3. Control over the enterprise does not pass to the creditors in a (transitory) crisis, but instead upon (permanent) insolvency. As long as the corporation is solvent according to its break-up values, there is no reason for the directors to intervene. In case of insolvency under break-up values but with a positive going concern forecast, the directors have increased duties of monitoring. In case of insolvency under break-up values but with a negative going concern forecast, the directors have duties of information and action and creditors

152 Supra (note 23), p. 398 et seq; likewise *Eidenmüller* FS Canaris, vol. 2, 2007, p. 49.
153 *Verse* 9 German L.J. 1109 (2009); *Pentz* FS Hüffer, 2010, p. 747; critical *Spindler* JZ 2006, 839, 844 et seq.

have the right to file a petition for insolvency proceedings. In case of permanent over-indebtedness and at the latest upon cash flow-based insolvency, insolvency proceedings are commenced.

4. Directors are liable for the delayed filing of a petition for insolvency proceedings, but shareholders are only liable in exceptional cases. However, they are also entitled to the right to file a petition for insolvency proceedings in exceptional cases.
5. Disbursements from the corporation's assets are prohibited by the standard of a conservative balance sheet test. This applies equally to open dividends and hidden asset shifts. Further self-interested measures triggering insolvency by directors and creditors are likewise prohibited.
6. The concept of raising and maintaining capital should be retained with the following modifications:
   a. Statutory minimum capital should be abandoned for closed corporations.
   b. The capital in the articles of association should be retained as an option on a "collective liability commitment". It remains up to the shareholders to what extent their capital contributions are considered as "free" or "liable" capital.
   c. The subscribed capital forms a disbursement limit. The capacity to cover debts according to the balance sheet test specified in no. 5 above remains a further lower limit for all corporations.
7. Shareholder loans and free capital which has been paid out within the year before the commencement of insolvency proceedings can be the ordered to be repaid to the company. Shareholders loans have lower rank than third-party loans but enjoy priority with regard to "free" and "liable" capital.

Chapter 6 Formation, Management and Transfer of Shares*

Table of Contents

The preceding chapters have focused on conflicts (of interest) between the shareholders of a closed corporation, conflicts between shareholders and directors and conflicts between the shareholders or the corporation and third parties. The question we examined was which rules can be used to minimise the costs associated with these conflicts. In this Chapter, we instead focus on relatively technical, operative issues of business activity: the formation and management of a closed corporation and a change of shareholders. We concentrate not on the costs of conflict but rather on transaction costs and how to reduce them.[1]

In recent years, econometric research has demonstrated the importance of the costs and speed of formation with respect to the choice of legal form.[2] An attractive offer in this context is a key factor for the success of a legal form in international competition between corporate law systems. At the same time, empirical evidence has confirmed the correlation between simpler, faster and cheaper formation of corporations in a country on the one hand, and the number of new corporations formed and national economic growth on the other.[3] This

* The text is based on a draft by *Eidenmüller.*

1 This is not to say that conflicts and conflict costs do not play a role in the formation, management and transfer of shares. They do. However, they do not take centre stage here, other than in the preceding chapters.

2 *Becht/Mayer/Wagner* 14 J. Corp. Fin. 241 (2008).

3 *Djankov/La Porta/Lopez-de-Silanes/Shleifer* 17 Q. J. Econ. 1 (2002); *Klapper/Laeven/Rajan* 82 J. Fin. Econ. 591 (2006); *Braun/Eidenmüller/Engert/Hornuf* Does Charter Competition Foster Entrepreneurship? A Difference-in-Difference Approach to European Company Law Reforms, 51

means that cheap and quick formation does not only influence the attractiveness of the legal form, but also affects the economic prosperity of the country in which the form is available for economic activity. High-speed formation also reduces the legal problems and, in particular, the liability risks which business activities present for founders in the formation stage.

According to the regulatory goal formulated in Chapter 2 C.I., our analysis here will primarily concentrate on the welfare economics efficiency effects of different regulatory models. This means, first and foremost, that transaction costs associated with the formation and management of a corporation and the change of shareholders should be kept as low as possible. Such transaction costs reduce welfare – and it is thus important to restrict the losses associated with them. Low transaction costs also have the positive ancillary effect that they ease negotiation processes and accordingly promote an efficient allocation of resources.[4]

As regards content, regulations on the formation, management and share transfer should in principle be default rules and provide for what reasonable parties would have agreed on if they had considered and explicitly regulated the relevant problem (replication of a hypothetical negotiation solution[5]). Only default rules allow for the correction of the statutory "offer" through party autonomy if the latter does not reflect the preferences of the market participants in an individual case. However, mandatory provisions are justified where private negotiation processes do not result in fair outcomes due to information asymmetries, irrationality or negotiation weakness of one participant.[6]

A Formation

The following considers the formation of a closed corporation as a formation from scratch. Consequently, transformation processes are not considered. We furthermore do not address issues related to the stipulation and raising of a certain share capital. These issues centrally affect creditor protection.[7] Conceptually, formation involves firstly *substantive requirements*, and secondly *formal procedure(s)*

Journal of Common Market Studies 399 (2013). See also *van Stel/Storey/Thurik* 28 Small Bus. Econ. 171 (2007).

4 See Chapter 2 C.II.1.

5 Chapter 2 C.II.2.

6 Chapter 2 C.III.1.

7 Chapter 5.

in which compliance with these requirements is examined.[8] The requisite time and costs incurred for formation are a function of these two variables: the higher the number of substantive requirements to be complied with and the greater the number of procedures in which these are examined, the longer the formation will tend to take and the more expensive it will tend to be.

I Existing Models

From a global perspective, we can say that the formation of a (closed) corporation at least generally presupposes the signature of a formation document by the founder(s), the submission of this document to a (public) register and the registration of the corporation. This at least is true for Europe,[9] but it also applies to the United States: according to the relevant statutes in the individual states, a *corporation* comes into existence when the *secretary of state,* as the competent public authority, stamps the *articles of incorporation* as "filed" (see Section 2.03 (a) MBCA) or – in other states – when he/she provides the founders with a certificate of incorporation.[10]

Apart from these commonly shared fundamental and structural characteristics, there are considerable differences between the formation procedures of different jurisdictions. These, for instance, concern the necessary number of founders (i.e., permissibility of formation by one person), the formal compliance requirements (i.e., written form, notarisation), the competent supervisory body and the scope of control prior to the registration of the corporation (i.e., notary and/or public authority, individual substantive formation requirements).[11] Furthermore, a fundamental issue is whether fully electronic high-speed formations within minutes should be possible. Some countries, such as the United Kingdom and Denmark or, outside Europe, particularly New Zealand, have made this possible or are currently in the process of doing so. We will return to this later.

8 This assumes a "system of statutory provisions" under which the formation of a corporation is a freedom right if the stipulated conditions are complied with. The "concession model", which was typical in the past, no longer conforms to the free legal systems of Western character.
9 See *Gesell/Flaßhoff/Krömker* in: Van Hulle/Gesell, European Corporate Law, 2006, p. 25, 28.
10 See *Bainbridge* Corporation Law and Economics, 2002, p. 40; *Merkt/Göthel* US-amerikanisches Gesellschaftsrecht, 2nd ed., 2006, p. 196.
11 For the EU Member States, see *Gesell/Flaßhoff/Krömker* in: Van Hulle/Gesell, supra (note 9), p. 28 et seq.

II Regulatory Goals

For a closed corporation, the process of formation is *prima facie* a procedure that can involve high transaction costs and therefore bears a corresponding potential for savings. For this reason, the European Council rightly passed decisions on 23 and 24 March 2006 indicating which aims are definitely deemed achievable: the Member States should establish a *one-stop shop* for setting up a company, formation should not take longer than one week, and start-up fees should be as low as possible.[12]

Accordingly, the aim is surely to develop the simplest possible procedure in which the formation of a corporation may not be obstructed by bureaucratic hurdles, unless these are objectively justified as mandatory (discussed below). The involvement of modern technology and systems in the formation process is in any case self-evident if they are established and widespread, as well as cheap and legally certain in use. The *mandatory* involvement of intermediaries (e.g., formation agencies, notaries, etc.) must be critically scrutinized, especially if their involvement means that the time, effort and cost of formation increases due to repeated examinations.

What then are legitimate substantive requirements for formation? This question is hardly an easy one to answer. These requirements should not primarily be administrative or public-law requirements (for instance, under tax law). With regard to transparency, simplification and costs, the formation process should not be burdened by the instrumentalisation of aims outside corporate law. By contrast, it is undisputed that a corporation must at least have shareholders, directors, a registered office, a business name and stipulated capital.[13] The necessity of an expressly stated "object" of the firm is more doubtful here.[14/15] If there is no

12 Council of the European Union, Presidency Conclusions of the Brussels European Council (23/24 March), EU Doc. 7775/1/06 REV 1, fig. 30.

13 It is an entirely different question whether there should be a minimum amount of capital. See Chapter 5.

14 On the distinction between *the object of the firm* and *the purpose of the firm* (*aim of the corporation*) in German law, see, for instance, *Ulmer* in: Ulmer/Habersack/Winter, Komm. z. GmbHG, 2005, § 1 margin no. 4 et seq. Other European legal systems are unfamiliar with this distinction. At a European level, Art. 3(1) and Art. 5c) EEIG Regulation contains both concepts. However, Art. 9(2) of the 1st Company Law Directive and Art. 2b) of the 2nd Company Law Directive refer to the object of the firm, and the aim of the firm is not mentioned.

15 S. 31(1) Companies Act 2006 therefore also waives a statement from the founders regarding the *objects of the company* for the United Kingdom. Likewise *Bachmann* ZGR 2001, 351, 359 et seq. The Draft SPE Regulation remains silent on the object of the firm, which is probably

ultra vires doctrine in relation to third parties, it can at least contribute to informing them about the corporation's field of activity and, furthermore, it fulfils an important function in restricting the respective powers of the organs within the corporation.

Prior to the formation of the corporation, it must be examined whether these requirements have been *formally* satisfied. This, however, does not in any way address the question of what further *substantive* requirements exist with regard to these characteristics and whether these additional requirements should be examined in the course of the formation process (i.e., number and (dis)qualification of the shareholders/directors, permissible object, registered office, business name etc.). Such further requirements are indeed indispensable. For example, certain persons are unsuitable as directors (e.g., those individuals with prior criminal convictions), certain objects of the corporation are illegal (e.g., those which serve criminal activities) and certain business names are impermissible (e.g., those which are already legitimately used by another corporation). However, when corresponding requirements are stipulated, then it makes sense to investigate compliance with them even before the corporation's formation and to prevent the founders from falling into a trap. It is nevertheless advisable here to keep the time and effort for a compliance test as low as possible, in order to save transaction costs.[16]

A special problem relates to the requirement of instructing and cautioning the corporation's founders. The Member States' legal systems acknowledge a great variety of activities which private persons can undertake with great liability risks without any state or state-guided communication about the existence of these risks. At the same time, one can also find specific transactions for which such instruction and cautioning is considered necessary, e.g., in Germany upon the formation of a GmbH pursuant to Sec. 2 GmbHG by the officiating no-

---

attributable to the English influence; see *Hügel* ZHR 173 (2009), 309, 317. See also *Hirte* FS Hüffer, 2009, p. 329, 333 et seq.

16 With regard to the number and (dis)qualification of shareholders/directors, automatic checks (register inspection) or assurances are easy in the formation process. The permissibility of the chosen registered office can also easily be checked automatically. The same applies with regard to the business name if, for instance, an alphanumeric code is required, as is the case with, for example, the Spanish *Sociedad Limitada Nueva Empresa* Artículo 131 Ley 2/1995, de 23 de marzo, de Sociedades de Responsabilidad Limitada, añadido por Ley 7/2003, de 1 de abril, de la sociedad limitada Nueva Empresa. However, transaction costs savings at formation also reduce the brand and advertising value of a "good" trade name here. Additional time, effort and expenditure is, in any case, required for checking the legality of the object of the firm, because it cannot be dealt with merely by automatic controls or assurances.

tary. This particularly aims to protect shareholders and third parties.[17] No consistent legal policy line is evident here either in the individual Member States or between them when compared to similar transactions. In Germany, the articles of association for a general partnership (*offene Handelsgesellschaft*) can, for example, be concluded orally. The history of the GmbH also makes the contingency of the notarisation requirement clear.[18] Formation of a closed corporation usually does not involve extraordinary (in the sense of existential) risks necessitating and justifying particular instruction and cautioning. Anyone wishing to seek professional advice in this context can obtain it at any time. A mandatory instruction and cautioning requirement would only be justified if we had to assume that the majority of the founders systematically underestimated the very limited liability risks and would only be encouraged to take stronger contractual precautions in the articles of association by instruction/advice. However, there is no empirical evidence on this point. This would, however, be necessary for such a serious regulatory encroachment. Written form is, in any case, sufficient for evidence and publicity purposes.[19]

III Investigating Authority and Register

On this basis, we can now look at an initial structural question of the formation procedure: which authority bears responsibility for investigating the fundamental requirements? In this context, relevant issues are the centralized or decentralized organizational setup, as well as the involvement of state or private agencies. State agencies can be further differentiated into public authority and judicial organs. Specific models to be considered are (i) centralised investigation by a specialised public authority (like *Companies House* in the United Kingdom), (ii) investigation by designated courts – centralized or decentralized, depending on the political system – and (iii) the involvement of semi-public or semi-private

17 See *Roth* in: Roth/Altmeppen, Komm. z. GmbHG, 6th ed., 2009, Sec. 2 margin no. 24.

18 The draft by *Oechelhäuser* ("father of the GmbH Act") considered written form to be satisfactory for formation. See *Fleischer* Münchener Komm. z. GmbHG, 2010, Introduction margin no. 55.

19 This line of legal policy probably dominates in the meantime. See *Hadding/Kießling* WM 2009, 145, 155 for further references.

agencies, such as formation agencies or notaries, in which a decentralized form of organization is implied.[20]

The structural question of the investigating authority is also linked to the register issue. It makes sense for the substantive investigation of formation and the register to be combined. Aspects of professionalism and scale economies argue in favour of a centralized form of organization. Public authority processing may be preferable to judicial organisation regarding flexibility and costs, and also due to the development potential for such an office to become a service centre for firms.[21] This would suggest a model similar to that of *Companies House* in the English system. On the other hand, established judicial structures are of great value and should not be replaced by a new system (which inevitably includes high (one-off) formation costs) unless absolutely necessary. Use of these established structures at relatively low cost is therefore a good decision from a legal policy point of view.

The same applies to the delegation of the investigation to numerous notaries or other semi-public or semi-private professionals or institutions. Notaries, in particular, currently fulfil important functions in some Member States in the formation process for corporations. In other Member States, however, this is not the case. In any case, these Member States will not introduce the profession of notary for the purpose of investigating formation nor extend its tasks accordingly. A decentralized organization also tends to make less sense in light of what has been said above. In any case, multiplication of the time, effort and expenditure required for formation through the involvement of both a state institution (public authority or court) *and* a private or semi-state/semi-private institution (notary) is not recommended. The Commission proposal for an SPE Regulation chose the right direction in this context. In accordance with that proposal, Member States can make the registration of an SPE dependent either on the examination of the legality of the documents and statements by a judicial or administrative public authority, or on certification of the documents and statements (by a notary) (Art. 10(4) Draft SPE Regulation).[22]

20 Notaries argue *de lege ferenda* in favor of an exclusive substantive law investigation of formation by (German) notaries: *Wachter* Wissenschaftliche Vereinigung für Unternehmens- und Gesellschaftsrecht (VGR) 12 (2006), 55, 92 et seq., 96.
21 See *Reichel* ZRP 2004, 184, 185 et seq.
22 Unfortunately, the European Parliament later distanced itself from this approach. According to Art. 10(4) of the Draft SPE Regulation proposed by the Parliament, registration by the Member States must be made dependent on *at least* one of the two forms of control. See European Parliament Resolution of 10 March 2009, EU Doc. T6–0094/2009.

IV Formation Procedure

Acceleration (and simplification) of the formation procedure can be achieved by using modern electronic communication methods. Today, we already often conduct significant transactions via the Internet (e. g., booking a trip, buying a car or furniture, etc.), and we will engage in such transactions more frequently in the future. E-Commerce remains the fastest growing form of sales.[23] The starting-point is therefore to *enable* the fully electronic/online formation of a closed corporation, although it is clear that the extent of flexibility and structural freedom permitted by such a formation procedure is necessarily limited. It must be pointed out, however, that the practical requirements for such flexibility and structural freedom are, in any case, few in number. Empirical studies in Germany and the United Kingdom have shown that the overwhelming majority of GmbH and limited liability corporation formations are standard formations without the need for individual contracts.[24] This conclusion is now also confirmed by the great success of entrepreneurial corporation (*Unternehmergesellschaft* – "UG") formations in Germany by means of model articles.[25] In addition, there are no credible arguments for precluding the offering of fully electronic formation as an option alongside conventional formation "on paper" with greater structural freedom.[26]

Today, there are numerous models which could serve as examples of fully electronic formation. The United Kingdom, Denmark and Poland are particularly noteworthy in Europe. In the United Kingdom, the Companies Act 2006 has brought about considerable deregulation of the formation process (see s. 7 et

23 See the GfK study on E-Commerce sales development in Germany, available at http://www.gfk.com/imperia/md/content/presse/pressemeldungen2010/100303_webscope_dfin.pdf (in 2009 German consumers bought goods to the value of EUR 15.5 billion through the Internet, approximately 14% more than in the previous year).

24 See *Karsten* GmbHR 2006, 57 et seq. (evaluation of approx. 250 GmbH articles of association for craftsmens' businesses in Chemnitz shows that they are predominantly standard formations; notaries' instructions and cautioning is largely unnecessary); *Cheffins* Company Law: Theory, Structure and Operation, 1997, p. 26 note 82 (95% of incorporations in the United Kingdom are carried out by *company formation agents* on the basis of *standard terms*).

25 See *Bayer/Hoffmann* GmbHR 2009, R 225 et seq. (in the first seven months after the entry into force of the Gesetz zur Modernisierung des GmbH-Rechts und zur Bekämpfung von Missbräuchen (MoMiG), more than 10,000 UGs were already formed in Germany; of the UGs formed in Thuringia, 78% were formations with model articles); *Bayer/Hoffmann* GmbHR 2010, R 161 et seq. (as of 1 May 2010 more than 30,000 UGs existed). UG formation by model articles can take place for approx. EUR 120 (EUR 100 for the register court, EUR 1 for the announcement, EUR 20 for notary costs). See *Wachter* GmbHR Sonderheft Oktober 2008, 25, 27 et seq.

26 On option models, see Chapter 2 C.III.1.

seq., 1068 et seq.). Whilst direct online formation is not yet possible via the Internet (*webfiling*),[27] electronic formation is possible to the extent that the necessary documents are submitted via email in a prescribed form (*software filing*).[28] Special software is required, as well as an authentication code, for the corporation to be formed. Both will generally only be available through an incorporation agent, so that the end-user remains dependent on the intermediary services of such an agent.[29]

Denmark has already gone one step further in this context. As of 2003, free digital signatures for official communication with public authorities were successively issued to citizens all over the country (OCES – *Public Certificate for Electronic Services*).[30] These can be used for identification in "real time" formation of corporations via the Internet.[31] A recent reform of the Polish law on limited liability companies also permits fully electronic formations within 24 hours.[32]

The New Zealand formation procedure is comparable to the Danish and Polish procedures in speed and simplicity, although without a digital signature and therefore not "purely online."[33] The formation documents are prepared automatically on the basis of information provided online and sent via email to the founders. They must then be signed and returned by e-mail or fax to the author-

---

27 However, important documents of an existing corporation can already be submitted in this way. See http://www.companieshouse.gov.uk/infoAndGuide/faq/webFiling.shtml. For this purpose, the corporation must have a security code sent to it by E-mail and an authentication code received by normal post.

28 See http://www.companieshouse.gov.uk/toolsToHelp/efilingfaq.shtml.

29 The guidelines cited in note 27 contain the following information on the allocation of authentication codes: "If the incorporation is in paper format, the newly incorporated companies can be allocated codes as already described. Alternatively, you may request that a given code is allocated against all companies incorporated by yourselves. You should inform Companies House in writing if you wish to invoke this option. If the incorporation is in an electronic format then a facility exists to specify a company authentication code with incorporation details." Variation 1 aims at prior written information to Companies House by the corporation regarding the code to be used in the future. Variation 2 relates to incorporation agents who form many corporations with the same code. In Variation 3, the registration agent can freely choose a code for the newly formed corporation together with the formation documents, and can then state it. The code then applies for all future submissions of the newly formed corporation.

30 See http://www.epractice.eu/en/document/288210.

31 Incorporation takes place through the Danish Consumer and Companies Agency, which makes use of a special service in this context (*Webreg*). See http://www.eogs.dk/sw21281.asp; http://www.webreg-portal.dk/home.asp.

32 On the new law see *Makowicz/Romanowski* RIW 2012, 497.

33 See http://www.companies.govt.nz/cms/how-do-i/form-a-new-zealand-company/Register-your-company.

ities. Registration of the corporation takes place within a few hours. Founders receive assistance in the form of a short demonstration video.[34] The American *model law* also provides for electronic submission of the formation documents (See Sec. 2.01, 1.40(5), (7 A), (22 A) MBCA).

The legal situation outlined here and the legal practice in the above-mentioned states demonstrate what is technically possible today and the direction further development will probably take: a closed corporation can be formed online "in real time" if the identification problem has been satisfactorily resolved, as is already the case in Denmark and Poland.[35] The clarifying information considered necessary is likewise provided online through official documents or correspondingly visible information. The forms to be filled out online are conceived in such a way that all substantive preconditions for registration[36] can be automatically checked. The measure of flexibility in structuring the corporate law relationships achieved in this way is limited, however, because applicants must work with forms made available online. More flexible individual formation will therefore still make the electronic submission of signed formation documents necessary in the future, as in New Zealand and in Art. 10(1) and (2) Draft SPE Regulation. However, the specific example of New Zealand shows that the signature of the formation documents by the shareholders is – or can be – sufficient as proof of identity. As a result, there is no serious risk of abuse and there have been no reports of such abuse. A further personal check, in addition to the signature as proof of identity upon formation, is unnecessary.

B Management

The operative management of a closed corporation involves questions such as expression of the shareholders' will (e.g., shareholders' meetings, exercise of voting rights or passing of resolutions, etc.), their competences and those of

34 See http://www.companies.govt.nz/cms/animated-demonstration-library/incorporate_skin.swf/nomenuview.

35 Germany is lagging behind other European countries such as, for example, Denmark, by about ten years in this context. The evaluation of pilot projects has just recently led to the introduction of a new identity card with electronic ID and electronic signature function on the one hand and a "De-Mail" service on the other hand, which enables simple, forgery-proof and legally binding electronic communication across the country. See the De-Mail Act of 28 April 2011, Bundesgesetzblatt (BGBl.) I/2011, p. 666 (see *Roßnagel* NJW 2011, 1473) and (on the identity card) the German Act on Identity Cards and Electronic Proof of Identity and for the Amendment of Further Provisions of 18 June 2009, Bundesgesetzblatt (BGBl.) I/2009, p. 1346.

36 See A.II. above.

the directors, reporting and accounting duties, but also any registration fees or taxes payable (*franchise fees and taxes*). In this context, numerous regulatory tasks and problems arise which are rooted in agency conflicts between shareholders, between shareholders and directors and between shareholders and the corporation and third parties. These regulatory tasks and problems have already been investigated in Chapters 3 to 5 and do not represent the focus here.

These issues of operative corporate management not only involve agency conflicts and costs. They can also be considered in light of the aim of minimising transaction costs. This approach involves keeping the unnecessary "friction losses" associated with the operative management of a closed corporation as low as possible. The differences between legal systems in the Member States are considerable in this respect.[37]

Fundamentally, the relevant regulatory tasks can and should, to the greatest possible extent, be left up to the shareholders' private autonomy in structuring the articles of association. They themselves know best how to minimise the transaction costs involved in operative corporate management, and they also have every incentive to do so. In particular, shareholders will wish to use the technically and economically most efficient means of communication regarding the exchange of information, expression of will and contact with state public authorities. Legislation can therefore in principle restrict itself to permitting the use of these means of communication and creating the necessary preconditions (i.e., electronic register, possibility of electronic communication with the register, etc.). However, certain mandatory provisions regarding form are justified for the purposes of proof and publicity.

Given the aim of minimising transaction costs, registration fees or taxes must *prima facie* be judged critically. However, to the extent they reflect the actual cost of public authority services, they are not objectionable. On the contrary: in competition between different regulators and regulatory systems, they fulfil the essential function of competitive pricing, i.e., signalling the scope and quality of service, providing incentives to reduce costs and counteracting distortions of competition.[38]

A special problem for the corporation's management relates to the scope of the directors' power of representation. Transaction costs of the business activity are minimised if this power is unrestricted, at least in relation to third parties, or

---

37 See *Gesell/Flaßhoff/Krömker* in: Van Hulle/Gesell (supra note 9), p. 30 et seq. on *recurrent costs and efforts*.

38 This topic has to a large extent "been dealt with" *de lege lata* for the EU in Council Directive 69/335/EEC of 17 July 1969 concerning indirect taxes on the raising of capital. See also *Schön* 42 Common Market Law Review 331, 337 et seq. (2005).

if any restrictions can be discovered without considerable investigation, time, effort and expenditure. This particularly applies to cross-border business activity. Consequently, Art. 33(1) and (2) Draft SPE Regulation rightly provide for the articles of association of an SPE to merely stipulate sole or joint power of representation, but further restrictions are irrelevant in relation to third parties. Acts outside the objects of the firm also bind the corporation. The *ultra vires* doctrine no longer has a place in a modern statute for closed corporations.[39]

C Transfer of Shares

In addition to tax aspects, the degree of flexibility of organisation and liability issues, the transferability of shares itself is frequently cited as the fourth main reason for the choice of a particular legal form.[40] In fact, the questions involved in this regard have great economic and legal significance. Free, cost-effective transfer of shares is a precondition for the efficient allocation of rights and duties associated with shareholdings (Coase Theorem). At the same time, it is an important instrument of minority protection (*exit* instead of *voice*). On the other hand, there may be a legitimate need to demobilise shares through contractual restrictions on transferability, particularly with the aim of preserving a group of shareholders familiar with one another and willing to cooperate.[41] Answers to the relevant questions mainly depend on how the shareholding and its transfer are legally conceived. In this context, the existing solutions world-wide diverge significantly from conceivable, conceptual solutions.

I Current Models

A share is often structured as an *uncertificated right* transferred from seller to buyer – possibly subject to requirements of form (i.e., written form, notarisation) – by contract. This, for example, is the concept underlying German law (Sec. 5, 15 GmbHG). Registration in the list of shareholders included in the Commercial Register merely legitimates the registered party as a shareholder in relation to the corporation (Sec. 16(1) GmbHG) and can form the basis for an acquisition in good faith (Sec. 16(3) GmbHG). However, neither the registration in the list

39 See also Art. 10 of the 1st Company Law Directive 2009/101/EC, the scope of which is, however, not quite clear.
40 See *Bainbridge* supra (note 10), p. 832.
41 See Chapter 2 A.

of shareholders nor the registration as a shareholder in the Commercial Register is a constructive part of the acquisition. This model is, for example, found in a similar form in Austrian GmbH law, albeit without the possibility of an acquisition in good faith[42], as well as in the Swiss law of obligations; however, the latter stipulates that written form is sufficient for share transfer (Art. 785(1) OR).

Other legal systems also follow this in principle, but they attach greater importance to registration in the list of shareholders or in the Commercial or Companies Register to the extent these registrations influence the validity of the transfer in certain legal relationships (i.e., that the legal effect of the transfer is split). In France, too, the transfer of shares in a SARL can, in principle, be performed by formless contract. However, for the transfer to be valid in relation to the corporation, a notary's act or a private deed is necessary, and for the transfer to be valid in relation to third parties, registration of the transfer in the Commercial and Companies Register is also necessary.[43] The legal position is similar in English law (ss. 544, 768 et seq. Companies Act 2006). The buyer acquires equitable title to shares of a *private company limited by share*s with a transfer contract, which is valid without fulfilling particular form requirements, i.e., entitlement under equity. He or she acquires *legal title* when he or she is registered as the new shareholder in the register of members on the basis of a written transfer deed and after the handover of a share certificate (documentary evidence) – to the extent *certificated shares* are concerned.[44] The Draft SPE Regulation pursues a comparable concept, specifying that shares can be transferred by written agreement (Art. 16(2) Draft SPE Regulation). However, a transfer is only valid against the corporation when the shareholder notifies the transfer to the SPE, and is valid in relation to third parties when he or she is included in the register of members pursuant to Art. 15 (Art. 16(4) Draft SPE Regulation). In all of these aforementioned models, transfer rules centre on the agreement between seller

---

42 See Sec. 76 GmbHG and *Kalss/Schauer* Die Reform des österreichischen Kapitalgesellschaftsrechts, 2006, p. 729 et seq.; *Kalss/Nowotny/Schauer* Österreichisches Gesellschaftsrecht, 2008, margin no. 4/307.

43 See *Arlt* in: Kalss, Die Übertragung von GmbH-Geschäftsanteilen in 14 Rechtsordnungen Europas, 2003, p. 89, 97 et seq. Art. L223–17, L221–14 Code de commerce require written form for the transfer of shares in a SARL. Case-law focuses on the failure to comply with form requirements, but does not declare nullity to be the consequence. Instead, in the relationship between the transferring parties, it considers the transfer valid even in case of a mere (formless) agreement. See Cass.com., 10 mars 1992, JCP G 1992, II, n° 21962, p. 432. The transfer is in any case only valid against the corporation when it has been notified to the corporation and only valid against third parties when register publicity has also occurred.

44 See *Davies* Gower and Davies' Principles of Modern Company Law, 8th ed., 2008, p. 935 et seq., 939 et seq., 950 et seq.

and buyer, which may need to fulfil formal requirements. Registration in a list of shareholders or in a Commercial or Companies Register also determines *legal title* (UK) or validity in relation to third parties (France, SPE).

On the basis of these models, further development is particularly conceivable in two directions: either (1) the certification of the share in a share certificate, which is then elevated from documentary evidence to a negotiable instrument – and correspondingly transferred – or, (2) a constitutive register solution in which registration is a constitutive requirement for the transfer *generally*, not just in certain legal circumstances. The conception of shares as *certificated rights* can also be found in Scandinavian legal systems. Both Swedish and Finnish law traditionally have had no independent statute for the closed corporation – even under more recent statutes – but only one standard corporate form in two variations: a public corporation and the closed corporation.[45] If – as is usual – the shares are certificated, then they can be transferred by endorsement.

It appears that a constitutive *register solution*, by contrast, has not hitherto been realised for closed corporations in any major European legal system. However, it has recently been made possible by s. 783 et seq. Companies Act 2006 in the United Kingdom. Under this legislation, rules can be passed "... for enabling title to securities to be evidenced and transferred without a written instrument" (s. 785(1) Companies Act 2006). In a system with a constitutive register solution, the transfer of a share would take place by agreement between seller and buyer and its constitutive registration in the Commercial Register or Companies Register. This would be similar to how land is currently transferred under German law (Sec. 873, 925 German Civil Code (BGB)).[46] At the same time, the incorrect registration of a person in the Commercial or Companies Register would mark the reference point for acquisition in good faith. Given the system conformity of a register solution (transfer by agreement and registration in the register) with transfers of rights (*in rem*) in many legal systems and the fact that such register-based systems are gaining popularity worldwide in different fields (particularly in loan collateral security law[47]), a detailed examination of this potentially promising model is especially worthwhile.

---

45 In Sweden, there is the "privat aktiebolag" and the "publikt aktiebolag", see 1 kap. 2 Sec. Aktiebolagslag (2005:551), in Finnland the "yksityinen osakeyhtiö" (closed corporation) and the "julkinen osakeyhtiö" (public corporation), 1 luku 1 Sec. Osakeyhtiölaki 21 July 2006/624.
46 For this proposal, see *Eidenmüller* in: Eidenmüller, Ausländische Kapitalgesellschaften im deutschen Recht, 2004, Chapter 1 margin no. 27; *Eidenmüller* ZGR 2007, 168, 202.
47 See the contributions in Eidenmüller/Kieninger, The Future of Secured Credit in Europe, ECFR Special Volume 2 (2008).

II Regulatory Goals

Here again, however – like the discussion about the formation procedure for a closed corporation – it is necessary to acquire some certainty about the aims pursued regarding the conception of the transfer rules. As we have already mentioned, transaction costs play an important role. The lower the costs of the transfer procedure, the higher the likelihood of a share actually being held by the person who can derive the greatest benefit from it. Relevant transaction costs include costs of searches and information (above all with regard to the seller's entitlement) and costs of contract conclusion and implementation.

It is now argued, however, that there is no need for freely tradable GmbH shares or even their marketability on the stock exchange.[48] Instead, it is argued that the legitimate aims in structuring the law of the closed corporation include keeping shares of a closed corporation away from the capital markets by suitable provisions. For this purpose, certain costly requirements of form, such as notarisation of the transfer act, are claimed to be advisable. The mere requirement of written form is, by contrast, unsuitable to prevent lively internet trade.[49] The aim of directing equity capital only into the market segment whose structure fulfils the guiding principles of investor protection can and should, however, be achieved by the rules applying to this legal segment, i. e., capital markets law. If, accordingly, shares in a closed corporation are not tradable, further corporate law regulation such as artificial inflation of the cost of transfer becomes unnecessary. The desire to prevent a grey market for such shares[50] also overshoots the mark, because, due to the typical interests involved in closed corporations and the corresponding contract structures, the development of such a market is, in any case, not anticipated (restrictions on transferability).[51/52]

48 See the considerations – which ultimately failed on the grounds of a lack of "demand" – in the 1980s in Germany on easing flotation on the stock exchange for small and medium-sized firms, in particular, Ministerium für Wirtschaft, Mittelstand und Technologie Baden-Württemberg, Bericht der Kommission "Zweiter Börsenmarkt": Börsenzugang für kleine und mittlere Unternehmen (Stuttgart, 1987); Ministerium für Wirtschaft, Mittelstand und Technologie Baden-Württemberg, Bericht der Kommission "Zweiter Börsenmarkt": Konkrete Gestaltungsvorschläge, 1989; *Kecker* Die Fungibilisierung von GmbH-Anteilen, 1991, in particular p. 165 et seq.

49 See *Kalss/Schauer* supra (note 42), p. 734 et seq.; *Kalss/Trenkwalder/Eckert* in: Kalss, supra (note 43), p. 1, 8, 16 et seq., 21 et seq; see also *Wilhelm* Kapitalgesellschaftsrecht, 3rd ed., 2009, margin no. 53 (citing the materials to the German GmbHG 1982).

50 *Kalss/Trenkwalder/Eckert* in: Kalss, supra (note 43), p. 1, 21 et seq.

51 See also C.IV.

52 See also *Behrens* Wissenschaftliche Vereinigung für Unternehmens- und Gesellschaftsrecht (VGR) 12 (2006), 195, 200 et seq.

However, the transfer rules should be conceived in a way that promotes legal certainty to the greatest extent possible and also offers a simple connecting factor for acquisitions in good faith. It is hardly disputed that acquisitions from a non-entitled party should be made possible in principle under certain circumstances.[53] Transaction costs are significantly reduced if every purchaser need not conduct costly research into the history of the shares in order to ensure that the planned transaction is valid.[54] The time, effort and expenditure necessary for structuring the contract are also reduced by the possibility of an acquisition in good faith. However, if this is to be introduced in principle, then such a structure should be as efficient as possible.

Necessary considerations regarding the instruction and cautioning of a seller or buyer are also the same considerations which apply in connection with the formation of the corporation.[55] There is no convincing reason for the mandatory involvement of a third (notarising) person in light of the risk involved in the purchase or sale of shares. Nor is there predominant practice in this regard in the Member States. Written form is sufficient for evidence and publicity purposes.[56]

A particular problem relates to the issue of publicity as a constitutive requirement for the transfer or – more generally – dispositions of the shares. It is often argued that there is no interest in disclosing encumbrances of shares or capital and financing structures generally. Transparency in this respect is said to be "undesirable". According to this view, the transfer rules must therefore be structured in such a way that corresponding disclosure is not necessary. For this reason, acquisitions in good faith *free of encumbrances* must not be introduced.[57] However, this view is hardly a sound one. Publicity of share encumbrances contributes to credit markets' ability to correctly assess risks and accurately reflect them in loan prices. Well-secured commercial banks have an individual

---

53 Arguing against the possibility of acquisition in good faith, *Zöllner* Wissenschaftliche Vereinigung für Unternehmens- und Gesellschaftsrecht (VGR) 12 (2006), 175, 182 et seq., 190 et seq. (where it is argued that there is a lack of a suitable bearer of legitimacy verification (*Rechtsscheinsträger*) – but this is not the case, see following text).

54 Naturally, on the other hand, it must be taken into consideration in structuring the prerequisites of a good faith acquisition that the party actually entitled must incur costs to avoid an undesired loss of rights.

55 See Chapter 6 A.II. above.

56 This legal policy line is probably dominant in the meantime, see *Hadding/Kießling* WM 2009, 145, 155 et seq. with further references.

57 See the discussion report of *Rodewig* in *Grunewald/Gehling/Rodewig* ZIP 2006, 685, 691. See also *Gehling* supra, p. 689: disclosure of third-party rights "... weakens the attractiveness of the GmbH as a legal form for medium-sized businesses."

interest in keeping their collateral as secret as possible; but this does not mean that the economy has the same interest.

III Transfer Rules

On this basis, the advantages and any difficulties of a constitutive register solution regarding the transfer of shares (i.e., transfer by agreement and registration in a Commercial or Companies Register) become clear. According to this solution, entries in the Register would be made electronically in a decentralized way by users with authorized access.[58] The Register would therefore automatically work on the basis of special software and would not be manually "served" by competent persons. Registrations would take place in real time, i.e., congruent to the respective information entered. Due to the lack of any time delay for the purchase, there would be no need for an "electronic priority notice" or similar measures. The problem of identification would be resolved by electronic codes or digital signatures generally available to the public or – where this is not the case – provided *ad hoc* for a particular transaction. Acquisition in good faith would be tied to incorrect entries (i.e., positive publicity).

Such a model would naturally presuppose the establishment of a corresponding electronic register and would therefore potentially involve considerable one-off costs. The costs of operation (including servicing and care) would, by contrast, be very low. The example of New Zealand once again demonstrates this point. An electronic register for security rights for movables was established in 2002. Register establishment costs had already been fully redeemed by 2006; the register is operated by a single part-time employee.[59]

Today, there are certain cost-induced differences between a register for security rights for movables and a register for shares. In particular, a register for shares must offer a high guarantee of accuracy with regard to the possibility of acquisitions in good faith, so that some examination of the entries is indispensable.[60] However, this examination can be formalized to a large extent and therefore take place automatically (i.e., pre-registration of the seller, formal consent of the seller, permissible disposition content from a catalogue of permissible dis-

---

58 Agreement would be formless and would be notified upon registration – if it was already reached before then – or would be implied in the registration procedure.

59 See *Kieninger* AcP 208 (2008), 182, 211 et seq.

60 See *Grunewald/Gehling/Rodewig* ZIP 2006, 685, 686. This was the decisive reason why this solution was not pursued within the framework of the latest GmbH reform in Germany. See *Seibert* ZIP 2006, 1157, 1160 ("additional burden on the register courts").

positions, etc.), similar to today's examination by the Land Registry in Germany for the registration of real estate rights.[61] The costs associated with this should therefore remain within reasonable boundaries. At the same time, persons who are negatively affected by register content must be given the opportunity to achieve a register block. This should also be possible in a formalized or automatic – and therefore cost-effective – procedure, for instance, on the basis of an electronic affidavit.

This would not only prevent a loss of rights through acquisitions in good faith, but also increase the guarantee of accuracy of the register.

Such a system for an electronic transfer of shares would presumably make legal transactions with shares considerably easier. It would also install a form of transfer that is both modern and offers greater legal certainty. Acquisition in good faith would be linked to the register entry and would therefore depend on a simple criterion, which is easily recognised and can be fixed in time. This criterion is far superior to other bearers of legitimacy verification such as the current German solution of a "list of shareholders included in the Commercial Register". According to this solution, the list must – in relation to the entitlement to the share – either have been incorrect for at least three years or less than three years but attributable to the entitled party as incorrect, in order to enable acquisition in good faith (Section 16(3) GmbHG). The (relevant) point in time of inclusion in the Commercial Register is not clearly evident. Moreover, subsequent investigations regarding the accuracy of the list remain necessary (i.e., has the present entry been *incorrect* for three years? Is a shorter period of incorrectness *attributable* to the party affected?). Further, there is no transfer free from encumbrances.[62/63] Even an improvement in the status of the list of shareholders to a bearer of legitimacy verification similar to the Land Register and administered by notaries[64] would only go half way towards a "real" and modern electronic

---

61 See *Eidenmüller* ZGR 2007, 168, 203 et seq.

62 See *Eidenmüller* ZGR 2007, 168, 201 et seq.; *Altgen* 9 German L.J. 1141, 1146 et seq. (2008); *Wachter* GmbHR Special Issue 10/2008, 51, 59 et seq.; *D. Mayer* ZIP 2009, 1037, 1039.

63 In addition, the protection of good faith pursuant to Art. 16(3) p. 2 Draft SPE Regulation is also completely muddled. According to it, "... the provisions of the applicable legal provisions of the respective Member State for the protection of persons who purchase shares in good faith apply in this context." For the German GmbH law, this would be fruitless, because the SPE list of shareholders is kept by the management organ according to Art. 15(3) Draft SPE Regulation and is not submitted to the Commercial Register (see Sec. 16(3) GmbHG). But the reference would also be fruitless in the case of legal systems that construe the rules of transfer (and consequently also the protection of good faith) completely differently from the SPE Regulation, for instance, because they focus on constitutive register entries for the legal effectiveness of a transfer.

64 See (the notary) *Wegen* FS Lüer, 2008, p. 321, 332 et seq.

Commercial or Companies Register. The solution proposed here for the transfer of shares within the framework of an electronic register system is also superior to securities law certification and transfer of shares. Possession of physical objects is an antiquated bearer of legitimacy verification (i.e., "de-materialisation" already characterises the *status quo* today and particularly the future of securities trading), an expensive one (i.e., issue of certificates, transfer, investigation of a chain of assignments, etc.) and certificated shares are, in any event, no less susceptible to forgery or manipulation than electronic entries.[65]

A further advantage of an electronic register and transfer system in the form described would be that any transaction taxes – similar to the case of stock exchange-listed securities – could be charged automatically. To the extent doubts about such a system derive from considerations of a closed corporation not accessing the capital markets, the publicity of dispositions and/or an instruction or cautioning of the necessary participants, reference can be made to the foregoing discussion.[66] Overall, an electronic register and transfer system would considerably modernise the law on closed corporations.

IV Restrictions on Transfer

The issue of recognising or overcoming restrictions on transfer must be discussed separately. It has already been mentioned that there can be legitimate interests in a restriction on transfer in spite of the fundamental economic and minority protection function of freedom of transfer.[67/68] In closed corporations, trust and the identity of the partners frequently play an important role. It should be possible to ensure that all shareholders have the necessary (management) competences. Shareholders frequently also have only little interest in selling shares because the shareholders are linked to one another by family ties or have made significant investments specific to the corporation, such as in particular competences or training. Ultimately, drastic and sudden changes in control should be prevented (for instance in 1/3 – 1/3 – 1/3-corporations).

From this typical set of interests, which is reflected in contractual practice in a restriction of transferability, we can deduce that the share sale – as a default

65 In this context, see also the discussion report by *Rodewig* in *Grunewald/Gehling/Rodewig* ZIP 2006, 685, 690.

66 Sec. A.II and C.II

67 See Chapters 2 A and 6 C.

68 See in the following also *Cheffins* supra (note 24), p. 50, 285 et seq.; *Bainbridge* supra (note 10), p. 811.

statutory rule – should be dependent on the consent of the remaining shareholders,[69] but that this consent cannot be inequitably refused without objective reasons. As the rule would not be mandatory in nature, parties could give effect to divergent interest positions by respective contractual arrangements. Clauses would have to be recognised which authorize the directors to grant consent or stipulate the majorities necessary for a transfer in divergence from the statutory regulation. Put options should also be recognized, and a participant could use put options to secure a certain exit scenario.[70] The same applies to the *drag-along* and *tag-along* clauses, which are especially widespread in the venture capital sphere.[71]

Current statutory practice in various European and non-European countries predominantly corresponds to these considerations.[72] In Switzerland, Art. 786 OR specifies a largely optional restriction on transferability by statute. In Germany, restrictions on transfer are not default statutory rules, but are permissible under private autonomy and represent usual practice (transferability can even be excluded altogether).[73] This corresponds to Art. 16(1) Draft SPE Regulation and – for the United States – Section 6.27 MBCA. In the United Kingdom, too, "[t]he extent of the restriction ... is solely a matter of construction of the articles of association."[74] Likewise, France, in principle, permits contractual restrictions on transfer; statutory provisions even provide for a general mandatory restriction

---

69 See also *Kroeze/Wezeman* Reform of Dutch Private Company Law, in: McCahery/Timmerman/Vermeulen, Private Company Law Reform: International and European Perspectives, 2001, p. 181, 187; *Kalss/Schauer* supra (note 42), p. 751. According to the typical interest position, a requirement of unanimity should apply to the default statutory rule with regard to consent. Comparatively, the interest position and legal position relating to the American LLC is also interesting. Here, the assets can be transferred without the consent of the other shareholders, but the management rights cannot. See *Ribstein* The Rise of the Uncorporation, 2010, p. 182 et seq. This split is doubtful. However, this leads us to the conclusion that the international trend in the direction of mobilisation of the shares also applies to closed corporate forms. This is a further reason for the *default* nature of the rule proposed in the text.

70 See *Cheffins* supra (note 24), p. 65 et seq.

71 *Drag-along* clauses give a (majority) shareholder willing to sell the right to "pull along" other shareholders, whereas *tag-along* clauses conversely give such shareholders the right to sell if another (majority) shareholder sells. For a discussion of such clauses from an institutional economic point of view, see *Saez Lacave/Gutiérrez* 11 Eur. Bus. Org. L. Rev. 423 (2010).

72 Overview of the European legal systems in *Kalss/Trenkwalder/Eckert* in: Kalss, supra (note 43), p. 1, 13 et seq.

73 See *Reichert/Weller* Münchener Komm. z. GmbHG, 2010, Sec. 15 margin no. 1, 358.

74 *Davies* supra (note 44), p. 942. See also *Lembeck* in: Kalss, supra (note 43), p. 223, 238 et seq.

on transfer of shares regarding transfers to third parties. It is the mandatory nature of the rule that must be viewed critically.[75]

If a share is blocked from transfer by statute or the articles of association, this should be noted in the electronic Commercial or Companies Register and – in case of an intended transfer – lead to an automatic block and notification of the parties to the transaction, as well as the third party protected by the consent requirement. If the note on the restriction on transfer is missing in the electronic register – i.e., the register is substantively incorrect – then, according to the logic of the system for acquisitions in good faith developed above, the purchaser in good faith overrides the block on transfer.

D Results

1. Costs for the formation and management of a corporation and for changes in the shareholder composition not only reduce welfare *per se*, but are also important indirectly: they are a decisive competitive factor in decisions on the choice of legal form. The possibility of simple, cost-effective formations also has a positive effect on economic growth. Rules on the formation, management and a change of shareholders should therefore primarily be conceived with the goal of ensuring the lowest possible transaction costs.
2. Requirements of formation should not be instrumentalized for purposes outside corporate law. Such requirements can be restricted to the essential characteristics of a corporation: shareholders, directors, registered office, business name and stipulated capital.
3. The formation of a closed corporation does not involve excessive liability risks even when compared to other transactions with no formal requirements. For this reason, the conclusion of the shareholder agreement should not be subject to a particularly strict form, such as notarization. Written form is sufficient for the purposes of evidence and publicity.
4. In formation procedure, the examination of the substantive formation requirements should take place in an automatic (formal) way, if possible. Examination and register maintenance should be brought together. If no other established and functioning structures exist, then a central and specialized public authority is advisable. Formation should be possible in electronic form and without significant time delays (i.e., through online formation).

75 Art. L223–14 C.com. However, the procedure is structured in such a way that the shareholder willing to sell is ultimately able to sell his or her share, albeit not necessarily to the person he or she first had in mind.

5. Regulatory tasks regarding the corporation's management can to a large extent be left to the private autonomous structuring of the articles of association by the shareholders. Registration fees (*franchise fees*) should only be charged to the extent they do not exceed the administrative costs.
6. A change of shareholders should be organised so that a transfer is as legally safe as possible. Transaction costs in particular can pose risks in light of extensive research into the history of the shares. Transfer should be conceived as a constitutive electronic register solution, in real time by agreement and registration in an automatic register. Acquisition in good faith would be possible and could rely on incorrect entries (positive publicity). Restrictions on transfer would be shown in the register and lead to a block.

Chapter 7 Regulatory Features of a European Closed Corporation*

Table of Contents

* The text is based on a draft by *Bachmann*.

A Why a Supranational Closed Corporation?

I Starting-Point: the Problem of Multiple Regulators

The considerations until now were based on the perspective of ideal legislation which stands for itself. In this context, it could be assumed that the necessity of a closed corporation does not have to be justified *per se,* because the need for such a legal form is universally accepted. Likewise, the power and the capacity of legislation to create such a legal form were not called into question. The discussion in this context could be restricted to the issue of the substantive structure of the legal form.

With regard to the *supranational* closed corporation, we must depart from this simple analysis framework. The question is no longer how a closed corporation *per se* should be structured, but rather which functions an *additional* closed corporation can fulfill in a multilevel system and which regulatory challenges arise in this context. For this purpose, the perspective must be changed in two directions. Firstly, the *number of participating regulators* increases. A supranational legal form presupposes at least *three* regulators on at least *two* levels: two national regulators on a lower level and a federal regulator on the upper level.[1] This multiplication brings into play additional (political) interests which have no role in the considerations to date.

We then no longer assume an ideal regulator, but instead a *specific regulator.* As such, we look to the European Union (EU). The reason for this is less the circumstance that supranational legal forms have, in particular, become established in Europe, than the fact that the diversity of conceivable multilevel systems excludes working through all possible variations within the limited framework

1 A multilevel model in which an upper and only one lower regulator create competing law products is probably only theoretical in nature. Federal legislature also must not automatically be institutionalised, but can instead comprise (contractual) cooperation by parallel regulators. These constellations are ignored here.

of this publication. Just as the fundamental model of the EU is comparable to that of other federal systems, the findings here can be transferred to other legal systems. This fundamental model is characterised by numerous “lower” regulators with divergent legal systems, and one “upper” regulator which, decisively, is not completely independent of the lower regulators and is significantly influenced by them.[2]

II The “Added Value” of a European Closed Corporation (ECC)

As the lower regulators, the Member States of the EU, all have their own closed corporations (Ltd., GmbH, Sprl, etc.), the central issue is whether a supranational statute is necessary at all.[3] More specifically: *what can a European closed corporation (ECC) do that a national closed corporation is not capable of?*

1 Debate on the Pros and Contras of an SPE

The discussion on the “added value” of a supranational European legal form was already intense in the 1960s.[4] It was revived with the draft of a *Societas Privatae Europaea* (SPE) demanded by the European Parliament, which the European Commission submitted in 2008[5] and which has subsequently been altered several times but never passed.[6] If we consider the debate about the pros and cons of such a legal form, we recognise the arguments which already played a

---

2 This distinguishes the EU from federal countries like the Federal Republic of Germany or the USA, in which the influence of the individual federal states on federal legislation is smaller. Even there, the federation cannot act completely autonomously. For more detail, see B.II. below.

3 The primary question from the legal point of view, namely whether a central statute *can* be passed (question of competence), is subordinate from a functional point of view and in addition depends on what is expected of such a legal form. It is treated in further detail below (see C.I. below).

4 Cf. the description in *Ch. Teichmann* Binnenmarktkonformes Gesellschaftsrecht, 2006, p. 234–238.

5 Proposal for a Council Regulation on the Statute for a European private company, COM(2008) 396 final. Available at http://ec.europa.eu/internal_market/company/epc/index_en.htm.

6 Individual references to the extensive literature on the SPE must be waived here. See, e.g. (with further references): *Davies* FS Hopt, 2010, p. 479; *Fleischer* ZHR 174 (2010), 385, 403 et seq; *Hügel* ZHR 173 (2009), 309, 319; *Uziahu-Santcroos* in: Zaman/Schwarz/Lennarts/de Kluiver/Dorresteijn, The European Private Company (SPE) – A Critical Analysis of the EU Draft Statute, 2009, p. 1. See too the references above, Chapter 1 note 7.

central role in the earlier discussion about the introduction of a European public stock corporation:

Supporters of the SPE especially hope for reduced transaction costs if only one legal regime must be taken into consideration for entrepreneurial activities across Europe.[7]Additionally, reference is made to the possibility of the easier relocation of a registered office across borders. Psychological advantages such as the demonstration of a "European brand" or the neutrality of the legal form in case of cross-border joint ventures are repeatedly cited as well. In this context, the interests of the countries which have recently joined the EU as members are invoked, because they are not (yet) able to use a legal form of their own "capable of export". Lastly, a revival of the competition of ideas in corporate law is anticipated.[8]

Critics counter that foreign activities could be realised equally well by a network of branches, at least by the use of one national legal form across the European Union (e. g. Ltd., GmbH).[9] The freedom of establishment guaranteed by the Treaty on the Functioning of the European Union (TFEU)[10] permits founders of corporations to use national legal forms at home and abroad in the EU if the country of formation permits the "export" of its legal form.[11] Decisive parameters for the choice of law, such as tax law, in any case remain unaffected by the single legal form.[12] Less clearly articulated but omnipresent, and the real reason for the failure of the SPE to date, is the fear of undermining national minimum standards and an associated "undertow". If the supranational legal form is particularly attractive, this can lead to a drying-out of the national reservoir of legal forms and, thereby, to a loss of control by the Member States.[13]

---

7 See in particular the Commission's *Impact Assessment* published as an accompanying document to the Draft SPE Regulation and the *Feasibility Study* (2005), both available under http://ec.europa.eu/internal_market/company.

8 See *Fleischer* supra (note 6), 385, 403 et seq, 409 et seq; *Fleischer* AcP 204 (2004), 502, 510 et seq, 518 et seq.

9 See the opinion of the German *Bundesrat* [Federal Council, representing the 16 German *Länder*], resolution of 10 October 2008, Drucksachen des Deutschen Bundesrates 479/08, p. 3.

10 See http://eur-lex.europa.eu/LexUriServ/LexUriServ.do?uri=OJ:C:2008:115:0047:0199:en:PDF.

11 See ECJ Case C-210/06 Cartesio [2008] ECR I-9641; ECJ [1988], 5483 – Case 81/87 (*Daily Mail*).

12 See *Davies* supra (note 6), p. 479, 481, according to which the SPE is very popular in surveys because, although its availability did not greatly benefit those interviewed, it also cost them nothing.

13 See *Bundesrat*, resolution of 10 October 2008, Drucksachen des Deutschen Bundesrates 479/08, p. 3. From the viewpoint of the German administration see *Neye* FS Hüffer, 2010, p. 717, 720: "From a legal policy point of view, the undermining of recently modified standards for the GmbH at a European level through the formation of an SPE must be prevented."

2 Evaluation of the SE

Before we consider these criticisms in detail, we should look at the experience gained by the *Societas Europaea* (SE), the European public stock corporation which already exists. The Regulation forming the basis of this corporation was passed in 2001 and since been made "usable" by all Member States of the EU by corresponding implementation provisions. In the meantime (as of 19 March, 2012), 1,123 enterprises in Europe have chosen the legal form of the SE.[14] This figure is high when compared to earlier prophecies of doom which saw the SE damned to insignificance. By contrast, the figure is low when compared to the absolute number of national stock corporations in Europe.

According to the evaluation instruction resulting from Art. 69 of the SE Regulation, the European Commission has taken efforts to discover the reasons for the choice of the SE (or decisions against such choice) and possible subsequent improvement. Supported by preliminary work from academia[15] and practice[16] and by a consultation procedure, the Commission submitted an evaluation report on this topic on 17 November, 2010, which emphasises the motives for the choice of the SE and the possible need for reform.[17]

The report primarily cites the *European image* as a motive for the choice of legal form, which, in particular, plays a role in smaller countries and in the Eastern European Member States. This correlates with experience in Canada, where image reasons contributed to the success of the reform of the form under federal law.[18] A further motive cited is not having suffered "defeat" in the case of international mergers.[19] The possibility of *relocating the registered office*, retaining the identity, or cross-border mergers, is also mentioned, although the number of ac-

---

14 Continuously updated figures are available under www.worker-participation.eu/European-Company/SE-COMPANIES/Facts-and-Figures.

15 See here in particular the empirical investigations of *Eidenmüller/Engert/Hornuf* 11 Eur. Bus. Org. L. Rev. 35 (2010); *Eidenmüller/Engert/Hornuf* 10 Eur. Bus. Org. L. Rev. 1 (2009); *Eidenmüller/Engert/Hornuf* AG 2008, 721; see also *Bayer/Schmidt* AG 2007, R 192 and AG 2008, R 31. For a normative evaluation see *Casper* ZHR 173 (2009), 181.

16 See here in particular Ernst & Young: "Study on the operation and the impacts of the Statute for a European Company (SE) – Final report (9 December 2009)", available under http://ec.europa.eu/internal_market/company/se/index_en.htm.

17 Report of the Commission to the European Parliament and Council on the application of Council Regulation (EC) No 2157/2001 of 8 October 2001 on the Statute for a European company (SE), COM(2010), 676 final. Critical analysis in *Kiem* Corp. Fin. L. 2011, 134.

18 See *Daniels* 36 McGill L.J. 130, 189 (1991); *Cumming/McIntosh* 22 Int'l J.L. & Econ. 277, 299 et seq (2002).

19 Commission Report, supra (note 17), p. 3; see also *Eidenmüller/Engert/Hornuf* 10 Eur. Bus. Org. L. Rev. 1, 28 (2009).

tual relocations of registered offices appears to be relatively low and the merger option has probably lost importance as a central motive of the implementation of the Merger Directive.[20] The possibility of selecting *alternative governance structures* is also a particular motivation in countries which, to a great extent, have a mandatory corporate constitution, namely, Germany. This primarily affects the regime of codetermination, which can be negotiated away or frozen for the SE and also, less significantly, the option of installing a monistic instead of a dualistic management structure.[21]

In addition to the empirical evaluation, there are considerations on how the legislative framework of the SE could be improved. In particular, a need for change is seen for the formation procedure which is considered *cumbersome*. Criticism is particularly levelled at the *numerus clausus* of the formation variations, but also, at the multi-state requirement, the tandem measure of the administrative headquarters, the seat of the articles of association, and the negotiation of codetermination involving time, effort and expenditure.[22] There is a general complaint about the, in part *unclear, dovetailing with national law* which results from the complicated reference technique.[23]

In addition, concerns about the supranational legal form are expressed. Trade unions fear that the national codetermination rules will be undermined by a flight into the SE.[24] The grant of more structural freedom intensifies competition with the legal forms in the Member States, which could provoke political resistance.[25] Concern about the reputation of the legal form, which could be harmed in case of very strong deregulation, is also articulated.[26] It remained un-

---

20 See Commission Report, supra (note 17), p. 4; see also *Eidenmüller/Engert/Hornuf* AG 2008, 721, 725.

21 See Commission Report, supra (note 17), p. 4 et seq; see also *Eidenmüller/Engert/Hornuf* AG 2008, 721, 728.

22 See Commission Report, supra (note 17), p. 7 et seq; see also *Arbeitskreis Aktien- und Kapitalmarktrecht* 10 Eur. Bus. Org. L. Rev. 285 et seq (2009); *Kiem* supra (note 17), 134; in detail, *Casper* supra (note 15), 181, 189 et seq, 208 et seq.

23 See Commission Report, supra (note 17), p. 7; *Casper* supra (note 15), 181, 185 et seq.

24 See Commission Report, supra (note 17), p. 9.

25 See Commission Report, supra (note 17), p. 9.

26 From the point of view of a (German) legal advisor – *Kiem* Corp. Fin. L. 2011, 134, 143: The SE with German character "enjoys its excellent standing not least due to the rigid regulatory structure to which it is subjected. The strict rules on the raising and maintenance of capital secure is a good reputation in advance which would possibly be swiftly lost in case of a noticeable loosening of the regulatory structure."

clear whether the advantages of the SE would be appreciated, not only by the initiators of the choice of legal form, but also by investors and stakeholders.[27]

The Commission itself dampens the hope of liberalisation of the regulation by concluding that the SE Statute was the "result of a precarious compromise reached after long negotiations".[28] In its recent (December, 2012) Action Plan outlining possible fields of future EU-corporate law reform, the Commission notes that respondents to a consultation in 2012 were supportive of revising EU legal forms in general.[29] However, as the expected benefits of a revision, in terms of simplification and improvement of both Statutes, would not outweigh the potential challenges involved in reopening the discussions, the Commission declared that it does not plan to revise them in the short term. Instead, the Commission will focus on improving the awareness of companies and their legal advisers about the SE (including the aspects related to employee involvement) in order to encourage them to opt for these legal forms more often.[30]

3 What should European Legislation do?

Given the pros and cons of the introduction of an SPE, and in view of the ambivalent evaluation results on the SE, how should European legislation deal with the issue of the European closed corporation?[31] The simplest answer would not be to pursue the SPE project any further but to turn back to legal harmonisation of national company laws.[32] In spite of the halting process of the SPE-cre-

---

27 See *Eidenmüller/Engert/Hornuf* 11 Eur. Bus. Org. L. Rev. 35 (2010).

28 Commission Report, supra (note 17), p. 11.

29 61 % (307 out of 496) in favour.

30 Action Plan: European company law and corporate governance – a modern legal framework for more engaged shareholders and sustainable companies (Communication from the European Commission to the European Parliament, the Council, the European Economic and Social Committee and the Committee of the Regions), COM(2012) 740 final, at 4.5. (p. 14). Available at http://eur-lex.europa.eu/LexUriServ/LexUriServ.do?uri=COM:2012:0740:FIN:EN:PDF.

31 The EU-Commission has once again explicitly raised the issue of the "added value" of an SPE for debate, see Consultation on the Future of European Company Law of 20.2.2012, http://ec.europa.eu/internal_market/consultations/2012/company_law_en.htm. The recent Action Plan concludes that "the Commission will continue to work on the follow-up to the SPE proposal with a view to enhancing cross-border opportunities for SMEs" (supra, note 30, at 4.4, p. 14). Most recently, the Commission has lanced a Consultation on a "*Single Member Company*" (SMC) to be created via harmonisation of member states law. It has then repealed its proposal for an SPE-statute and announced that it considers to present a new proposal in this area, see COM (2013) 685 final.

32 Cf. *Sandberg/Skog* AG 2010, 580, 583; see also *Report of the Reflection Group on the Future of EU-Company Law* 2011, p. 29 (with differing views); *Davies* supra (note 6), p. 479, 498: "Should not have been undertaken in the first place"; sceptically with a view to the results of the SE

ation, this should not be the last word in our view. Instead, we should take a step backwards and discuss the fundamental issue of which functions a European closed corporation can sensibly fulfil.

B The Functions of a Supranational Closed Corporation

The arguments of those in favour of an SPE, but also the findings from the evaluation of the SE, show that the issue turns on not one, but *several*, functions of the supranational legal form. In contrast, the arguments of the critics express reference to *functional equivalents*. This is important because an ECC can only succeed if we bear in mind alternative solutions.

I "Classical" Function: Cross-Border Vehicle

The basis for the idea of a European legal form is the fact that different corporate law regimes constitute hurdles for the cross-border development of entrepreneurial activity and, therefore, for the development of the "Single Market" (Art. 26 TFEU). The supranational legal form can remove them. This could involve cross-border relocation (see 1. below) or a group of enterprises operating throughout Europe (see 2. below).

1 Mobility (Transfer of Seat, Cross-Border Mergers)

a) Functions – Functional Equivalents – Problems

The possibility of transferring the registered office across borders in a way which preserves the identity of the company, i. e. without dissolution and new formation, was "one of the most important grounds for the development of the idea of a corporation under European law".[33] This need is no longer so pressing in view of the generous interpretation of the freedom of establishment guaranteed under European primary law (Art. 49 TFEU). According to the relevant case-law of the European Court of Justice (ECJ), corporations legally formed in one member state can move their headquarters across the border without the need to dis-

---

evaluation *Kiem* supra (note 17), 134, 139 (necessity of further supranational legal forms doubtful); more hopeful *Andenas/Woolridge* European Comparative Company Law 2009, p. 416 ("should be given serious attention").

33 *Lutter* Europäisches Unternehmensrecht, 4th ed., 1996, p. 719.

solve, if the home country so permits.[34] Thus, a British Ltd. registered in London may operate exclusively in Germany. Even without such permission by the home country, the transfer of seat is possible if the corporation is willing to accept the legal form of the host country and the latter accepts the change of legal form.[35] The host state is not allowed to generally refuse to convert foreign companies moving in its territory to national corporate forms if it enables its own companies to convert their legal form.[36]

Although the TFEU itself does not provide a detailed framework for transfer of seatincurring a change of legal form (like the Regulation on the *Societas Europae* does),[37] it can be made available by harmonisation in the form of an EU-Directive on the transfer of seat. Corresponding drafts have been prepared and wait to be passed.[38] In practice, provisional use is made of the instrument of cross-border merger, which was harmonised by the so called Tenth Directive,[39] and which allows for similar results. With the use of a foreign vehicle formed or acquired solely for this purpose, relocation with a change of legal form can be implemented without serious difficulty. As this route, in some cases, involves fewer obstacles (especially as regards worker's codetermination law) than the formation of an SE, the latter has, to date, not become important as an instrument for the transfer of registered offices or for cross-border mergers.[40]

Therefore, the need for a supranational legal form only exists to the extent to which neither the freedom of establishment nor the Merger Directive guarantees

34 Cf. ECJ 1999, I-1495 – C-212/97 (*Centros*), allowing a British "brass-plate" company to do business exclusively in Denmark via its Danish "branch office". Whether such foreign letter box companies are still possible is now disputed as the ECJ recently emphasized that "the concept of establishment within the meaning of the Treaty provisions on the freedom of establishment involves the actual pursuit of an economic activity through a fixed establishment in the host Member State for an indefinite period", see ECJ 2012, I-C-378/10 (*Vale*). However, since the court did not explicitly give up its *Centros*-rule, it still seems to be good law.
35 See ECJ 2008, I-9641 – C-210/06 (*Cartesio*), para. 112.
36 See ECJ 2012, I-C-378/10 (*Vale*).
37 See Art. 8 SE-Regulation.
38 See the recent consultation on the cross-border transfer of registered offices of companies by the EU-Commisson (http://ec.europa.eu/internal_market/consultations/2013/seat-transfer/index_en.htm). See also the European Parliament resolution of 2 February 2012 with recommendations to the Commission on a 14th company law Directive on the cross-border transfer of company seats (2011/2046(INI) – P7 – TAPROV(2012)0019).
39 Directive 2005/56/EC of the European Parliament and of the Council of 26 October 2005 on cross-border mergers of limited liability companies, OJ L 310 of 25.11.2005, p. 1 et seq.
40 See Commission Report, supra (note 17), p. 4; *J. Schmidt* 1 Asian J.L. & Econ. 15 (2010): ("has taken away a unique selling point for the SE"); *Dorresteijn/Uziahu-Santcroos* 5 Eur. Co. L. 277, 279 et seq (2008); *Uziahu-Santcroos* supra (note 6), p. 17 et seq.

relocation without a change of legal form. Instead, a Member State remains entitled to withdraw legal capacity from corporations formed under its laws and relocating away from its territory.[41] European law would therefore not prevent Germany from prohibiting a German GmbH from relocating to Great Britain with the "threat" of compulsory dissolution. Yet German law does not do this because, like many other European countries, it permits its corporations to have their registered office abroad.[42] This resulted from the ECJ case-law already mentioned, on the generous interpretation of the freedom of establishment which permits foreign legal forms to establish themselves in Germany.[43] This in particular benefits the British limited liability corporation. German legislation sought to avoid this "competitive disadvantage" by permitting the "export" of the GmbH as a legal form.[44] If this impulse is not enough to encourage all other Member States to open up on a similar way, European legislation could still resort to the instrument of harmonisation of the conflict of laws in corporate law.

If we summarise these considerations, the supranational legal form today is not an *exclusive* but rather an *alternative* mobility vehicle for corporations in Europe. Their function is less the facilitation of cross-border relocation (the original idea in the 1960s) and more the extension of the relevant toolbox for cross-border strategies. The GmbH tired of Germany can therefore choose, if it wishes, to "emigrate" to Great Britain by making use of the freedom of establishment (Art. 49 TFEU), to merge with a British Ltd. under the rules of cross-border mergers harmonised under EU secondary law or to transform into a supranational legal form such as an SE or SPE and then (or afterwards) move to Great Britain.

From the viewpoint of shareholders and directors, cross-border relocation harbours no particular difficulties. A change of legal form may be involved, but this is also possible in a purely national context. However, from the point of view of third parties, questions are raised which do not arise in a purely national context. In essence, there are three regulatory challenges: (1) Relocation abroad makes recourse by the existing creditors to the corporation's assets more difficult, at least in practical terms. (2) Relocation involving a change of legal form makes the corporation a corporation under foreign law. In principle, this also means that rules of codetermination attaching to the legal form fall away. (3) Relocation with retention of the existing legal form confronts the

41 See ECJ 2008, I-9641 – C-210/06 (*Cartesio*), para. 110.

42 See, e.g., *Bachmann* in: Spindler/Stilz, Komm. z. AktG, 2nd ed., 2010, Section 262 para. 75 et seq; *Weller* Münchener Komm. z. GmbHG, 2010, Introduction para. 379 et seq.

43 See supra (note 34).

44 Technically this was achieved by deleting the requirement that statutory seat and "real" seat of a GmbH must coincide.

(new) creditors in the country of arrival with a foreign legal form with which they are not familiar.

b) Regulatory Consequences

Whereas the last of the three problems specified above must, in principle, be accepted in a Single Market, the first problem can be mitigated by prohibiting relocation of insolvent corporations or corporations ready for dissolution and ordering *perpetuatio fori* for claims which arose before relocation. The SE Regulation makes provision for this accordingly (see Art. 8(15) and (16) SE Regulation). Council Regulation (EC) No. 44/2001 of 22 December 2000 on jurisdiction and the recognition and enforcement of judgments in civil and commercial matters provides assistance by declaring that, in case of claims, both the seat of the articles of association and the administrative headquarters give rise to competence, thereby making the mere relocation of the one or the other irrelevant (see Art. 60 Council Regulation (EC) No. 44/2001).[45] In addition, existing creditors will have to accept that a natural debtor can disappear abroad and that they have to take precautions against this in private autonomy.

The second problem is familiar from national and/or harmonised transformation law. There, a protective model has been established which served as a role model both for the SE Regulation (Art. 8 SE Regulation) and for the Directive on cross-border mergers. It also appears to be suitable for the Directive on the relocation of a registered office.[46] It provides for a process in stages which comprises elements of a plan (for office relocation) to be made public, a report, a resolution, a formal investigation, a registration procedure and creditor protection provisos (e. g. the provision of collateral). In the same way, a transfer model has emerged for employee codetermination. The formation of a negotiation body on the employees' side is required, which negotiates a codetermination regime for

---

45 When the SE Regulation was passed, this already raised the question of whether the order of *perpetuatio fori* in Art. 8(16) SE Regulation is dispensable. It was subsequently made the subject of the evaluation process mentioned above (A.II.2.). In its evaluation report, the Commission tends towards this view, but at the same time sees no urgent need for change (Commission Report, supra (note 7), p. 9 et seq).

46 See *Arbeitskreis Europäisches Unternehmensrecht* (AKEur), NZG 2008, 897 (www.akeur.eu). On this protective model, see *Hommelhoff/Riesenhuber* in: Grundmann, Systembildung und Systemlücken in Kerngebieten des Europäischen Privatrechts, 2000, p. 259; prior to the harmonisation *Wiedemann* Gesellschaftsrecht, Volume I, 1980, p. 875 (distinguishing between preventative and repressive models).

the new legal form with the management. If no agreement is reached, default rules apply which are oriented towards the previous status.[47]

As the supranational legal form is only an alternative vehicle for the solution of cross-border problems, it is not surprising that the proposal for an SPE Statute is based on the regulatory model which was developed for the other cross-border strategies. For example, a prohibition on the relocation of a registered office for the SPE in case of insolvency and *perpetuatio fori* are provided for.[48] The procedure for the relocation of a registered office is also oriented towards the model described.[49] In both cases, there are no significant differences from the SE although the SPE-model is in part more liberal.[50] Codetermination causes particular problems. Although the negotiation model with default rules has established itself as a general model, details are contested for every legal act. Here too, the SPE appears to follow a model which is more liberal than that for the SE, but which is nevertheless not concerted and which threatens to bring about the failure of the entire legal form.[51]

As an *interim result*, we can say that the supranational legal form as a vehicle for mobility meets with the same challenges as its functional equivalents (relocation of registered office, cross-border merger) and, therefore, relies on similar protection precautions in favour of third parties (creditors, employees). The decisive question is whether there are specific regulatory requirements which affect

47 See Council Directive 2001/86/EC of 8 October 2001 supplementing the Statute for a European company with regard to the involvement of employees, OJ L 294 of 10 November 2001, p. 22; Directive 2005/56/EC of the European Parliament and of the Council of 26 October 2005 on cross-border mergers of limited liability companies, OJ L 310 of 25 November 2005, p. 1.

48 As in the Draft SPE Regulation (Art. 35(2) and (4) of the Commission proposal = Art. 36(2) and (4) Swedish compromise proposal, see below (note 50), which in this context follows the example of the SE Regulation, see Art. 8(15) and (16) SE Regulation).

49 See Art. 37, 38 SPE Regulation of the Commission proposal and Art. 37, 38 SPE Regulation of the Swedish compromise proposal with fundamentally the same wording.

50 It is politically disputed whether the SPE Regulation should follow the example set by the SE Regulation and link the seat of the articles of association and the registered administrative office to one another, see the compromise proposed by the Swedish presidency of the EU-Council (precept of a link for a limited time), Council of the European Union, 16115/09 ADD1, DRS 71, SOC 711, available under www.europeanprivatecompany.eu.

51 There is dispute here, amongst other things, about the threshold value beyond which the codetermination rules apply, see also the Swedish compromise proposal, supra (note 50), p. 3 (at least 500 employees, of whom at least half are employed in the country in which provision is made for a (higher) codetermination regime). The proposal was refused by Germany. For a detailed discussion of the codetermination problem, see *Dorresteijn/Uziahu-Santcroos* 6 Eur. Co. L. 152, 157 et seq (2009); *Hommelhoff* ZEuP 2011, 7; *Hommelhoff* in FS Schneider, 2011, p. 547.

either the supranational legal form alone or can only be realised through it. Both must be answered in the affirmative.

The risks which may arise for third parties from a cross-border change of legal form reduce to the extent to which the legal form on both sides of the border is the same. This was the consideration which made early proponents of supranational legal forms believe that those forms are an ideal tool for relocation across borders. They still assumed that the articles of association of such a legal form would be standard across the European Union, so that cross-border relocation would lead to a change of the registered office, but not to a change of the memorandum and articles of association. This is, unfortunately, not the case with the SE. Although it retains its legal form through the cross-border relocation, it is subjected to a *de facto* change of legal form due to the numerous references to national corporate law (Art. 9 SE Regulation). Regardless, the theory remains that the supranational legal form should have an *independent* Statute if possible, i.e. without recourse to national provisions. This would render any special regulatory devices protecting existing creditors largely obsolete and new creditors would not be confronted with a legal form with which they are unfamiliar.

If the supranational legal form is ideally able to deal with the problem of cross-border relocation better than its functional equivalents, it conversely faces particular challenges. These arise because excessive susceptibility to insolvency or abuse for untrustworthy purposes can lead to a *loss of reputation* of the legal form.[52] This is more dangerous for the supranational closed corporation than for the pseudo-foreign corporation. Even if a particular national legal form which is attractive from a founder's perspective should acquire the reputation abroad of being a "junk" legal form, this does not adversely affect the legal form. It would still be capable of acting in its home country, which has learnt to live with it, and to tackle a deplorable state of affairs there. The situation is different with a supranational legal form. If it loses its universal trustworthiness because, rightly or wrongly, it has acquired a reputation as a suspicious vehicle, it loses its specific function as a cross-border instrument of mobility.[53] This circum-

52 *Müller-Graff* Europäisches Währungssystem (EWS) 7/2008 (Editorial).

53 *Brems/Cannive* DK 2010, 629, 638; *Freudenberg* NZG 2010, 527, 528; *Hommelhoff/Teichmann* GmbHR 2009, 36. A look at the pseudo-foreign Ltd. operating in Germany is instructive. There are not only reports of its high susceptibility to insolvency (see *Niemeier* ZIP 2007, 1794 et seq). It is also conspicuous that it is used frequently for suspicious business models. Providers of so-called "Internet cost traps" were organised as Ltds in virtually all cases known to the courts, see for example OLG Frankfurt, NJW 2011, 398.

stance acquires particular weight because the image is a decisive reason for choosing the European legal form at all.[54]

This consideration may justify the establishment of a *stricter creditor protection regime* and/or *higher access hurdles* than would be indicated for the closed corporation if considered in isolation.[55] Thus, the SE links the seat of the articles of association to the registered headquarters of the main administration in a mandatory way (see Art. 7, 64 SE Regulation), which makes mobility more difficult but prevents the creation of "letterbox companies" with a bad reputation. It is politically disputed whether similar provision should be made for the SPE.[56] Yet it must be noted that the reason for such precautions is not to provide a higher degree of protection for creditors of the supranational legal form than would be necessary according to general considerations (see Chapter 5 above), but to protect the supranational legal form itself, i.e. safeguarding *the institution*. The situation is comparable to the prohibition on insider dealing in capital markets law. Some brand it as inefficient, but it promotes trust in the capital market as an institution, thereby keeping it operable.[57] In addition, stricter creditor protection can allow founders to signal legal quality.

2 Uniformity (European Group Subsidiary)

a) Function – Functional Equivalents – Problems

As described, the transfer of registered office can be carried out with the aid of supranational legal forms, but it can also be achieved using different means. The driving force behind current endeavours to create an SPE is, therefore, less the relocation of a registered office than the idea of a *uniform vehicle* to be used as a building block for groups of companies, in particular, of medium-sized businesses acting across the European Union.[58] The establishment and management of such a group of enterprises would be made considerably easier by a uniform legal appearance. Similar arguments are used to pursue endeavours towards an (optional) uniform European sales law regime or other (optional) genuinely Eu-

---

54 See supra (note 19).

55 In particular *Hommelhoff/Teichmann* supra (note 53), 36; *Hommelhoff* GesRZ 2008, 337, 341 et seq.

56 In further detail, *Hommelhoff* FS Roth, 2011, p. 269.

57 See *Fleischer* Informationsasymmetrie im Vertragsrecht, 2001, p. 188 et seq.

58 Emphasised in *Hommelhoff* ZHR 173 (2009), 255, 256 et seq with further references ("model which has characterised the discussion right from the start").

ropean law instruments, namely the European patent.[59] It is easy to see, and not seriously disputed, that such an (optional) uniform regime can achieve significant savings on transaction costs, even if not all legal framework conditions have been harmonised.

The existence of functional equivalents, with which critics attempt to argue that supranational legal forms are unnecessary,[60] does not alter this.[61] Those functional equivalents do not achieve the comparative cost advantages made possible by a European closed corporation. This is clear for *branches* which do not allow for efficient asset partitioning and must, therefore, be excluded as a serious alternative to a single legal form. The same holds true for the cross-border use of national legal forms (e.g. Ltd.). Although guaranteed by the TFEU's freedom of establishment, it creates frictional losses because the interaction of the foreign legal form with local law has not been adequately solved and cultural resistance may challenge these guarantees.[62]

This could only be counteracted with a more or less comprehensive *full harmonisation* of the laws on closed corporations in Europe. Apart from this being politically incapable of realisation,[63] the creation of a supranational legal form is the legally and factually preferred instrument. It leaves the participants the choice between different legal forms and does not stifle the horizontal competition of ideas. This way is predominantly viewed as preferable, not only for legal reasons (principle of subsidiarity, Art. 5 TEU), but also for economic reasons.[64] Finally, the reference to different tax laws is unhelpful. The fact that the costs of doing business in a foreign country cannot be reduced to zero does not justify not reducing them at all.

---

59 For the draft of a European Sales Law Regulation see Proposal for a Regulation of the European Parliament and the Council on a Common European Sales Law of 11.10.2011 COM (2011) 635 final; for the European Patent see REGULATION (EU) No 1257/2012 OF THE EUROPEAN PARLIAMENT AND OF THE COUNCIL of 17 December 2012 implementing enhanced cooperation in the area of the creation of unitary patent protection.

60 Supra A.II.1.

61 For a convincing assessment of the economic benefits of a SPE see Impact Assessment, supra (note 7), p. 13 et seq.

62 See *Teichmann* supra (note 4), p. 65 et seq; *Klöhn* RabelsZ 76 (2012) (English version available at ssrn.com under the title: "The case for market-mimicking supranational legal forms in Europe").

63 On the problems of full harmonisation, see *Gsell/Herresthal* (ed.), Vollharmonisierung im Privatrecht, 2009; on the proposal for a far-reaching harmonisation of the single-member corporation by a harmonised sample contract, see the recent EU Action Plan *infra* (note 30).

64 See *Schön* ZHR 160 (1996), 221, 249; more recently, *Fleischer* supra (note 6), 385, 405; from an economic point of view *Holzgräbe* Höchstrichterliche Finanzrechtsprechung (HFR) 1999, 69, 79; *Röpke/Heine* Jahrbuch für die Ordnung von Wirtschaft und Gesellschaft (ORDO) 56 (2005), p. 157, 161, 172.

As shareholders indirectly participate in these costs savings as well as consumers, no contrary interest can be seen in this context.[65] (Foreign) directors may find themselves in an unaccustomed role, for example, if they are used to particular advantages in the legal forms at home (e.g. liability restrictions) which do not exist in the supranational legal form. However, adaptations to different legal settings are generally expected of a manager in an international group. It has already been said that the freedom of establishment requires similar adjustments by the creditors of a company.[66]

Employee interests give rise to more serious problems. Whereas the legal form of the employer does not affect their employment law relationships, this does not apply to corporate codetermination. As already mentioned, codetermination has proven to be a stumbling block on the path to a supranational legal form in Europe.[67] This touches on the fundamental problem of reaching political agreement on supranational Statutes within the EU. Even if agreement exists that a uniform legal form saves transaction costs, this does not necessarily mean agreement on what the uniform law should look like.

b) Regulatory Consequences

Regarding the uniformity function (saving transaction costs) of a supranational company, the central regulatory strategy must also focus on the creation of a Statute which is *as self sufficient as possible*, i.e. independent of the respective national corporate law systems. References to national law must be avoided as far as possible. As the basic building block for a group of enterprises operating across the EU, the ECC will usually be a *single-member corporation*. This means that majority-minority conflicts do not arise, which renders the necessity for corresponding regulation obsolete and reduces the need for such regulation as between shareholders and directors. As a consequence, as far as shareholders and their relationship with the directors is concerned, the ECC as a group element can be conceded a far-reaching *degree of freedom for the articles of association* and rely on optional rather than mandatory law.

---

65 The creation of an SPE is therefore demanded by business in particular and is at least not opposed by consumer associations.

66 Supra B.I.1.

67 Supra, at note 47.

3 Summary

As a European cross-border vehicle, the supranational legal form has lost some of its importance. Once the Directive on the transfer of registered offices was passed, the mandatory need for it would fall away. On the other hand, this is no reason not to make it available as an *alternative* mobility vehicle. As such, an ECC could use its comparative advantages to the full if its regulation and would be as self sufficient as possible, but also exhibits characteristics which preserve its reputation as a "European brand". These could comprise a creditor protection regime which is stricter than those of national legal forms plus (moderate) access restrictions.

As a building block for a group of enterprises operating throughout Europe, an ECC would be more useful. Here, a self sufficient Statute would also be an advantage. As a single-member corporation, its regulation could be largely optional.

II The Modern Function: Enlargement of the Legal Forms on Offer

1 The Function

Recently, the idea of the creation of a supranational legal form to enlarge the range of legal forms and, thereby, to encourage the competition for the "best" corporate law, has come to the fore.[68] As shown in the preceding chapters, this idea is *prima facie* supported by the fact that there are often various theoretical tactics for the regulation of closed corporations, the advantages and disadvantages of which only emerge in practical experience. One might argue, that a broad range of legal forms is, therefore, desirable.[69] Not surprisingly, national corporate law systems already correspond to this idea by offering a, more or less, wide range of legal forms. This is supplemented by the option of choosing a foreign legal form as opened up by the freedom of establishment.[70] Why do we then need an additional, supranational alternative?

The question can be parried with a counter-question: Why not? Theoretically, it cannot be judged whether an ECC will be successful in the market for corporate forms and what benefit it will have for the economy, just as it is impossible to

68 For a detailed discussion see *Fleischer* supra (note 6), 385, 403 et seq, 409 et seq.

69 It is not discussed here whether the freedom of assembly (Art. 9 German Constitution, Art. 11 European Convention on Human Rights) results in the obligation to provide such a range, see *Fleischer* supra (note 6), 385, 397.

70 Supra, note 34 (*Centros* case).

judge from theory whether consumers will like a new product.[71] It is, therefore, advisable to simply create the supranational legal form and then observe its acceptance: if it is chosen, then the market has answered the demand-question positively; if it is not chosen, the Statute remains a dead but harmless law.[72] Only the costs of market introduction must be taken into account, i.e. the time, effort and expenditure (including the opportunity costs) involved in designing an ECC.[73] Since those costs have already been incurred they may be neglected.

2 Problems

We should not shy away from the question why we need a supranational Statute conceived as a mere additional alternative. If there is a legal form with a potentially high demand, there must be reasons why it is not already on offer in the Member States themselves. These reasons may contribute to the supranational form not being realised in its ideal constellation. As mentioned at the outset, the proposal submitted by the European Commission in 2008 for a SPE which, at least in part, followed the considerations developed in this book, failed. In search of an explanation, it is helpful to take a closer look at the different camps which have formed in the public debate about advantages and disadvantages of an SPE:

Entrepreneurs (including the associations which represent them) very predominantly argued, and still argue, *in favour of* the introduction of an ECC.[74] The SPE is also favoured by internationally oriented lawyers,[75] legal academics,[76] and the newer (mostly East-European) EU member states.[77] By contrast, *doubts*

---

71 A possible example is Apple's iPad. Although viewed with scepticism at its launch, it later proved to be a much-imitated market bestseller.

72 See *Bachmann* ZGR 2001, 351, 372; *Eidenmüller* JZ 2009, 641, 652; *Fleischer* supra (note 6), 385, 401 et seq; *Schön* ZHR 160 (1996), 221, 249.

73 Opportunity costs mean the welfare losses arising from legislation dealing with the European private company and thereby being prevented from tackling other projects. See, e.g., *Davies* supra (note 6), p. 479, 481.

74 Cf. the results of the consultation process "Synthesis of the Comments on the Consultation Document of the Internal Market and Services Directorate-General on a Possible Statute for a European Private Company", available under www.europeanprivatecompany.eu.

75 See DAV (German Lawyers Association), NZG 2008, 138; DAV, NZG 2009, Supplement to no. 7, p. 1.

76 See *Arbeitskreis Europäisches Unternehmensrecht* supra (note 46).

77 See *Radwan* 18 Eur. Bus. L. Rev. 769, 771 (2007); *Lamandini* 3 Eur. Co. L. 272, 274 (2006); Impact Assessment, supra (note 7), p. 6.

are voiced by (German) trade unions,[78] (German) notaries[79] and groups of those Member States which have an established, in part mandatory, law on the closed corporation.[80] If we analyse these two camps from the political economy viewpoint, they reflect the anticipated negative or positive vested interests of the participants.[81] The SPE opens up a further structural option for entrepreneurs and managers, provides large law firms with additional advisory business and gives legal academics a platform for transnational discussion. These groups have nothing to lose. The opponents fear the loss of codetermination (trade unions), of notarial business (notaries) or of possibilities for national government to influence corporate law making in a traditional way (Member States).[82]

From a welfare perspective, one might be inclined to declare the opponents' arguments irrelevant because they are determined by private (egoistic) motives, not by concern about overall economic welfare.[83] Such motives, and their influence on corporate law legislation, were, therefore, deliberately left out of consideration in the preceding chapters.[84] However, they must be included here. Whereas particular interest groups (lobbies) are able to block innovations in a single state context, they cannot prevent the creation of the limited liability legal form as such. For reasons to which we will return soon, this is different in a supranational context. The question must, therefore, be raised: whether the concern about the erosion of national standards of protection is justified and, if so, how it can be countered.

78 See Frankfurter Allgemeine Zeitung (FAZ) of 4 November 2008: "*Mitbestimmungsstreit behindert Europa-GmbH*" ["Struggle for Co-Determination blocks Euro-GmbH"].

79 See Frankfurter Allgemeine Zeitung (FAZ) of 11 March 2009: Notaries fear circumvention of the duty of notarisation; statement by the German Notaries Association of 31 July 2008; from the point of view of the German Federal Chamber of Notaries see *Bormann/König* RIW 2010, 111 et seq.

80 See supra (note 17). Critically, *Hommelhoff/Teichmann* GmbHR 2009, 36.

81 For this approach specifically for corporate law, see *Macey/Miller* 65 Tex. L. Rev. 469 (1987); *Carney* 26 J. Legal Stud. 303 (1997); *Heine* Regulierungswettbewerb im Gesellschaftsrecht, 2003, p. 167 et seq.

82 It is remarkable that objections are not only raised by Member States which have a regime that tends to be strict, but also by those with a long tradition of a liberal regime (e.g. the UK), because they too risk a loss of influence through the European legal form. For a revealing discussion, see *Davies* supra (note 6), p. 479, who does not give the SPE project a chance for this reason.

83 On the standard of overall welfare, see Chapter 2 C.I., supra.

84 This is not to say that particular interests – such as the notaries' interest in fees or the will of functionaries to retain power or structure organisation – do not play a considerable role in national legal policy.

In fact, it is not only possible, but even likely, that supranational corporate law forces national corporate law to adapt and even displaces it.[85] After all, if the European legal form is to fulfil the role of an attractive additional alternative envisaged for it, it must display characteristics perceived as positive by those choosing the legal form (i.e. the shareholders) which are *not* available in this form or at this price in the national range on offer.[86] If this is the case (because the EEC-statute, for example, waives any minimum capital requirements) it can unleash a "run" on the European legal form which forces diverging national law to adapt to the level of regulation, even if it is sub-optimal from their point of view.[87] This is not merely a theoretical assumption, as we can see from recent corporate law reforms in Europe. Forced by a "run" on the British Ltd. (made possible by the ECJ's very liberal interpretation of the freedom of establishment clause), most member states have imitated the example of the Ltd. by reducing or abolishing their minimum capital requirements.[88] In Canada too, the introduction of a federal corporate law reform quickly caused the provinces to adapt their own corporate law accordingly.[89]

It is rightly pointed out in a national context that the "protection of species" cannot be an argument against the provision of more attractive legal forms.[90] It is correct that national legislation should not allow itself to be deflected from optimising a legal form (such as the German AG) because other legal forms (such as the GmbH) would lose some of their attractiveness as a result. In a transnational context, however, things are different. Whereas national legislation (and the interest groups influencing it) can stand the loss of attraction of one of the legal forms it offers,[91] the same result at a transnational level means a politically problematic loss of control of the jurisdiction affected.

This was the reason for erecting artificial access restrictions for the SE (*numerus clausus* of the types of formation, requirement of a cross-border-element, high minimum capital). Today, their removal is increasingly demanded in the lit-

---

85 Clearly seen and articulated in the feasibility study, supra (note 7).

86 This situation must be distinguished from the one where the legal form is intended to exclusively fulfil cross-border functions. Then it can develop its advantages even if it has no original regulatory structure.

87 There is the fear of such undertow effect in favour of the SPE, see for example *Hommelhoff* GesRZ 2008, 337, 341.

88 See *Fleischer* Münchener Komm. z. GmbHG, 2010, Introduction, at 228.

89 See *Daniels* 36 McGill L.J. 130, 151 (1991): "Dramatic success".

90 *Windbichler* JZ 2008, 840, 844 (relating to the displacement of the GmbH by a deregulated AG); particularly on the SPE, see *Hügel* ZHR 173 (2009), 309, 312.

91 German liens on real estate serve as an example: as between the alternatives mortgage and land charge, the latter has *de facto* displaced the former to a large extent.

erature because unrestricted competition between national and supranational legal forms is considered desirable.[92] The EU Commission followed this path, when it presented an extremely liberal draft of an SPE Regulation, which waives all access barriers.[93] As expected, this advance was considerably weakened by the European Parliament and then blocked in Council by the Member States.

The Commission argued that the creation of the SPE leaves national corporate law "largely untouched".[94] From a purely legal point of view this is correct – but is it also true from an economic viewpoint? To answer this question, one must scrutinize the conditions under which competition between national and supranational legal forms takes place (or could take place). Neither supporters nor opponents of the SPE have done so. We will try to find some answers.

3 Pre-Conditions for Regulatory Competition

The preconditions and consequences of a so-called competition of corporate laws are now extensively discussed in Europe.[95] The discussion focuses on horizontal competition, which must be considered before we can take a look at the special features of vertical competition.

a) "Regulatory Competition"

In horizontal competition between legislatures, the different laws of the individual states compete for demand, with the federal level (Federal Republic, Union) assuming a position similar to that of an arbitrator. Two issues must be discussed:

The first is whether the *preconditions* for such competition exist in Europe. They are, apart from the existence of at least two different legislatures (suppliers), the freedom of choice by customers (demand side) plus sufficient adjust-

---

92 Speaking for many, *Casper* supra (note 45), Art. 2, 3 SE Regulation para. 3. Sceptical: *Hommelhoff* GesRZ 2008, 337, 341 et seq.

93 The draft makes no provision for minimum capital or notarisation requirements and provides only voluntary restrictions on distributions. It also permits the seat of the articles of association and the registered administrative headquarters to be in different places and leaves the issue of codetermination solely up to the country where the registered office is located.

94 According to the grounds for the proposal for an SPE Regulation, supra (note 5), fig. 5 (p. 4).Critical *Uziahu-Santcroos* supra (note 6), p. 1 et seq.

95 See only *Eidenmüller* FS Heldrich, 2005, p. 581; *Schön* 43 Common Mkt. L. Rev. 331 (2005); *Heine* supra (note 81), p. 85 et seq; *Röpke* Gläubigerschutzregime im europäischen Wettbewerb der Gesellschaftsrechte, 2007; *von Hein* Die Rezeption des US-amerikanischen Gesellschaftsrechts in Deutschland, 2008, p. 572 et seq. Generally, *Kieninger* Wettbewerb der Privatrechtsordnungen im Europäischen Binnenmarkt, 2002.

ment incentives for the supplier.[96] The freedom of choice is guaranteed at the latest since 1999, when the freedom of establishment clause (Art. 49 TFEU) was liberally interpreted by the ECJ. In accordance with it, citizens of the Member States are free to choose the corporate law form which appears most favourable to them, even if the corporation does not develop any activities in the state of formation.[97] By contrast, it was long doubted that European countries which, other than the notorious Delaware, do not depend on levying corporate tax (franchise fee) have sufficient incentive for the "customer-friendly" enactment of legal provisions.[98] In view of recent experience, this can fundamentally be affirmed.[99] The possibility opened up by the ECJ of resorting to founder-friendly foreign alterative legal forms has encouraged such demand, particularly for the British Ltd., to which competing providers of legal forms have reacted with corresponding liberalisation of their "products".[100] To be fair, there are different views on whether this is "genuine" (proactive) or merely passive (defensive) competition.[101] Nevertheless, at least some form of competition for corporate charters has evolved in Europe. How it will develop in the long run is an empirical question still to be answered.[102] It remains to be seen whether the increase in corporate formations resulting from deregulation has ultimately generated welfare advantages or not.[103]

96 See *Eidenmüller* JZ 2009, 641, 643; in detail *Kieninger* supra (note 95), p. 56 et seq.

97 See ECR 1999, I-1495 – C-212/97 (*Centros*).

98 See *Kieninger* supra (note 95); *Körber* Grundfreiheiten und Privatrecht, 2004, p. 30 et seq; *Merkt* RabelsZ 59 (1995), 545, 554 et seq; *Teichmann* supra (note 4), p. 397 et seq.

99 See *Eidenmüller* ZGR 2007, 168 et seq; *Fleischer* supra (note 88), Introduction GmbHG para. 227; *Zimmer* FS K. Schmidt, 2009, p. 1789, 1795 et seq; see also *Cheffins* Company Law, p. 435–440.

100 The fact that national legislation and the interest groups influencing it also have incentives to market their regulations even without franchise fees is illustrated in Germany by the "Bündnis für deutsches Recht" (Union for German Law), see *Gehb* DRiZ 2008, 222: "The export of law is a competition we have to face". See www.lawmadeingermany.de.

101 In the latter sense, see *von Hein* supra (note 95), p. 590; *Klöhn* supra (note 62); B*ratton/McCahery/Vermeulen* How does Corporate Mobility Affect Lawmaking?, ECGI Law Working Paper No. 91/2008 ("Responsive, not competitive lawmaking"); for a reserved view, see *Schön* 42 Common Mkt. L. Rev. 331, 343 et seq (2005). Generally on the distinction between proactive and passive regulatory competition, see *Cumming/McIntosh* 20 Int'l Rev. L. & Econ., 141, 144 et seq (2000).

102 *Eidenmüller* JZ 2009, 641, 649.

103 See *Hornuf/Eidenmüller/Engert/Braun* Does Charter Competition Foster Entrepreneurship? ECGI-Finance-Working Paper 308/2011: "While the reforms have evidently fostered the creation of new firms, we have little to say about their quality. It may be that lowering the regulatory costs of incorporations lures mostly incompetent or unproductive entrepreneurs".

More important to us is the second issue. This is the (normative) question of how the competition between legislatures is to be *evaluated*. Anyone used to considering competition as something fundamentally positive will tend to answer it in the affirmative. However, in contrast to the product market, the law market faces three fundamental problems:

The first is to find an example by which to judge whether a particular law product, here the regulation of a closed corporation, is to be considered "better" or "worse" than comparable products. If we do not wish to go round in circles, this problem cannot be "solved" by looking at the results of (hypothetical) regulatory competition.[104] Instead, an external example is required like the one described at the outset of this book: the quality of a law product is *inter alia* measured according to its welfare economic consequences. Rules which cost more than they are worth must be evaluated more negatively than those which do not.[105]

The second problem is that the selection process on the market for corporate laws may be more strongly influenced by market shortcomings than the selection process on the product market: Market failure may play a significant role. There are indications that "customers" of corporate law products (managers, founders) pay special attention to short-term advantages such as low minimum capital without including long-term (ancillary) effects of the choice of legal form in the equation.[106] In addition, it is important that third parties worthy of protection (in particular small creditors and tort creditors) do not participate in the choice of legal form (negative externality), that managers making the choice do not necessarily have the interests of shareholders or other stakeholders in mind (principal-agent conflict), that the choice of law permits cherry-picking, or that providers of corporate law end up in a ruinous downward spiral due to collective action problems ("race to the bottom").[107] Conversely, it cannot be excluded that market forces are, at least in the long term, able to heal those shortcomings. Thus, it is conceivable that the persons choosing the legal form voluntarily opt for a re-

104 See supra Chapter 2 C.I.

105 See supra Chapter 2 C.I. It is conceded that this does not permit us to determine one "right" solution.

106 Illustrated with the example of the German Ltd. boom in *Fleischer* supra (note 88), Introduction GmbHG para. 221 and 312; *Niemeier* ZIP 2007, 1794.

107 See *Eidenmüller* JZ 2009, 641, 649 et seq; *Schön* 42 Common Mkt. L. Rev. 331, 343 et seq (2005).

stricted legal form in order to win the trust of creditors, investors and customers ("signalling").[108]

The third problem, which is frequently ignored, turns on political theory. In the legal market, those permitted to choose a law product are not identical to those affected by the consequences of the product.[109] However, the identity of those choosing the law and those affected by the law constitutes the fundamental idea of democracy. Continuing with the example above, the (mandatory) provisions of the British Companies Act are democratically legitimated, but not by those who are confronted with the Ltd. outside Great Britain.[110] This circumstance becomes more explosive if both, those choosing the legal form and those affected by it, are not located in the state of formation – the classical problem of the pseudo-foreign company. This problem becomes particularly relevant where the welfare increasing effects of legal provisions cannot be ascertained or where competing values come into play, such as in the case of corporate codetermination.[111] However, even from the point of view of political theory, regulatory competition can be useful because it gives citizens a way to ward off the influences of powerful lobbies.[112] It must also be recognized that in the EU the principle of the Single Market partly overrides the idea of national democratic sovereigns.

We conclude that the welfare producing effect of regulatory competition presupposes both the removal of market imperfections and concordance with democratic principles. Therefore, as with any market, a regulating order is required that guarantees the functioning of market forces and, at the same time, defines its limits.[113] In the EU, this order consists of a complex interaction of choice-of-law rules, acts of private law harmonisation and basic freedoms (freedom of establishment, free movement of capital, etc.) which the ECJ must balance out.[114]

108 Optimistic in this sense, *Röpke* supra (note 95), p. 133 et seq, 182 et seq; in detail *G.H.Roth* ZGR 2005, 348, 376 et seq.

109 On this problem, see *Eidenmüller* JZ 2009, 641, 648; in greater detail, *Bachmann* FS Hommelhoff, 2012, p. 21, 26 et seq; ignoring this problem: *Klöhn* supra (note 62), who identifies the "citizens" choosing the law with those choosing the legal form.

110 The fact that we nevertheless accept foreign legal forms in Germany is connected to the Single Market principle and the idea of free trade increasing welfare, which may admittedly clash with the idea of national sovereignty.

111 See *Bachmann* Private Ordnung, 2006, p. 51; *Uziahu-Santcroos* supra (note 6), p. 12 et seq.

112 See *Eidenmüller* JZ 2009, 641, 648 et seq; *O'Hara/Ribstein* The Law Market, p. 21 et seq. Critically *Peters* VVDStRL 69 (2010), 7, 28.

113 This is known to be the fundamental view of the (German) ordo-liberal school, see *Eucken* Grundsätze der Wirtschaftspolitik, 6. Aufl., 1990, p. 254 et seq.

114 See *Bachmann* supra (note 111); *Grundmann* ZGR 2001, 783, 803 et seq.

Now we will turn to the issue of how the relevant order for vertical regulatory competition is structured and which conclusions must be drawn from this for the structure of an ECC.

b) Peculiarities of Vertical Regulatory Competition

Even authors who are critical of the idea of horizontal regulatory competition generally welcome the creation of supranational legal forms, because they also anticipate an enrichment of the "competition of ideas".[115] The unspoken expectation is that vertical regulatory competition will produce food for thought and possibilities for selection which national legislation cannot create, and remove the fear of a race to the bottom. But is this really true?

More detailed scrutiny shows that the special features of vertical regulatory competition have not been examined in detail either in the corporate law or private law literature.[116] Some have analysed the competitive effects of the creation of the SE.[117] However, this analysis focuses solely on competition between different national forms of SE (intra-SE competition) which is made possible by the circumstance that the SE-Regulation makes extensive reference to member state law (cf. Art. 9 SE-Regulation). It does not focus upon vertical competition between the SE and its national counterparts (AG, SA, etc.).

To gain insight into the functions of vertical regulatory competition, it may be helpful to look to the USA, where the phenomenon of the competition of corporate laws has been intensively disputed for a long time. This debate, however, deals with horizontal competition between the individual states. The issue of a competing federal corporate law form is seldom raised there. Firstly, because in the USA no federal corporate law form exists, and secondly, because the success of the Delaware corporate law form gives no rise to a call for a stimulating federal law form. Although a demand for federal corporate law is voiced now and again, the supporters of such a solution usually do not envisage an *alternative* parallel federal legal form, but rather wish to remove the perceived deficits

---

115 As an example *Kieninger* supra (note 95), p. 377 et seq, 384 and *Teichmann* supra (note 44), p. 353 et seq.

116 *Fleischer* supra (note 6), 385, 413 ("academically unenlightened"). Further-reaching approaches in *Röpke/Heine* supra (note 64); *Schön* 42 Common Mkt. L. Rev. 331, 360 et seq (2005); *Klöhn* supra (note 62); *Bachmann* supra (note 109); *Hommelhoff* GesRZ 2008, 337, 342.

117 See *Enriques* 4 J. Corp. L. Stud. 77, 84 et seq (2004). Empirically, regulatory arbitrage has, however, not to date been found within the different national sample SEs, see *Eidenmüller/Engert/Hornuf* 10 Eur. Bus. Org. L. Rev. 1, 27 (2009). A reason for this may be that a free choice of law is not possible due to the requirement of having the office and the statutory seat within the same country (Art. 7, 64 SE Regulation).

in horizontal competition by the *prerogative* of federal corporate law.[118] As some have noted, the threat of such federal provisions may have motivated states such as Delaware to make "voluntary" adaptations of their regulatory systems in individual cases.[119] This interaction, however, is not competition in the genuine sense. Few authors have expressed the idea of *optional instruments* being created at federal level in favour of which the solution offered by state corporate law can be opted out of.[120]

More helpful might be a glance at Canada. As opposed to the USA, a federal corporate law form exists that competes with the corporate law forms created by the Canadian provinces.[121] Entrepreneurs are free to choose whether to incorporate in a province or to choose the federal law form. As in Europe, corporations formed at the lower (provincial) level are free to act in the entire federal territory so that provincial and federal legal forms genuinely compete with one another. Unlike in the USA, the need for a federal legal form emerged because a market leader like Delaware did not exist. Ultimately, vertical competition has led to provincial corporate law, more or less, aligning itself with the model of federal law.[122] Whether this was intended by the federal legislation or was a spontaneous consequence of (vertical) regulatory competition is not clear.[123] In any case, it seems that Canadians have learnt to live with the vertical coexistence of corporate laws and also accept the factual predominance of the federal form.

If federal legislatures on the other side of the Atlantic are trusted practically (Canada) or theoretically (USA) to ensure attractive supplements to the individual state range of legal forms, this would appear to confirm the primarily positive evaluation of vertical regulatory competition in Europe mentioned above. This

118 See (critically) *Romano* Foundations of Corporate Law, 2nd ed., 2010, p. 117 et seq; pleading for a genuine federal corporate law form, *Dent* 35 J. Corp. L. 499 (2010).

119 On this form of vertical competition, see *von Hein* supra (note 95), p. 501 et seq; *Schön* 42 Common Mkt. L. Rev. 331, 361 (2005); *Roe* 117 Harv. L. Rev. 588 (2003); *Roe* 118 Harv. L. Rev. 2491 (2005); *Coffee* 8 Cardozo L. Rev. 759, 766 (1987).

120 See most prominently *Bebchuk/Ferrell* 87 Va. L. Rev. 111, 131 et seq (2001) (relating to takeover law); see also *Schön* 42 Common Mkt. L. Rev. 331, 362 (2005).

121 The basis of the federal corporate law form is the *Canada Business Corporations Act* of 1975. For a more detailed description see *Kieninger* supra (note 95), p. 181 et seq; most recently *Klöhn* supra (note 62).

122 See *Cumming/McIntosh* 20 Int'l Rev. L. & Econ., 141, 147, 153 (2000); *Ziegel* in: Cumming, Harmonisation of Business Law in Canada, 1986, p. 1 et seq. By contrast, Australia has waived competition between corporate laws and only granted the relevant legislative competence to the federal level, as in Germany, see *Klöhn* supra (note 62), with further references.

123 In the latter sense *Daniels* 36 McGill L.J. 130 et seq (1991); in the first sense *Cumming/McIntosh* 20 Int'l Rev. L. & Econ., 141, 158 et seq (2000).

view is supported by the fact that, due to considerable language, cultural and legal differences horizontal competition in Europe will not bring about a European Delaware in the foreseeable future.[124] Therefore, a "federal" European corporate form, as in Canada, would probably enjoy considerable popularity.

The obvious consequence would be to plead for vertical competition of the corporate law forms to be as open as possible and untouched by political disruption factors.[125] Accordingly, supply and demand would identify not only the preferable legal alternative, but also the optimal regulatory level (EU or Member States). Competition would work, in a Hayekian sense, as a discovery procedure.[126] At the same time, the European subsidiarity principle (Art. 5 EU-Treaty), according to which the upper-level legislator that can only regulate if regulation on the lower (state) levels does not work properly, would receive a new and dynamic interpretation. The proper legislative level would no longer be allocated in accordance with an abstract legal principle, but would have to be determined in market processes.[127]

This competition-friendly approach has much to recommend it in view of what we know about positive welfare effects of competition. Nevertheless, it appears to be in need of supplementation. In most models of vertical competition the institutional design of the upper-level legislator either remains a black box or is only perceived as a disruptive factor. This overlooks the fact that this design characterises the constitutional framework which every type of regulatory competition needs, as we have noted above. Therefore, we should not rest here with the acknowledgement of positive effects of competition in general, but go on to ask about the conditions under which regulation takes place at the upper (federal) legislative level. To do so, we will first *abstractly* describe the characteristics which distinguish the superior regulator in a federal system from its inferior competitors. We will then take a look at the *specific* framework conditions for legislation in the EU from which regulatory consequences can then be drawn.

Let us start with the abstract view. Amongst the specific characteristics of a federal legislature, two are particularly important: the circumstance that can act with a greater degree of freedom from *path dependency*, and a dilution of the in-

124 See, e.g., *Tröger* Choice of Jurisdiction in European Corporate Law (Working Paper 2004, available at ssrn.com), p. 64 et seq (also published in 6 EBOR 2005, 3–64).

125 So *Röpke/Heine* supra (note 64), p. 178; *Röpke/Heine* in Jahrbuch Junger Zivilrechtswissenschaftler (Jb.J.ZivRWiss) 2004, p. 265, 278; tending towards this, also *Fleischer* supra (note 6) 385, 421 et seq; *Schön* 42 Common Mkt. L. Rev. 331, 361 et seq (2005); *Klöhn* supra (note 62).

126 *Röpke/Heine* supra (note 64), p. 173; *Röpke/Heine* supra (note 125), p. 272 et seq (with reference to Hayek); *Fleischer* ZHR 174 (2010), 385, 415.

127 *Röpke/Heine* supra (note 64), p. 174 et seq; *Röpke/Heine* supra (note 125), p. 273 et seq.

fluence of local *interest groups.*[128] Independent of individual fiscal incentives, it can make use of its entire store of economic and comparative insights and possibly come closer to the ideal legal form than the lower legislative levels. In addition, in relation to horizontal competitors it has the advantage of a broader basis of legitimacy, because it is not only elected by the citizens of the state which provides the most attractive range of legal forms from the founder's point of view (which may be tiny), but by everyone potentially affected. Finally, even if its legal products are identical to those created on the lower level, they do not face the same language barriers.[129]

Upper-level law making also has several disadvantages not to be ignored. They are a reduced sense of responsibility resulting from increased distance to the parties directly affected by the laws, possible bureaucratic overzealousness and a lower capacity and sensibility for embedding the legal form in the context of national provisions.[130] Whereas the individual state must at least argue its model before the home audience and correct it in case of undesirable developments (and can easily do so), this is not guaranteed in case of the superior legislature. At the same time, the upper-level legislator has an artificial competitive advantage. Anyone deciding in favour of a foreign legal form must also take on all language, cultural and legal eventualities which are inevitably linked to such a choice of law.[131] These natural barriers are at least in part surmounted by the choice of a supranational legal form. This competitive advantage is partly balanced by the lack of positive network effects of new federal forms.[132] Once the supranational legal form has established itself and reached a "critical mass",

128 This argument is also used in the USA in favour of federal corporate law, see *Bebchuk/ Ferrell* 87 Va. L. Rev. 111, 149 et seq (2001); critically *Romano* supra (note 118).

129 This circumstance naturally plays no role in federations that do not face internal language barriers, notably in the USA. Its influence on regulatory competition, which should not be underestimated is therefore continuously neglected in US scholarship. In a European context it can be decisive: A Greek limited liability corporation, however attractively modelled, will hardly be able to succeed in the competition of corporate laws. Here, England has a natural competitive advantage since English is the mostly used language. British company forms may therefore succeed in a regulatory race even if they are less efficient than foreign forms. A European legal form might contribute to compensating this unwarranted advantage.

130 The latter problem can also affect horizontal competition in the same way.

131 This is not the case in the USA due to the homogenous nature of the states, which is why federal corporate law is less urgent there from *this* point of view.

132 *Fleischer* ZHR 174 (2010), 385, 422; *Hügel* ZHR 173 (2009), 309, 314.

this disadvantage will disappear. Positive network effects will now work in favour of the supranational form.[133]

The advantage of federal regulation which lies in its distance from the roots may, alternatively, be viewed as its decisive disadvantage. Whereas competitors in horizontal competition have the same structural strengths and weaknesses, legislatures with different incentives and capacities compete in the vertical model. For this reason, it cannot be excluded that an ambitious but inexperienced superior legislature might supply a legal form which forces lower-level legislatures to go on the defensive, although the supranational legal form is inefficient from an overall economic point of view. If the superior regulator is not in a position to then react swiftly and flexibly, a suboptimal law product may prevail.

As an *interim result*, we can say that a federal legal form could theoretically satisfy needs which the individual states are unable to fulfil for the reasons specified (language barriers, local lobby influence, path dependencies, and legitimacy deficits). On the other hand, the mere fact that the law form alternative is offered "from above" does not, in itself, guarantee that the problems of regulatory competition will disappear. Vertical competition, therefore, requires some form of constitutional framework. As the federation cannot play the role of arbitrator, since it is itself a party to the competition, the question is raised: how can federation and the individual states reciprocally influence their respective law form offers?

This question can be answered in an abstract way by attempting to formulate the conditions (meta-rules, constitution) under which regulation and regulatory competition *should* take place in federal systems.[134] This would lead us round in circles, because the modelling of the legislative procedure depends on the results expected and how they are evaluated.[135] A sensible answer would require a detailed discussion of theories of federalism and models of democracy, which would go far beyond the concept of this publication.[136] For this

133 See *Engert*, Archiv für die civilistische Praxis (AcP) 213 (2013), 321, 352 et seq; *Engert* in: Eidenmüller (ed.), Regulatory Competition in Contract Law and Dispute Resolution, 2013, p. 304 et seq.

134 Cf. *Röpke/Heine* supra (note 64), borrowing on the (competition-friendly) model of Weingast's "market-preserving federalism", see *Weingast* 11 J.L. Econ. & Org. 1 (1995); *Weingast* 21 J.L. Econ. & Org. 103 (2005).

135 Cf. *Bachmann* supra (note 111), p. 191 et seq with further references.

136 Attention would also have to be turned to other institutional arrangements which are or could be exposed to vertical competition, such as languages, social norms, currencies, etc. For a complete picture, private providers of such "products" would also have to be investigated.

reason, we restrict ourselves to a more specific perspective and focus on the conditions for law making by the EU.

c) Regulation in the EU

In the EU, the conditions of the superior legislature just described are found in the form of the *Commission*. As an institution from which the relevant regulation proposals emanate, it is more immune to local pressure groups than the lower level (i.e. member states). It does not pursue any particular or individual fiscal interests and is willing to listen to voices which garner little attention at the levels of horizontally competing legislatures.[137] Path dependencies also naturally play a lesser role at the Commission level. On the other hand, the Commission is less directly responsible to the electorate and, therefore, has a lower degree of legitimacy in relation to those affected by its proposals. In turn, it is subject to the influence of lobbies which are strong enough to be constituted at federal level. Their familiarity with the national statutory provisions environment and their capacity to make adjustments or additions is also lower.

It is therefore logical that corresponding counter-forces are integrated into the institutional structure of the EU.[138] The *European Parliament* is one of them and has higher legitimacy due to its direct election by the citizens of the European Union without owing the same duty to national interests as do the legislatures in individual states. It can influence the legislation process without being able to decide it. This role is allocated to the *Council*, which comprises representatives of the national governments and which must approve every regulation proposal.[139] If it must decide unanimously, which is the case for the creation of supranational legal forms,[140] each Member State is entitled to a veto right. If we initially leave aside the separate route of increased cooperation (Art. 326 TFEU),[141] each national legislature has the ability to slow down any vertical race it fears or make it dependent on concessions of its choice.

---

137 We therefore do not allege that the Commission would be immune to lobbying influences. However, it has no own economic interest in favouring a particular clientele (e.g. legal services providers). Global competition nevertheless creates an incentive to keep the European legal inventory attractive as a whole (see *Schön* ZHR 160 (1996), 221, 237).

138 For a detailed discussion, see *Haltern* Europarecht. Dogmatik im Kontext, 2nd ed., 2007, para. 136 et seq.

139 Transposed to Germany, the situation is comparable to that in which the *Bundesrat* (Federal Council = legislative body representing the governments of the 16 German *Länder* [states]) would be the decisive legislative organ.

140 See C.I. below.

141 See B.II.3. below at the end.

For the vertical competition, this design can have fatal consequences. Member States who see their own range of legal forms threatened "from above" will try to prevent this from the outset by using their influence in the Council.[142] Pressure to agree can arise even if there are veto rights. This stalemate puts the parties in a worse position than an agreement which may be considered suboptimal by one party.[143] This may, partially, be the case in corporate law because an attractive SPE may appear to some to be the lesser evil when compared with an attractive pseudo-foreign corporation. However, the existence of the supranational legal form is not essential for doing business at all. Things get more difficult because horizontal competition has recently caused many EU member states to modernise their laws on limited liability corporations, so that many see no need for competing supranational alternatives. The veto construction also has the disadvantage that a solution, once consented to, is just as difficult to alter or abolish, so that it threatens to become a fossil ("petrification effect"). Fearing this, the Member States which are, in principle, willing to consent to an SPE will consider very carefully whether and when they give their consent to a supranational Statute.

In view of all this, the voluntary agreement on European statutory alternatives which directly compete with those of the Member States may appear to be a miracle. Indeed, the agreement on an SE Statute reached in 2001 has been described as such. Admittedly, the "miracle" was bought by significant concessions, the most obvious of which is that the SE-Regulation has shrunk to a body which refers to national corporate law in central issues. After all we have said about the cross-border function, this "renationalisation" of the European Company was, rightly, the subject of serious complaint by supporters of a European solution. However, given that such inadequacies are pre-programmed by the European legislative procedure, complaints are unhelpful and solutions must instead be sought.

142 The Council has therefore been compared with a cartel, see *Schön* 42 Common Mkt. L. Rev. 331, 362 (2005); *Fleischer* ZHR 174 (2010), 385, 416. This comparison is inaccurate in that the Member States do not eliminate the competition between them, but merely prevent additional competition by a "joint venture". For a discussion of joint venture parallels, see *Fleischer* RabelsZ 76 (2012), 235 et seq.

143 Illustrated with the example of fishing and agricultural policy by *Haltern* supra (note 138), para. 215 – 234; generally *Eidenmüller* Unternehmenssanierung zwischen Markt und Gesetz, 1999, p. 489 et seq.

4 Regulatory Consequences

a) The EU as Provider of the "Ideal" Legal Form

An initial answer would be to simply ignore the political framework and to call upon the EU to create the "ideal" corporation as described in the preceding chapters.[144] In fact, we take the view that such a supplement would be desirable in the sense of the greatest possible freedom of choice and should, therefore, continue to be striven for. As the success of the SE shows, temporary stagnation at European level does not mean that a supranational legal form must be considered to have ultimately failed. However, as the example of the SE also teaches us, it is unlikely in view of the constitutional framework described that the SPE will be created in its "pure form". The fate of the ambitious Commission proposal evidences this.[145] If we wished to leave it at this answer, we would expose ourselves to the "Nirvana" objection: the submission of a concept which is theoretically perfect but can never be realized under the conditions of the real world.[146] The first answer, therefore, cannot be the last.

b) Reform of the European Legislative Process

A second answer could be to call for a fundamental reform of the European legislative process, namely, to plead for less influence by the Member States via the Council.[147] This would, however, entail the removal of the democratic deficits inherent in European legislation, a central problem of vertical regulatory competition in Europe.[148] Any such reform must ultimately result in transforming the EU into a federal state, something that seems illusory for the time being after the proposal for a European Constitution recently failed. For this reason, we do not choose this path, but will briefly discuss individual issues of improved legislation in the EU at the end of this chapter.

---

144 This is the proposal made by *Klöhn* supra (note 62). Klöhn admits that his proposal politically has no chance of success.

145 See Chapter 1, supra.

146 See *Richter/Furubotn* Neue Institutionenökonomik, 3rd ed., 2003, p. 549.

147 In this direction *Röpke/Heine* supra (note 64).

148 Proposals in *Bernholz/Schneider/Vaubel/Viber* Public Choice 118 (2004), 451. For a detailed discussion of the EU's democracy deficit, see *Haltern* supra (note 138), para. 259 et seq; particularly in the context of vertical regulatory competition, see *Bachmann* supra (note 109).

c) Alternatives to the SPE

The third way is to accept the existing constitutional restrictions as given and to search for possibilities to realise an ECC within these boundaries. This is a regulatory challenge, since the supranational Statute must be attractive enough to be chosen by law customers, but not to give rise to fears of complete displacement by the Member States. Compromise solutions and artificial access restrictions can be useful techniques here. We will discuss them in further detail below (C.). A different strategy is the search for alternative regulatory instruments to realise an ECC in a less invasive way.[149] Such alternatives will be briefly examined here:

The first consideration would be to abandon the idea of an SPE Statute which fulfils *all* possible functions and is applicable in all Member States.[150] Instead, *several* SPEs could be created, one of which, for example, would be suitable for a cross-border (single-member) group, whereas another could be a general purpose vehicle alongside the national limited liability corporations.

Alternatively, the range of application of an SPE-Regulation could be reduced to those Member States able to agree on a uniform Statute. The EU allows for this strategy by way of "*increased cooperation*" (Art. 326 TFEU), which is also taken into consideration for other supranational regulatory alternatives, such as the Common Consolidated Corporate Tax Base (CCCTB), and has recently been used for implementing the European Patent.[151] Although it is only conceived of as a "last resort" (Art. 20(2) EU), the ECJ exercises judicial self-restraint and respects the discretion of the Council in deciding on this precondition.[152]

In addition, the possibility of establishing a European model of the closed corporation, not by a directly applicable regulation, but with other instruments, must be pointed out.[153]A *Directive* could first be considered, which can be passed by the Council with a majority and is therefore easier to realise. A recent proposal to establish a "simplified single-member company template" was made particularly for the single-member corporation, which will probably be the chief case of application of an SPE in the European group of companies.[154] This would certainly be an advantage when compared to the previous situation. However, this

---

149 See the Impact Assessment, supra (note 7), p. 13 et seq, 37 et seq (discarding alternatives).
150 The EU Commission has already abandoned the idea of liberalising the SE Statute and *thereby* satisfying the need for an SPE, see *Uziahu-Santcroos* supra (note 6), p. 19 et seq; see also Impact Assessment, supra (note 7), p. 17.
151 See ECJ judgment of April 16, 2013, C-274/11, C-295/11.
152 ECJ, ibid.
153 See in particular *Uziahu-Santcroos* supra (note 6), p. 16–27.
154 *Reflection Group on the Future of EU-Company Law* supra (note 32), p. 66 et seq.

would not create a truly independent legal form.[155] This proposal also has no answers to the "hot questions" surrounding the SPE (minimum capital, real-seat-doctrine, notarisation obligations, and employee codetermination). Ultimately, there is no difference when compared to an SPE which relies on option solutions for these contentious issues and refers to national law to close the gaps.[156]

Finally, "softer" instruments of law adjustment come into consideration as alternatives. The so-called *open method of specific statutory provisions* is conceivable here, which aims at the establishment of "best practice" across the European Union.[157] If only the "European brand" is desired, *certification* could be an alternative.[158] In addition, the possibility of a *recommendation* directed at the Member States or a *model law* is also under discussion.[159] This can also produce innovative effects, as illustrated by the success of various model statutes of the United Nations (UNCITRAL).[160]

The advantage of these instruments is that they leave the sovereignty of the Member States largely untouched. The negative side is that the Member States can completely prevent their citizens from access to the range of models (by not implementing them). To the extent to which an international model has established itself as "best practice", it will be increasingly difficult for stubborn states to withhold this standard from their citizens. If there is free choice of law, the parties affected also have the possibility to choose another legal system which has implemented the model, and thereby initiate horizontal competitive pressure. Nevertheless, soft regulatory instruments can, at best, constitute a second best solution, nor do they replace an independent European legal form directly available to entrepreneurs.

5 Summary

Theoretical considerations and practical experience show that supranational legal forms can be a welcome enrichment of the law market. When compared with the alternatives, centralised standardisation and horizontal competition, the federal supplementary alternatives prove to be an elegant third way. However, the condi-

155 See de *Kluiver* 3 Eur. Co. L. 112 et seq (2008); *Uziahu-Santcroos* supra (note 6), p. 25 et seq.
156 See C.III. and IV. below.
157 See *Fleischer* ZGR 2012, 160 et seq.
158 *Uziahu-Santcroos* supra (note 6), p. 20 et seq.
159 Considered by *Sandberg/Skog* Die Aktiengesellschaft (AG) 2010, 580, 583 and *Uziahu-Santcroos* supra (note 6) , p. 24 et seq, both with reference to the model law project of *Baums/Krüger Andersen* (See supra Chapter 1 note 3).
160 Documented under www.uncitral.org.

tions under which vertical regulatory competition develops are difficult and have been mostly neglected in the discussion so far. Closer scrutiny shows that an upper-level regulator has strengths as well as weaknesses when compared to its lower-level competitors. In order to compensate for the weaknesses, the EU federal system leaves the decision about "when" and "how" of vertical competition in the hands of the competitors (Member States). This may be regrettable, but must be accepted as political fact. There are various strategies to overcome resistance from individual states and simultaneously counter potential deficits of the federal alternatives. These include artificial access barriers as well as compromise or option solutions and a restricted sphere of application.

III Other Functions

Other functions that an ECC might fulfil overlap with those already discussed in detail. Therefore, they will only be briefly touched on here:

An ECC Statute may provide a *stimulus* for national corporate law legislation and for scholarly discussion. Both gain new illustrative material and a platform for discussion. Although academic curiosity is not enough to justify the creation of a supranational legal form, it is a welcome side-effect.

The idea of a *European brand*, which was the reason for choosing the SE for many corporations, is becoming more important not only in a cross-border context. Even a corporation which is only active in one country may be interested in giving itself a European touch. However, the risk of abuse which may be associated with such a touch must be pointed out here and may, in turn, be a reason for access restrictions.[161]

Finally, an efficient supranational corporate form may not only benefit individual corporations in Europe, but also the *European economy* as a whole. This insight becomes important when we discuss the power to legislate.[162]

IV Interim Result

The question raised at the outset about the added value of an ECC must be answered in the positive. Although it has lost its exclusive status as an instrument for crossing borders, it is still a possibly attractive alternative to cross-border

161 See C.II. below.
162 See C.I. below.

mergers. It also promises efficiency benefits as a uniform element of groups operating across the European Union and as an innovative vehicle which supplements the existing range of legal forms available at Member State level.

Despite these obvious advantages, the creation of an SPE has proven extremely difficult in political reality. In its cross-border function, it is primarily reliant on a self-sufficient Statute for which unanimous consent necessary in the Council, as for the SE, cannot be achieved.[163] As an innovative optional instrument, it provokes fears in the Member States that their own legal forms will fall into disuse. Viewed in this light, the attempt by the EU-Commission to create an ECC which fulfils all possible functions at the same time was doomed in the first place. If we do not wish to completely abandon the idea of an ECC,[164] the political hurdles must be accepted and the techniques to deal with them must be discussed.

C Specific Problems of European Corporate Law Forms

In the preceding Chapters (§§ 2–6), it could automatically be assumed that the respective legislature is legally and factually able to create a closed corporation. It could also be assumed that institutions, such as courts, are in place that can interpret, complete, or adapt the relevant statutory provisions as and when required. With regard to a supranational European company, things are different. After having discussed the features of European law making in a more abstract way, we now turn to specific problems of creating an ECC.

I Regulatory Competence

1 Competence Entitlement

Federal systems are characterised by constitutional norms allocating the powers to legislate either to the upper (federal) or to the lower (member state) level.[165] The same holds true for the EU. According to the "principle of conferral" (Art. 5 para. 1 TEU), the EU can only legislate where legislative powers have been explicitly conferred upon it by the treaties (TEU and TFEU). Regarding

163 From an insider's point of view: *Neye* FS Hüffer, p. 717 (on resistance to the Commission's proposal); *Sandberg/Skog* AG 2010, 580 (on the failure of the Swedish compromise proposal).
164 See references, supra (note 6).
165 For a market model of allocating regulatory powers in federal systems see *Röpke/Heine* supra (note 64).

the creation of an ECC, two entitlements might be relevant: on the one hand Art. 114 TFEU, which permits measures for the approximation of such provisions "which have as their object the establishment and functioning of the internal market" with a qualified Council majority, and on the other hand, the so-called rounding-off competence in Art. 352 TFEU, which, as a catch-all clause, requires unanimity in the Council.[166]

There are good reasons for seeing Art. 114 TFEU as the suitable basis of competence.[167] However, after the existing supranational corporate forms (SE, SCE, EEIG) were all based on Art. 352 TFEU, and after the ECJ has explicitly acknowledged this,[168] the issue has practically been settled. Consequently, the current proposal for an SPE-Regulation is also based on Art. 352 TFEU. As a result, every Member State has the power to veto the creation of an ECC. Due to its own constitution, Germany must make use of its veto right unless a two-thirds majority resolution empowering its consent in the Council has been passed by the *Bundestag* and the *Bundesrat*.[169] In view of the sharp criticism of the Commission's liberal SPE draft by the German *Bundesrat*,[170] this has probably sealed its fate. An SPE-Statute with German participation can only be realised as a compromise solution, if at all.[171]

2 Principle of subsidiarity

Another problem is the barrier created by the subsidiarity principle (Art. 5(3) EU). According to this principle, the EU may only act in areas which do not fall within its exclusive competence if the objectives of the measures "cannot be sufficiently achieved" by the Member States (negative test), but can, by reason

166 Art. 352 TFEU reads: "If action by the Union should prove necessary (...) to attain one of the objectives set out in the Treaties, and the Treaties have not provided the necessary powers, the Council, acting unanimously on a proposal from the Commission and after obtaining the consent of the European Parliament, shall adopt the appropriate measures".

167 See *Müller-Graff* in: Hommelhoff/Helms, Neue Wege in die Europäische Privatgesellschaft, 2001, p. 289, 295 et seq. The proposal for a Common European sales law (supra, note 59) is based on Art. 114 TFEU. Critics claim that it must be rather based on Art. 352 TFEU.

168 See ECJ, EuZW 2006, 380 – C-436/03 (*SCE*).

169 See Section 8 *Integrationsverantwortungsgesetz*. According to the case-law of the German Federal Constitutional Court, this requirement results from the German Constitution, see Entscheidungen des Bundesverfassungsgerichts (BVerfGE) 123, 267 (Treaty of Lisbon), para. 328 and 417; for a critical view of this, see *Fleischer* ZHR 174 (2010), 384, 400 ("overlooked consequences for European corporate law").

170 Supra (note 9).

171 See *infra* C.II. and III.

of their scope or their effects, be "better" achieved at the Union level (positive test). Some argue that this is the case here since the Member States are not in a position to create a supranational legal form at all.[172] This could be countered by the argument that the abstract character of supranationality as such is not important (which can really only be created at EU level), but rather the *functions* of which the supranational vehicle is capable. The European Commission, therefore, applies a so-called added value test when examining the subsidiarity principle.[173] In this context, it is important to distinguish between the different functions an ECC may fulfil.

Regarding the cross-border function of an ECC, it is easy to see its added value. Some argue that there is no need for an ECC since the freedom of establishment allows for the cross-border use of national forms.[174] As already mentioned, this is not convincing.[175] In regard to the function of extending the choice of corporate forms available, the question is more difficult. Even authors who are principally open to the idea of an ECC are doubtful here.[176] In order to accord due weight to the subsidiarity principle, they demand the inclusion of a *transnational element* in the Statute to prevent the ECC to directly compete with national closed corporations. This may be advisable from a political point of view,[177] but it does not appear mandatory from a legal perspective.[178]

Whilst commentaries on Art. 5(3) TEU repeatedly refer to "transnational aspects" which the measure in question must display,[179] this does not mean that European optional uniform law must necessarily be restricted to cross-border transactions.[180] There are several arguments against this: firstly, the protective function of Art. 5(3) TEU loses importance where the Member States are entitled to a veto right, because they are then themselves able to resist centralistic pre-

---

172 See *Schön* ZGR 1995, 1, 25, 28: "per definitionem" not to be realised by means of national law.

173 See *Calliess* in: Calliess/Ruffert, EUV/AEUV, 4th ed., 2011, Art. 5 TEU para. 40.

174 E.g. *Bloemarts* 3 Eur. Co. L. 265 (2006).

175 See B.I. above.

176 See *Müller-Graff* Europäisches Währungssystem 7/2008 (Editorial); *Dorresteijn/Uziahu-Santcroos* 5 Eur. Co. L. 277, 279 et seq (2008); *Dorresteijn/Uziahu-Santcroos* 6 Eur. Co. L. 152, 154 et seq (2009); *Hommelhoff/Teichmann* GmbHR 2008, 897, 900.

177 See C.II. below.

178 *Fleischer* ZHR 174 (2010), 385, 421; *Hügel* ZHR 173 (2009), 309, 319 et seq.

179 See *Calliess* supra (note 173), Art. 5 TEU para. 34, 38.

180 See *Schön* ZGR 1995, 1, 25 et seq. However, the proposed framework for a Common European law of sale does this, see Proposal for a Common European Sales Law, supra, note 59, at p. 13 and p. 28 (Art. 4; see also Art. 13).

tentions of the Commission.[181] As already mentioned, such a veto right is conferred within the framework of Art. 352 TEU. Secondly, Art. 5(3) TEU was drafted in the light of *alternative* legislative competences. As the Member States lose their law making competence where the Union has made use of it (see Art. 2(2) TFEU), it is plausible to control the EU's desire for competence by a strictly understood subsidiarity principle. However, if, as here, only the creation of an *additional* law form offer is at stake, the subsidiarity principle can and must be interpreted more generously. The Member States are not robbed of their corporate law competence, but are merely exposed to competition which, in any case, exists at a horizontal level by virtue of primary law (freedom of establishment).[182]

A further aspect is often overlooked in the discussion: the existence of an attractive ECC not only encourages the activities of European corporations within the Single Market but also strengthens their competitiveness *outside the Single Market.*[183] It is noteworthy that the EU has explicitly declared the strengthening of such competitiveness as one of their objectives: In order to guarantee the competitiveness of its industry, the EU must endeavour to create a "favourable environment" for the initiative and further development and cooperation in particular of small and medium-sized enterprises (Art. 173(1) sentence 2 TFEU). This mission becomes increasingly important if we consider that, in spite of the freedom of choice of law guaranteed by the freedom of establishment (Art. 49 TFEU), the European industry has no "Delaware" available to it, which makes the advantages of a uniform corporate form even more obvious. All this argues in favour of giving the EU the competence to create a closed corporation even if its formation is not made conditional on a strict multi-state principle.

---

181 See *Schön* ZGR 1995, 1, 24 et seq: "Whether a European legal form is desirable does not turn on Art. 3b(2) EC Treaty (now: Art. 5(3) TEU), but is decided on the legal basis of the Community organs."

182 See supra, at note 34–36 (referring to ECJ case law).

183 Correctly acknowledged by *Drury* 3 Eur. Co. L. 267 (2006): "It is just as important to consider the relevance of a possible European Private Company to trade flows outside the EU and the competitive position of the EU in the world markets".

II Access Restrictions

1 Necessity of Access Restrictions?

In principle, a closed corporation should be open to all interested parties for all purposes.[184] "Artificial" access barriers limiting the use of an ECC to certain purposes or certain persons restrict the freedom of choice and, therefore, require justification. Such justification can be undertaken with legal, economic or political arguments. *In legal terms* access barriers are, above all, justified with competence considerations, which is hardly convincing for the reasons already specified.[185] From an *economic* point of view, access restrictions are a double-edged sword. They may help to guarantee that an ECC is not formed or used for questionable purposes and thus guard the reputation of the supranational legal form.[186] However, they also block the preferential choice of entrepreneurs and prevent positive network effects from arising. Depending on how much we trust vertical competition,[187] access barriers can be more or less useful. Access restrictions can also be advisable for *political* reasons if the necessary unanimity in the Council can only be achieved in this way.

2 Models for Access Restriction

In view of the economic ambivalence, access restrictions should be structured so that they do not constitute a serious hurdle for the respectable entrepreneur. Were this otherwise, very few, or none at all, would choose the supranational legal form. A *numerus clausus* of the formation form appears less suitable because it would hamper the use of the supranational closed corporation as a group vehicle and, thus, one of its main functions.[188] The same rule applies to *purpose restrictions.* Neither is present in the current drafts of an SPE Statute.

The requirement of a *transnational component* appears more open to debate. If the corporation is intended for use as a cross-border vehicle,[189] fulfilment of this requirement usually harbours no difficulties. The repertoire of conceivable

184 Section 1 of the German GmbH-Gesetz is paradigmatic: "Corporations with limited liability can (...) be established for any legal purpose by one or more persons."

185 Supra C.I.

186 Supra, at note 52.

187 Supra B.II.

188 A numerus clausus of formation forms is characteristic for the SE, which cannot be formed "from the scratch" but only by transforming or merging already existing companies into an SE, or by forming a joint venture or a holding company, cf. Art. 2 SE-Regulation.

189 Supra B.I.

solutions is broad and cannot be debated in detail here.[190] We need only point to solutions which appear unsuitable from this point of view. Demands for the presence of shareholders from several Member States should no longer be made. This would prevent the formation of a single-member corporation and prevent the group operating throughout the European Union from running its subsidiary at home as an SPE.[191] The requirement that cross-border activity must have already taken place is also doubtful, because the closed corporation often serves as a legal form for start-ups whose (cross-border) activities are just being established. Finally, the "punishment"of mandatory transformation into a national legal form in case the transnational element is no longer fulfilled seems impractical.[192] By contrast, it appears acceptable to require that there be the intention of cross-border activity at the time of formation or a cross-border object of the enterprise let this be sufficient.[193] It, admittedly, makes clear a central problem of any requirement of transnational elements: it is easy to circumvent and difficult to enforce. For precisely this reason, its abolition is advocated for the SE.[194]

Overall, the reasons against artificial access hurdles predominate. If we want an ECC at all, we must allow it to form a sufficient "critical mass". At best, therefore, (moderate) access hurdles could be considered for an initial phase, until the SPE has established itself as a trustworthy corporate form. In view of the special role which reputation plays for the European legal form, elements of creditor protection in the form of a (moderate) minimum capital or a binding solvency test are conceivable.[195]

---

190 For a list of several solutions see *Hommelhoff* GesRZ 2008, 337, 345 (cross-border object of the enterprise, members residing in different countries, place of registration and business headquarters in different countries, discrepancy between the place of the registered office and the registered office of at least one significant participating shareholder). For specific formulation proposals see DAV (German Lawyer's Association), NZG-Beil. 7/2008, para. 12; Arbeitskreis Europäisches Unternehmensrecht (AKEur), NZG 2008, 897, 899 no. 20. See also the proposal of the European Parliament (Art. 3(1) ea) Draft SPE Regulation EP, Art. 3(1) ea) Draft SPE Regulation EP and the Swedish compromise proposal (Art. 3(3) Draft SPE Regulation), which, however, only requires the cross-border element "at the time of registration".

191 See *Fleischer* ZHR 174 (2010), 385, 422; *Hügel* ZHR 174 (2010), 309, 314.

192 According to the proposal of the European Parliament, see Art. 9(3) Draft SPE Regulation EP, available under www.europeanprivatecompany.eu. Rejected by *Fleischer* ZHR 174 (2010), 385, 423.

193 According to the Swedish compromise proposal, supra (note 50).

194 See *Arbeitskreis Aktien- und Kapitalmarktrecht* ZIP 2009, 698 = 10 Eur. Bus. Org. L. Rev. 285 (2009); *Casper* ZHR 173 (2009), 181, 189 et seq (on the SE); on the SPE, see *Hügel* ZHR 173 (2009), 309, 316 et seq; Impact Assessment, supra (note 7), p. 25 et seq. Arguing in the opposite direction *Bachmann* ZEuP 2008, 32, 53; *Fleischer* ZHR 174 (2010), 385, 423.

195 See supra (reputation) and *infra* (creditor protection).

III Compromise Solutions

1 Pressure to Compromise

As regards content, a supranational Statute is not intended to take a deliberately experimental direction. Instead it should orient itself towards the welfare economics optimum.[196] Guiding lines for this have been offered in the preceding Chapters, to which reference can be made here. However, we again face the political problem of the required Council unanimity. When trying to work out common legal standards, Member States orientate themselves less towards functional criteria, and more towards the reference point of their own law. This makes it hard to reach agreement. As the history of European corporate law shows, overambitious projects are doomed to fail. In order to surmount this difficulty, the use of certain regulatory techniques is helpful, which have become particularly characteristic of European corporate law in general and the European supranational legal forms in particular.[197]

2 Compromise Techniques

It is *not* advisable to *cumulatively* adopt national models, for example to concentrate all creditor protection elements to be found in the different laws on limited liability corporations. This would produce a regulatory monster that neither entrepreneurs nor lawmakers would find attractive. Instead, it could be advisable to concede to the supranational legal form all options which the individual legal systems grant their own closed corporations in the sense of a *most-favoured-nation* clause.[198] However, whether such a model, theoretically attractive as it might be, has the capacity for realisation, seems doubtful. Apart from this, such a solution would lead to legal uncertainties which are disadvantageous in particular to a supranational legal form whose success heavily depends on legal certainty.

A classical compromise route would, in contrast, be a meeting in the middle. An example of this is the proposal made for the SPE of providing for a minimum capital at a level (specifically: EUR 8,000) in between the figures binding in the

---

196 *Eidenmüller* JZ 2009, 641, 652; *Klöhn* supra (note 62); on a substantive level, also Impact Assessment, supra (note 7), p. 20–35, where the different regulatory options are investigated with regard to the five criteria of standardisation, flexibility, legal certainty, effectiveness and political acceptability. The Commission obviously underestimated the significance of the last criterion, as the subsequent fate of its draft shows.

197 See *Fleischer* ZHR 174 (2010), 385, 406 et seq.

198 Considered for the SE (but ultimately abandoned) by *Kiem* Corp. Fin. L. 2011, 134, 144.

individual Member States.[199] However, this route cannot be taken if, as so often occurs, no "middle" can be found. In such cases, the right approach may be a "mixed" Statute which reflects the regulatory traditions of all Member States. The *Forum Europaeum Konzernrecht* – a transnational group of corporate law scholars chose such a strategy, thus trying to pave the way for harmonised law for groups of companies ("*Konzernrecht*").[200] For instance, they wanted to combine the French *Rozenblum*-doctrine with the German concept of "control agreement" and the British rule of "wrongful trading". This proposal, however, met with some interest from legal scholars but not in the political arena. Apart from this, it seems questionable whether individual elements of national legal systems can really be smoothly implanted into a supranational creation.[201] A "patchwork" ECC does not, after all, seem to be the ideal solution.

The use of *option models* would appear more promising.[202] This not only helped the European Takeover Directive, but ultimately also the SE to achieve a breakthrough. Examples are the options existing for the SE being able to choose between one-tier and two-tier board structure (cf. Art. 38b SE Regulation) and being able to replace the statutory codetermination regulation by a negotiated model (Council Directive 2001/86/EC of 8 October 2001 supplementing the Statute for a European company with regard to the involvement of employees). This regulatory technique is also found in the existing SPE proposals in various forms.[203]

Whereas such option techniques force the shareholders to make a choice, it is alternatively conceivable that the Member States could be left with a choice between different structural options (or to combine both ways). This route is also mentioned in the proposals for an SPE Statute, with regard to establishing minimum share capital.[204] The extent to which the member states make divergent use of this causes the uniform nature of the legal form model and, thereby, a major advantage of the supranational legal form, to be lost. However, the innovative character of the remaining body of the Statute can be retained. Although this may not be the ideal way, it is better than waiving the European

199 According to the Swedish compromise proposal, supra (note 50).

200 Forum Europaeum Konzernrecht, ZGR 1998, 672 et seq; for a critical account see *Windbichler* 1 Eur. Bus. Org. L. Rev. 265 (2000).

201 For a discussion of "legal transplants" from a German point of view see *Fleischer* NZG 2004, 1129 et seq.

202 *Fleischer* ZHR 174 (2010), 385, 406 et seq, 407; and generally above, Chapter 2 C.

203 The European Parliament, e.g., proposed to give founders of an SPE the choice between a minimum share capital or a solvency test, see 16(4) Draft SPE Regulation.

204 According to the Swedish compromise proposal, supra (note 50).

legal form altogether. It should be added that though Member States make use of options granted do them for the sake of compromise, they cannot be resented for doing so.[205]

The same applies to the technique of referring to national corporate law on issues which are not capable of consensus (*reference model*). This route is also a doubled-edged sword,[206] but, again, better than nothing.[207] Furthermore, the creation of not one, but several SPEs could be considered in order to do justice to the different functions and their sometimes incompatible requirements. For instance, it may be advisable to create a special Statute particularly for the single-member group subsidiary.[208] As this imposes lower regulatory requirements, agreement may be easier to achieve here.

Paving the way for the SPE by first *harmonising* major parts of the national limited liability corporation laws appears less advisable to us.[209] Apart from such harmonisation, in spite of the majority principle which applies to it, being even more illusory than agreement on a supplementary European limited liability corporation model, it would also give away precisely the advantages which characterise the supranational legal form as a regulatory alternative in relation to the standardisation of laws.[210]

3 Compromise Items

Certain items have emerged as recurring points of dispute in the discussion about the creation of European corporate forms and are, therefore, typical candidates for compromise solutions. They include the issue of minimum share capital, formation formalities, the scope of freedom of the articles of association, workers codetermination, the board structure and the choice of a registered office. These points could be clarified for the SE by agreeing on option models as was the case in relation to codetermination, the board structure and, in some cases, the formation formalities. In other points, the Member States agreed

205 See *Hopt* in: Hommelhoff/Hopt/von Werder, Handbuch Corporate Governance, 2nd ed., 2009, p. 59: "It is thoroughly normal that the Member States which have option rights make use of them. This is not necessarily (...) based in protectionist grounds, but can be based on (...) taking into consideration path dependencies (...)".

206 For more detail, see C.II.

207 See *Hügel* ZHR 173 (2009); 309, 346: "Filling gaps with national law is better than not filling gaps at all".

208 See *Hügel* ZHR 173 (2009), 309, 334 et seq.

209 Considered, for instance, by *Sandberg/Skog* AG 2010, 580, 583.

210 See B.I.2.a) above.

on a strict regime[211] which was, however, subject to the reservation of subsequent review (as regards the mainly mandatory character of the Regulation and the limited choice of registered office (real-seat-doctrine), see Art. 69 SE Regulation). In some cases, rules could be adopted which had already been harmonised by Directives and were, therefore, less prone to dispute (as regards the raising of share capital and in some cases forms of formation).

Finding a compromise has proved more difficult for the SPE. Here too the desire was to use the tried and tested technique of option models for the points specified. However, codetermination proved to be a point of contention once again. The German negotiators have accepted none of the compromise proposals presented to date. This is probably because an increasing number of German corporations use the options opened up to them by European law (SE, cross-border merger, *Centros* case-law) in order to escape the strict scheme of German codetermination law, a fact that particularly angers German trade unions. There is still no political consensus in sight.[212]

Agreement on *minimum share capital* is difficult, because, other than in relation to stock corporations, there is no corresponding harmonisation for the closed corporation. However, an optional model is starting to look like a solution capable of consensus. The Member States would then be free to stipulate a moderate level of minimum capital for corporations in their jurisdictions.[213] Willingness to compromise will probably be encouraged by the circumstance that various Member States have already moved on to optional minimum capital for their own legal forms. The option solution also leads the way with *formation formalities*. The idea here is to leave it up to registration states whether they ask for compulsory notarisation of the Articles of Association or not.[214]

More open is the fate of the so called real-seat-doctrine, according to which *registered office and head office* of a corporation must be in the same place, as is the case with the SE (see Art. 7 SE Regulation). The compromise proposal made for the SPE provides to stipulate this during the initial starting period of the Regulation, yet it has not met with undivided consent among the Member States. If the SPE Statute makes auxiliary reference to national law (as it does), the package of registered office and head office can make the establishment of a uniform group across Europe more difficult and block horizontal regulatory competition. On the other hand, it places national corporate law (applicable in an auxiliary

211 A strict regime is taken here to mean a regime which provides for comparatively high access hurdles and more mandatory law intended to protect minorities or third parties.

212 New compromise proposals in *Hommelhoff* ZeuP 2011, 7.

213 According to the Swedish compromise proposal, supra (note 50).

214 According to the Swedish compromise proposal, supra (note 50).

way) and the Insolvency Statute on an equal footing (see Art. 3, 4 European Insolvency Regulation), making it easier for the creditors to investigate the insolvency Statute *ex ante* with legal certainty and to assess its risks.[215] In view of this ambivalence, the real-seat-doctrine may be acceptable, at least for a transitional period.

IV Filling Gaps and Specific Regulation by Legal Provisions

1 The Problem of Gaps

Due to the difficulty to find compromises, a European (supranational) Statute will remain in need of supplement even in cases where national law typically provides answers. For the SE, this problem was solved by excessive reference to national stock corporation law. Whereas some see this as the key to the SPE as well,[216] others continue to call for an autonomous European solution.[217] There is probably agreement that a very detailed Statute like those common in national laws will initially remain utopian in view of the regulatory conditions described. Central tasks, therefore, include the search for suitable techniques to close gaps.

2 Techniques for Closing Gaps

For the analysis, it is helpful to distinguish between external and internal gaps along the lines of the nomenclature of the international law on the sale of goods.[218]

a) External Gaps

Externals gaps affect issues which are not covered by a Statute at the outset because they belong to other branches of the law, such as insolvency law or tort law. The problem of defining and filling such external gaps is not specific to supranational legal forms, but is familiar from international corporate law (choice of law). The regulatory task is to define the area covered by a statute as precisely as possible and synchronise it with other European regulations (e.g. Council

---

215 See *Casper/Weller* NZG 2009, 681, 682; *Veil* Kölner Komm. z. AktG, 3rd ed., 2011, Art. 7 SE Regulation para. 10.

216 E.g. *Hügel* ZHR 173 (2009), 309, 347.

217 E.g. *Bücker* ZHR 173 (2009), 281, 287.

218 See only *Schlechtriem/Ferrari* CISG, 3rd ed., 2000, Art. 7 para. 41.

Regulation (EC) No. 1346/2000 of 29 May, 2000 on insolvency proceedings). This may sound simple, but it harbours challenges which are often underestimated.[219] For every national statute is embedded in an existing environment of regulations and institutions and aligned to this. A legal form ripped out of this framework – like a corporation operating abroad and being subject to, say, foreign tort law, suffers from threatening latent over- or under-regulation. The same holds true for "artificial" supranational legal forms. However, as these are not genuine issues of the ECC, we cannot go into greater detail here, but must instead refer to the rich body of literature on conflict of laws.

b) Internal Gaps

We should look somewhat more closely at the gaps arising *within* the regulatory scope of a possible SPE-Statute. Those are gaps which, although of a corporate law nature, have not been explicitly answered in the statute, either because the legislator has not thought about them, or, more likely in a supranational context, due to the lack of political consensus.

The SPE Draft of the EU Commission presents an interesting technique for closing internal gaps by applying so-called *mandates to regulate* ("*Regelungsauftrag*"). According to this draft, issues requiring regulation are not answered by the Statute, but shareholders are instructed to find a solution themselves and set them out in the Articles of Association. For example, the draft SPE Regulation does not regulate whether the SPE is required to establish reserves but obligates shareholders to do so.

The charm of this solution is that member states do not have to agree on a compromise, nor do they have to resort to national law.[220] On the other hand, mandates to regulate produce legal uncertainty, because the parties risk making faulty, unclear or incomplete regulations, especially if they act without legal advice.[221] In this case, there must be a default regime if the corporation has already been registered and started business, because dissolution no longer seems a reasonable sanction.[222] Also, mandates to regulate force the parties to incur transac-

---

219 See *Engert* ZVglRWiss 104 (2005), 444 et seq.

220 *Bachmann* supra (note 111), p. 375 et seq, *Fleischer* ZHR 168 (2004), 673, 696 and supra, Chapter 2 B.III.3.d).

221 This shows that the choice of regulatory technique (to close a gap here) can prejudice the choice of other techniques (such as the use of preventative advice and control duties).

222 This is also the proposal of the European Parliament, see Art. 43a Draft SPE Regulation EP. The Commission's draft does not satisfactorily solve the problem. For preventative control, see Arbeitskreis Europarecht (AKEur), NZG 2008, 897, 898, fig. 13.

tion costs where the economic value of private ordering is doubtful.[223] This is the case where the statute calls upon the parties to regulate an issue, although they do not see a need for such regulation. For these reasons, the Commission Draft, which relies extensively on mandates to regulate, has rightly been criticised.

As an alternative, *sample Articles of Association* have been proposed.[224] According to this solution, shareholders would be able to simply refer to the sample articles provided by the European legislator. National legislation increasingly resorts to this technique too.[225] At first sight, it appears to remove the disadvantages of mandates to regulate. However, upon closer inspection, sample Articles of Association are just a variation of optional law. This becomes obvious if the application of the sample articles of association does not have to be explicitly agreed (opt-in solution), but instead applies automatically if the parties do not agree otherwise (opt-out solution).[226] As with optional law, the problem of the need for political consensus arises here. In order to avoid this, the sample must be kept lean, which in turn requires the use of additional techniques for closing gaps. A way out might be delegating the drafting of the sample articles of association to a body which can reach consensus more easily than the European legislature (such as a private body of legal experts).[227] This, in turn, raises fundamental legitimacy problems which may not be easily swept aside.[228] In summary, sample Articles of Association are not an ideal solution. Apart from this, like the mandate to regulate, they only come into consideration for matters for which private autonomy can be granted at all, i.e. they are of limited use if third party interests are affected.

223 Also critical for this reason DAV (German Lawyer's Association), NZG-Beil. 7/2009 para. 27 ("threatens the aim of a cost-effective legal form"); *Hadding/Kießling* WM 2009, 145, 153 ("makes every formation complicated and expensive").

224 According to the proposal of the European Parliament, see Art. 8(2) and Art. 43a Draft SPE Regulation EP; likewise Arbeitskreis Europarecht (AKEur), NZG 2008, 897, 898, fig. 14; *J. Schmidt* EMS 2008, 455, 456; from the viewpoint of advisory practice *Bücker* ZHR 173 (2009), 281, 307 ("clearly to be welcomed"). Such sample articles of association have already been prepared at the Commission's request, see the *working document* of the Advisory Board on Corporate Governance and Company Law of 23 July 2008, 1122/Drucksache 17.

225 For Germany, see for example Annex 1 to Section 60 Tax Code; Annex to Section 2(1a) GmbHG.

226 For a description of opt-out and opt-in models, see supra, Chapter 2 C.III.1

227 See *Hommelhoff/Teichmann* DStR 2008, 925, 930: "Legal policy specialist feedback body" with a model intended to have the "rank of statute justification"; see also *Hommelhoff/Teichmann* GmbHR 2008, 897, 899. The Advisory Board on Corporate Governance and Company Law (see note 224) established by the Commission is borne in mind here. See also Arbeitskreis Europarecht (AKEur), NZG 2008, 897, 898, fig. 14.

228 See *infra* C.V.

If neither the mandate to regulate nor the sample articles of association proves perfect, two techniques for closing gaps remain. Their pros and cons were already discussed when the SE was created, and they still divide legal scholars into two camps. One technique ultimately used for the SE is the auxiliary application of the *law of the state of the registered office* (reference to national law – "reference solution"). This solution can claim to motivate founders to choose a supranational legal form, because the link with familiar models of national law is not entirely severed. It also stimulates horizontal competition within the supranational model.[229] Most of all, however, it ensures legal certainty: it is relatively easy to determine the applicable set of rules, and those rules have been comprehensively put into action by the national institutions such as commentators or courts. The price is the re-nationalisation of the legal form already discussed, which gives away a good part of the efficiency gains from the standard legal form outlined above.

The second solution, originally conceived (but not realised) for the SE, is to refer to *general principles* of EU corporate law (*ius communitatis*) and/or of member states corporate law (*ius commune*).[230] The advantages and disadvantages of this solution mirror those of the reference model just discussed. A central problem of this approach, which finally led to it being abandoned for the SE, is the difficulty to distil general principles from the fragmentary European legal material and, primarily, to make such principles sufficiently specific to be applicable in concrete cases. Whereas the former may be achieved,[231] the success of the latter is doubtful because the principles are highly abstract.[232] In any case, an institution with the necessary authority, capacity and legitimacy is required to transform such principles into workable rules. Reference to general principles of European corporate law is not the last word, but leads directly on to the final point of our analysis.

V Is the EU good at legislating?

Whether the EU is good at legislating is a question that is often asked when it comes to harmonizing company law in Europe. Here, the issue was raised when

229 See supra note 117.

230 See *Bachmann* ZEuP 2008, 32, 48 et seq.

231 In further detail *Schön* FS Hopt, p. 1343; likewise in RabelsZ 64 (2000), 1 et seq; with special reference to the SPE *Bücker* ZHR 173 (2009), 281, 287, 308.

232 In further detail *Bachmann* ZEuP 2008, 32, 49 et seq, 53 et seq; *Bachmann* ZGR 2001, 351, 373 et seq; *Casper* FS Ulmer, 2003.

we discussed possible innovative functions of an ECC and talked about specific regulatory issues. It became clear that the institutional structure of the EU (which is very much dependent on political compromise) is designed to produce legal forms which are as original as they are imperfect. Since our task is not to discuss fundamental changes to this structure, the final question is: what can be done *within* the institutional framework of the EU to optimise legislation in particular in European corporate law? This question goes beyond the scope of this book, which is why we will only briefly outline some possible answers.

The starting-point is an extensive public *consultation procedure*. If we fear that supranational legislature is too far removed from the interests of those affected by the regulation and that vertical competition may be inadequate to correct this spontaneously,[233] the interests of all those affected by the regulation must be investigated to the greatest possible extent in advance. European legislative procedure is far more progressive here than German legislative procedure, which only involves the public once a statute draft is finished and then leaves it up to the discretion of the leading ministry.[234] European law, in contrast, obliges the Commission to carry out extensive hearings *before* proposing a legislative act.[235] The proposal for an SPE Regulation made by the Commission was not only based on thorough preliminary work and suggestions from the academic world and legal practice, but also on a survey of corporations affected and an extensive consultation process which was supplemented by a feasibility study and an assessment of the consequences.[236]

A problem frequently addressed in the context of European legislation is the so-called *fear of petrification:* due to the awkward nature of the European legislative procedure, it is often impossible to diverge from stipulations once made, in spite of better insights later.[237]A helpful remedy might be the use of so-called "sunset clauses", increasingly employed both in national and European law, according to which a statute enters out of force after a fixed period of time. This technique is only partly suitable for supranational corporate forms because enterprises seek for a stable legal environment. In Canada, for instance, precisely the resistance of the federal model to reform appears to have made it more at-

233 On this problem see supra Chapter 7 B.II.3.b).

234 Rightly criticised in OECD, Better legislation in Europe: Germany, 2010, p. 73 et seq; see also *Bachmann* ZGR 2001, 351, 368 et seq; *Schäffer* Theorie der Rechtssetzung, 1988, 145, 158 et seq.

235 See Art. 2 of the protocol on the application of the principles of subsidiarity and proportionality. See also generally Art. 11 TEU.

236 Documented under http://ec.europa.eu/internal_market/company/epc/index_en.htm.

237 See *Schön* ZHR 160 (1996), 221, 236 with further references.

tractive for business.[238]Alternatively, the Commission could be obliged to evaluate the success of European corporate form, as was done in the SE Regulation (s. Art. 69 SE Regulation). However, experience with the SE shows that carefully crafted compromises are only unwrapped unwillingly at a later date, even if the evaluation shows some reason for reform.[239]

The petrification effect is less dramatic for optional systems of rules than for acts of harmonisation, because those subject to the rule have an exit option.[240] The threat of petrification only becomes a serious problem if an optional ECC-statute, later acknowledged to need correction which is not possible due to a lack of consensus, leads to the drying out of national alternative forms. Due to the limited attractiveness of the supranational legal form in Europe, such drying out need not currently be feared. Nevertheless, this aspect should be borne in mind.

If we look for ways to make the European regulatory instruments more flexible, we come across the *committee process* ("Lamfalussy-procedure"), which is extensively used in European capital market law. The idea here is to delegate technical details of regulation to subordinate committees staffed by members from supervisory authorities or national experts. The commission process has reached vast proportions in EU-regulation, but is criticised for its lack of democratic legitimacy.[241] In view of its flexibility, its use may also be advisable in European corporate law. Yet by its very nature, corporate law is less suitable for bureaucratic standardisation than, for example, securities law. For this reason too, serious modifications would have to be considered before adopting the commission process for an ECC.

The committee process is not the only way to achieve adaptable European corporate law. In addition to the extension of the majority principle in the EC Treaty, which is currently illusory from a political point of view, the activation of *private expert knowledge* is a possible solution. Unspecific principles of European corporate law can be brought into a workable form, not just by the courts, but also by private expert groups. To achieve this, a common language, available with English, and a platform for discourse are necessary. Expert networks may supply solutions for specific case constellations in a more or less institutional-

238 The view taken by *Cumming/McIntosh* 20 Int'l Rev. L. & Econ., 141, 144 ff (2000).

239 Cf. supra note 28.

240 Pleading for an increased use of option models for this reason *Hertig/McCahery* ECGI Working Paper 78/2007 (ssrn.com/abstract=958247) = 3 Eur. Co. & Fin. L. Rev. 341 (2006).

241 See *Haltern* supra (note 138), para. 282f; for a less critical view *Schmolke* NZG 2005, 912; see also *Möllers* ZEuP 2008, 480; *Kasten* ZBB 2008, 238; *Sethe* Anlegerschutz im Recht der Vermögensverwaltung, 2006, p. 450 et seq. On recent reforms, see *Bremer* NZG 2011, 341.

ised form.[242] Competing private sets of rules, modelled on the "Draft Common Frame of Reference" (DCFR),[243] or various national or self-regulating codices would provide courts with decision-making aids as persuasive authority. The result would be a compromise between "fully nationalised" and the "purely European" legal form.

Finally, rule making by *courts* themselves has to be addressed. Regardless of the technique used to close gaps, courts are needed in order to authoritatively settle legal disputes. This raises the question of whether such settlement should be organised centrally or in a decentralised way. An advantage of a centralised solution at EU level is that it helps to reach legal uniformity plus the circumstance that national courts are overtaxed by extensive comparative work. However, as the ECJ is cumbersome and insufficiently specialised as a court of last instance, a decentralised solution also comes into consideration.[244] If we wish to retain the advantages of centralised decisions we should consider a *reform of the European courts system*, for example through the establishment of special divisions for commercial or corporate law.[245] Whether this is politically feasible is uncertain, as the attempts to establish a European patent court have shown.[246] Notwithstanding, extensive access to arbitration tribunals should be made possible for the ECC and those participating in it.[247] In any case, publication of the decisions accessible in translation or in a commonly-used language (English) should be required.[248] If the parties shy away from this, capacity for arbitration would have to be restricted or the reference to general European law principles abandoned. Neither would contribute to the attractiveness of a European closed corporation.

---

242 The establishment of the European Law Institute (ELI) provides a starting-point for this, www.europeanlawinstitute.eu.

243 The DCFR is a model for an optional European private law regime.

244 See also *Dammann* Materielles Recht und Beweisrecht im System der Grundfreiheiten, 2007 (for decentralised clarification of the fundamental freedoms of the TFEU).

245 In favour: *Eidenmüller* FS Heldrich, p. 581, 592; *Bachmann* ZEuP 2008, 32, 56 et seq; in detail *Völter* Der Lückenschluss im Statut der Europäischen Privatgesellschaft, 2000, 268 et seq with further references.

246 As attempts to create a patent court within the system of the TFEU failed, the European patent court will now be based on an international agreement ("Agreement on a Unified Patent Court") among some member states.

247 As in Art. 42a Draft SE Regulation of the European Parliament.

248 The approach in Art. 45(3) Draft SE Regulation of the European Parliament (list of court decisions).

D Results

1. A European closed corporation (ECC) fulfils three functions: it can be used (1) as a vehicle for the transnational transfer of seat and for cross-border merger; (2) as a uniform element of European groups of enterprises ("*Konzern*") and (3) to extend the range of corporate forms available in Europe. Although these functions can, in part, be achieved with national legal forms, the supranational legal form has comparative advantages making its creation desirable. By contrast, model laws or harmonisation of national laws of closed corporations are only a second-best solution.
2. The European Union owns the power to enact an ECC-regulation. However, its creation presupposes unanimity in the EU-Council and, therefore, the consent of all Member States.
3. In order to fulfil its functions as best as possible, the ECC should have an autonomous Statute, i.e. it should, as far as possible, avoid recourse to national corporate law.
4. Lack of reputation (due, e.g., to a strong susceptibility to insolvency) affects the ECC more strongly than national legal forms. To maintain the value of the "European brand", stricter creditor protection than economically necessary may be advisable, at least in the initial phase.
5. In many cases, the ECC will only have one shareholder. This reduces the need for regulation and allows generous use of default rules. In addition, a special statute for one-shareholder corporations may be advisable.
6. As a European alternative, the ECC competes with existing national legal forms. This is ambivalent from an economic point of view. The distance of European institutions to local lobbies and to national path dependencies nurtures the hope of a more efficient corporate form; yet, it is possible that the European corporate form will displace national competitors and stifle regulatory competition, although the ECC might have long-term deficits. "Curbed" competition seems preferable here. Unrestricted vertical competition makes changes to the institutional structure of the EU necessary which are not in view at present.
7. Artificially restricting the access to the ECC is problematic because it blocks the creation of a "critical mass". Access restrictions may only be used moderately, if at all. Cross-border requirements are easily circumvented. Comparatively strict insolvency protection should be sufficient to prevent the ECC from becoming "over-attractive".
8. Due to the veto power EU-Member States, the creation of an ECC heavily depends on compromise. To overcome political obstacles, we consider the use of option models particularly advisable.

9. A central problem of supranational legal forms is closing gaps. Various techniques are available, among which reference to national law and the use of general European legal principles in particular compete with one another. The latter is preferable in view of the desirable autonomy described (see 2.).
10. To guarantee good legislation and adjudication for an ECC, existing European institutions must be improved. Helpful are (1) institutionalised discussion platforms (European Law Institute), (2) the development of the European Court system (specialized ECJ-division) and (3) transnational access to national court decisions (data banks, translation of judgments).

Index